THE STUDY OF SOCIAL DIALECTS
IN AMERICAN ENGLISH

The Study of Social Dialects in American English

WALT WOLFRAM
Federal City College and
Center for Applied Linguistics

RALPH W. FASOLD
Georgetown University

Prentice-Hall, Inc., *Englewood Cliffs, New Jersey*

Library of Congress Cataloging in Publication Data

WOLFRAM, WALTER A
 The study of social dialects in American English.

 Bibliography: p.
 1. English language in the United States—Dialects.
2. Speech and social status. 3. Linguistic research.
I. Fasold, Ralph W., joint author. II. Title.
PE2808.W6   301.2′1   74-782
ISBN   0-13-858787-6

Printed in the United States of America.

10   9   8   7   6   5   4

ACKNOWLEDGMENTS: Figure 4–3 used by permission of Charles-James N. Bailey. Figures 4–4, 4–5, 4–9, and 4–10 are reproduced by permission of the publisher from Walt Wolfram, *A Sociolinguistic Description of Detroit Negro Speech* (Washington, D.C.: Center for Applied Linguistics, © 1969).   Figures 4–7 and 4–8 are reproduced by permission of the American Anthropological Association from *American Anthropologist 66*, No. 6 (Part 2), 1964.   Figure 4–11 is reproduced by permission of the publisher from Ralph W. Fasold, *Tense Marking in Black English: A Linguistic and Social Analysis* (Washington, D.C.: Center for Applied Linguistics, © 1972).   Table 5–8 is used by permission of Gillian Sankoff.

PRENTICE-HALL INTERNATIONAL, INC., *London*
PRENTICE-HALL OF AUSTRALIA, PTY. LTD., *Sydney*
PRENTICE-HALL OF CANADA, LTD., *Toronto*
PRENTICE-HALL OF INDIA PRIVATE LIMITED, *New Delhi*
PRENTICE-HALL OF JAPAN, INC., *Tokyo*

To our students
at Federal City College
and Georgetown University

CONTENTS

LIST OF ILLUSTRATIONS

PREFACE

During the past decade, interest in the use of language in its social context has grown rapidly. Studies which deal with language in society have commonly been subsumed under the title of *sociolinguistics*. The types of studies that are sometimes included under this rubric actually cover a rather broad spectrum of topics. One area deals with the interaction of large-scale social factors and language or dialect situations. This type of sociolinguistics is really a branch of the social disciplines that treat language systems as social institutions, and has sometimes been referred to as the *sociology of language*.

Another area of concern is the actual use of language as a type of "speech event." The focuses of study in this area include rules for the appropriate selection of speakers, relationships of interlocutors, topic, setting, and the like. One who studies these things is, in essence, concerned with how language is used to carry out certain functions. This area of interest is sometimes referred to as the *ethnography of speaking*. Although the detailed analysis of linguistic structures as such is not typically the concern of these studies, this type of descriptive interest may be seen to complement studies of linguistic structure per se. Traditionally, such studies have been consigned to the ethnographer who is interested in the functions of language, but recent developments in linguistics indicate that some of these areas cannot be avoided by the general linguist.

A third area of interest deals with language in its social context as a proper concern of *general linguistics*. From this perspective, the investigation of language in its social context is seen to be central to the solution of problems of linguistic theory. It is maintained that theoretical issues in linguistics can be solved only by looking at language variation in society. This concern is not seen as an interdisciplinary adjunct to the study of language but an indispensable consideration in the development of a theory of language. Since language is ultimately a social phenomenon, it stands to reason that one must look at the social environment in order to find answers to many problems which emerge in the study of linguistic structure.

The final area sometimes subsumed under the label of sociolinguistics involves the application of linguistic knowledge to social problems. Problems related to language planning and language standardization are concerns which may be considered in this area. We would also consider the application of knowledge about language variety to education under this area of interest, since education in most societies is ultimately a matter of socialization. This area has been referred to as the *ecology of language* since it deals with the relationship of language to its social environment.

Although one might consider this book to be sociolinguistic in nature, we make no claim to cover all the areas which could be treated under the rubric of sociolinguistics. Instead, we have taken a small area and applied it to language variation in American English. For the most part, we have totally ignored aspects of the sociology of language and the ethnography of speaking, and we have only dealt with selected aspects of general linguistics and the ecology of language. To consider anything more would take us far beyond the limitations of a single volume.

We have attempted in this book to introduce the student to the range of linguistic variation found in American English. This includes the presentation of a particular philosophical perspective on social dialects, procedures used in data collection, theoretical models for describing such data, a compendium of socially diagnostic linguistic forms, and a discussion of the consequences of language differences for American education. Since the book is designed as an introductory text, we have, for the most part, kept the technical linguistic terminology to a minimum. An introductory course in descriptive linguistics would be a helpful background for a full understanding of our vantage point, but most of the chapters do not presume any specific training in linguistics on the part of the reader. The possible exception to this is Chapter Five, where we present the linguistic models for handling linguistic variation. Although we consider this to be an important chapter for the student of linguistics, it may be omitted by the reader who is not interested in linguistic models for describing variation. The major portion of this book, then, may be used by the upper level undergraduate or graduate student in English, education, speech and hearing, or sociology who is interested in social dialects of American English. The need for specialists in these areas to become familiar with this topic should be apparent from Chapters One and Eight, where the philosophical and practical implications of linguistic diversity are considered.

While there is some introductory material that may be redundant to the linguist, we feel that this book holds considerable interest for the student in general linguistics who wants a survey of social dialects. Of particular interest to such a student are the chapters on field techniques, the theoretical approach to linguistic variation, and the compendium of socially diagnostic linguistic forms in American English.

Throughout the book we have used the term *dialect* in one of its popular senses rather than in its technical sense. The term is meant to indicate any combination of observable variable features of English. As we explain in Chapter Four, we see no reason to restrict ourselves to the technical definition of *dialect* involving bundles of geographical or social isoglosses. Whether or not the boundaries of several variable features are located at the same spot in geographical or social space is of little linguistic significance. The linguistically significant patterning of variable features is explained in Chapter Five. The concept of dialect as understood by laymen does not typically involve the technical notion of an isogloss bundle; rather, it refers to sets of differences, wherever they may occur, which make one English speaker's speech different from another's. This popular concept of dialect is very close to the technical definition of the term *lect* as used by Charles-James N. Bailey (1973). Our use of *dialect,* then, is technically more closely related to Bailey's use of *lect* than to the traditional linguistic definition of dialect.

There have been a number of individuals who directly or indirectly contributed to the contents of this book. We are particularly grateful to colleagues at our various institutional affiliations. These include Ronald Williams, M. Eugene Wiggins, and Orlando L. Taylor of Federal City College; Roger W. Shuy of Georgetown University; and Rudolph C. Troike of the Center for Applied Linguistics. Some of the above have read and commented on parts of the manuscript. As usual, they should be absolved of all responsibility for the remaining inadequacies. In the case of Mr. Fasold, the support of a National Science Foundation grant to the Sociolinguistics program at Georgetown University is gratefully acknowledged. Marge Wolfram and Jan McDonald graciously undertook the task of deciphering our rough draft in typing the manuscript. Finally, we would like to thank our students at Federal City College and Georgetown University who read and interacted with parts of the manuscript so that we might keep in touch with our audience. We do not claim to have produced a "student-proof" text, but we would like to let them know that we were thinking of them by dedicating this effort to our students.

WALT WOLFRAM
RALPH W. FASOLD

1

FOUNDATIONS
OF SOCIOLINGUISTICS

Most of us have had the experience of sitting on a bus and eaves-dropping on a conversation taking place behind us. As a matter of etiquette, we don't turn around and stare at the participants in the conversation, so we have no observational characteristics to support any impression we might get of the speakers. Nonetheless, we do get impressions. In part, these may be based on what the participants are talking about. The basis of our impressions, however, goes further than that. We make judgments about a person's education, origin, ethnicity, and social class based on *how* he is talking. If we have occasion to check out our impressions, we are often surprised at the accuracy with which we have categorized a person on the basis of his speech. Most of us can recall instances in which another person answers the telephone and tells us that an unidentified caller is on the line. Our immediate reaction is, "What does he sound like?" We may be told, "He sounds like a salesman," or "He sounds like a garage mechanic." In many instances, the identification of the caller turns out to be fairly accurate despite the fact that he has never been seen or spoken to previously. In these cases, whether a person realizes it or not, he is judging the social characteristics of an individual entirely on the basis of speech.

Judgments of social status based on speech are as inevitable as the social assessments we make when we find out where a person lives, what his occupation and educational background are, and who his friends are.

1

When one lives in a certain way, one is expected to talk in a manner that fits that life style. In the same sense that we can talk of social class in America, we can talk of social dialects. In fact, it has sometimes been suggested that a person's speech may be a more accurate indicator of social status than many of the current sociological indices used.

The entity designated as social class is, of course, not an isolated variable that will account for all varieties of English spoken in America. As we shall observe throughout the course of this book, there are a number of other variables that constantly interact with social status to account for speech differences. Most of us have engaged in the guessing game in which we try to identify the regional origin of individuals on the basis of their speech. Furthermore, no one needs to be told that different styles of speech are appropriate in formal and informal situations any more than he needs to be told that different styles of dress are appropriate for different social situations. And, of course, nobody really expects teenagers to talk like adults or vice versa. We could illustrate further here, but the various factors that interact with social class will be discussed in detail later. Suffice it here to say that many social factors interact with social status to account for socially significant varieties of American English.

Cultural Relativity and Linguistic Differences

The investigation of language in relation to social class must begin with a sociolinguistic perspective on language differences. The view of language differences current among linguists is historically derived from the anthropological tradition of *cultural relativism*. When anthropologists at the turn of the century reacted against the evaluative measures of their predecessors in describing non-Western cultures, they set the stage for a similar reaction in relation to language differences. American anthropologists such as Boas, Kroeber, and Herskovits insisted on viewing cultures descriptively rather than by some yardstick of evolutionary development. Such an approach precluded classifying a culture or language as "underdeveloped," "primitive," or inherently inferior simply because it is not associated with technological advances found in Western civilization. The notion of "primitive" culture or language was denounced as a product of ethnocentrism on the part of socially and technologically superordinate cultures.

Prior to this relativistic viewpoint, many language scholars simply followed the notions of nineteenth-century evolutionary anthropology, which considered different cultures as representative of different stages in the evolutionary development of language. For example, one popular typological classification in the nineteenth century was made according to whether languages were *isolating, agglutinative,* or *inflectional.* Isolating languages were those which had few or no inflectional affixes (Chinese was generally given as the sample of this type). Inflectional languages were those which used inflectional affixes to a considerable extent (Greek or Latin were generally given as the typical examples). Agglutinative was a transitional type (typified usually by Turkish or Swahili). Whereas inflectional languages were thought to fuse affixes and bases of words, agglutinative languages were thought to neatly separate the word base from the affixes. According to popular evolutionary theory of the middle nineteenth century, the more "primitive" a culture, the more isolating its language structure should be. The descriptive account of many preliterate Indian cultures in North and South American countries, however, showed that some of these languages were, by comparison, considerably more inflectional than either Latin or Greek. And by the same token, there were isolating languages that were characteristic of highly developed technological cultures. The empirical evidence simply did not support such an evaluative scheme. More important, perhaps, was the emergence of cultural relativity in twentieth-century anthropology, the discipline from which descriptive linguistics developed. The relativistic approach in linguistics simply paralleled that in cultural anthropology. Just as anthropologists rejected the Procrustean mold of Western civilization in describing other cultures, linguists rejected the mold of the classical languages in describing non–Indo-European languages. Thus, for example, in 1921, Edward Sapir wrote:

> The evolutionary prejudice . . . instilled itself into the social sciences towards the middle of the last century and . . . is only now beginning to abate its tyrannical hold on our mind. Intermingled with this scientific prejudice and largely anticipating it was another, a more human one. The vast majority of linguistic theorists themselves spoke languages of a certain type, of which the most fully developed varieties were the Latin and Greek that they had learned in their childhood. It was not difficult for them to be persuaded that these familiar languages represented the "highest" development that speech had attained and that all other types were but steps on the way to this beloved "inflective" type. Whatever conformed to the pattern of Sanskrit and Greek and Latin and German was accepted as expressive of the "highest," whatever departed from it was frowned upon as a shortcoming or was at best an interesting aberration. Now any classification that starts with preconceived values or that works up to sentimental satisfaction is self-condemned as unscientific. . . . If, therefore, we wish to understand language in its true inwardness we must disabuse our minds of preferred "values" and accustom ourselves to look upon English and Hottentot with the same cool, yet interested detachment.
> (1921:123)

Each language was to be described in terms of its own structure, without evaluative reference to other languages. Although some linguists still compare languages typologically using a refined measurement of the types of classification first suggested in the nineteenth century, value judgments are not made on this basis.

At first, the relativistic premises which were the basis of descriptive linguistics were mainly applied to languages compared across clear-cut cultures; later they became relevant to the comparisons of speech differences for social levels within the framework of a larger culture. For English, this meant that a relativistic standpoint was taken with respect to the different varieties of English, whether there were social or geographical reasons which accounted for these differences. In linguistics, this relativistic viewpoint probably reached its apex in Robert A. Hall's popular book, *Leave Your Language Alone,* published in 1950. In this treatment, Hall attempted to deal with many of the popular misconceptions about linguistic absolutism. The shock effect of some of his pronouncements was great; he suggested that "there is no such thing as good and bad (or correct and incorrect, grammatical and ungrammatical, right and wrong) in language" (1950:6). Although this may appear to be overstated (and, in terms of current linguistic theory, parts of it would be considered incorrect), it does reflect the objective detachment from evaluative norms that tends to be the hallmark of the linguist. More than one English teacher has angrily approached us with a remark something like "Anything goes with you linguists!" Conversely, linguists have constructed a fictional school teacher, Miss Fidditch, who has made her task the survival of an imaginary entity she has labeled "pure" English.

The debate concerning the inherent adequacy of language varieties used by members of lower social classes has not subsided; in fact, it has intensified in recent years along with the emphasis on improving the education of economically impoverished members of our society. Although linguists have, admittedly, not been the most courteous dissenters from popular misconceptions about the implications of language differences, their reactions against linguistic prejudice are based on some very fundamental notions about the nature of language. In looking at language from a sociolinguistic perspective, there are essentially two sets of premises that needs to be considered, one dealing with the cognitive function of language and one with the behavioral function. The cognitive function of language, language as *code,* has to do with the communicative capacity of language as a system of signs. The premises relevant to the behavioral function of language, language as *behavior,* deal with language as one aspect of cultural behavior through which societal roles are carried out. The first set of premises is generally considered within the proper limit of linguistics. Although these notions are generally given in any introduction to linguistics, their implications as applied to social dialects are often not spelled out. We shall there-fore review these fundamental notions and discuss them in relation to some of the current viewpoints concerning social dialects, particularly nonstan-dard ones. The second set of premises comes to light as we look at language in its social context. It is not enough to study only the form and structure of language as code; it is necessary to look at the social significance of acts of speaking themselves. Ultimately the form of language and the social context of its usage go hand in hand.

Language as Code

LANGUAGE AND LOGIC

At the foundation of human thought lie fundamental logical opera-tions that are basic to the use of language to express syllogistic reasoning. These include logical operations such as equivalence, implication, negation, conjunction, disjunction, and the like. All languages adequately provide for the conceptualization and expression of logical propositions, but the particular mode (i.e., grammar) for encoding conceptualization may differ among language systems. The linguist, therefore, assumes that the different surface forms for expression have very little to do with the underlying logic of a sentence. There is nothing inherent in a given language variety that will interfere with the development of the ability to reason.[1] This does not necessarily mean that particular language categories may not predetermine particular conceptualizations of the external world (the Whorfian hy-pothesis) or that a particular cultural conceptualization may not influence language categories. But there is no evidence that different language cate-gories or cultural conceptualizations will impede the fundamental processes that are the basis of human thought.

Although this premise is axiomatic to linguistics, it does not coincide with some of the current notions about nonstandard dialects of English on the part of both laymen and scholars in some disciplines dealing with language. It has sometimes been suggested that some nonstandard dialects impose certain cognitive limitations. Thus, it is claimed that some non-standard varieties of English are "illogical" in comparison with Standard English.

This can readily be illustrated by "double negatives" as they are used

---

[1] Throughout this section we refer to "normal" individuals. There are, of course, small numbers of individuals in any social group who are retarded in terms of their cognitive development and/or speech. It is essential to evaluate the speech deficiencies of these individuals in terms of the norms of their surrounding com-munity rather than in terms of some absolute norm.

in some nonstandard varieties of English. In Standard English, negative sentences that occur with an indefinite pronoun following the verb generally only express the negative at one point, either on the auxiliary or the indefinite. We can thus get *John didn't want anything* or *John wanted nothing.* If, however, a person should say *John didn't want nothing,* it can only be meant as a positive statement, because two negatives "logically" make a positive.[2] In this view, if a person uses the construction in a sentence such as *John didn't do nothing because he was so lazy,* he is using English in an illogical way. The speaker apparently means that John did not work, but by saying *John didn't do nothing* he actually affirms that John did something. Interpretations of this sort ignore a quite regular rule in some nonstandard dialects which roughly states that when you have a negative sentence with indefinites, you may add a negative element to every indefinite.[3] This means that we can have sentences like *We ain't never had no trouble about none of us pulling out no knife or nothing.* In this respect, Nonstandard English is simply like many other languages including Spanish, French, and Italian, in which one basic negative can be expressed at more than one point in the sentence. It is further like socially acceptable uses of English found in literature of the thirteenth and fourteenth centuries in England. In actual use, these sentences are always understood as having only one negative which is redundantly "spread" to the various indefinites in the sentence.

Essential to understanding the underlying proposition of the example sentence is awareness of the distinction between *abstract structure* and *surface structure* in language. Abstract structure is basically a system of propositions that express the meaning of the sentence. Surface structure is the expression of these propositions in sentences as they are actually spoken. For example, the sentence *John didn't go,* according to one kind of analysis of abstract structure, has a structure something like that of Figure 1-1a. The surface structure of the sentence as it is actually spoken is like that in Figure 1-1b. The knowledge of language involves the ability to assign abstract and surface structures, including phonetic interpretation, to an infinite range of sentences, with the appropriate mappings of abstract structures onto surface structures by grammatical rules.

To say that certain socially stigmatized varieties of English are illogical is only possible if one of the primary premises about the nature of language is naively disregarded. Ultimately, such notions are derived from predetermined ideas of what is "correct" in language, although philo-

---

[2] This sentence could, of course, be interpreted positively in a context such as *He didn't do just nothing; he was always busy.* Usually, however, there is a strong stress on *nothing* to indicate this intention.

[3] Our use of the word *rule* follows its linguistic rather than its popular definition. To a linguist, a *rule of language* is an account of how people actually *do* use language, not a regulation about how they *should* use it.

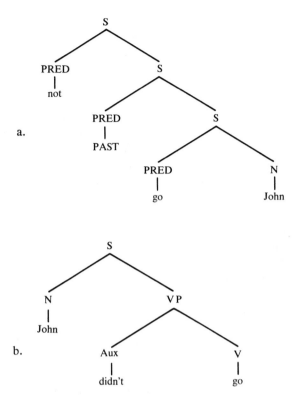

Figure 1-1. Abstract and surface structures of *John didn't go:* a. abstract structure; b. surface structure.

sophical dictums about the logical nature of certain rules of a language add a ring of authority to such pronouncements. All language varieties are equally capable of use in reasoning, abstracting, and hypothesizing. Middle-class dialects are no more or less inherently equipped to deal with abstract or logically complex reasoning processes than are lower-class dialects.

LANGUAGE ADEQUACY

Another premise of the linguist is that all languages or dialects are adequate as communicative systems. It is accepted as given that language is a human phenomenon which characterizes every social group, and that all language systems are perfectly adequate as communicative systems for the members of the social group. The social acceptability of a particular language variety is totally unrelated to its adequacy as a communicative code. The question concerning different language varieties is not the *what* but the *how* of communication. Thus, the consideration of the so-called disadvantaged child as "nonverbal," "verbally destitute," or drastically deficient" in his speech is diametrically opposed to this basic assumption. There are situations in which young children decline to talk very much because of the discomfort of the social situation or as a protective device against meddling by strangers, but this cannot be interpreted as meaning that the child is nonverbal.

As Labov (1970a) has pointed out, monosyllabic responses in situations involving a teacher and child might be an effective defense against a potentially hostile and threatening situation. But if a more comfortable social situation is set up, the same child who was judged as nonverbal in a formal test situation may be shown to be highly verbal. Linguists can show that the label *verbal destitution* cannot refer to vernacular language patterns in an indigenous setting, but rather to the impression of speech created by a contrived formal test situation.

The problem of language *use* should be kept separate from questions of inherent language ability. It is quite likely that there are syntactic constructions present in a child's grammar which he is not accustomed to use in ways necessary for functioning in school. Carl Bereiter provides a classic example of this, although he mistakenly gives it as an example of language disability. He observed that some disadvantaged four-year-old black children cannot perform "simple *'if–then'* deductions." He gives the following example:

> The child is presented a diagram containing big squares and little squares. All the big squares are red, but the little squares are of various other colors. "If the square is big, what do you know about it?" "It's red."
>
> (1965:200)

If the child cannot make the correct response, he is incompetent in using if–then constructions. But Bereiter himself goes on to admit:

> This use of *if* should not be confused with the antecedent-consequent use that appears in such expressions as, "If you do that again, I'm going to hit you," and which the child may already be able to understand.
>
> (1965:200)

In other words, even Bereiter would not deny that the child has the grammatical skill to at least interpret if–then constructions. One could even go further and show that a child who doesn't even use the word *if* still has mastered the if–then logic. A sentence like *You don't stop messin' wif me, I'ma hit you upside you head* demonstrates mastery of if–then logic just as surely as *If you should continue to annoy me, then I should beat you about the head*. What Bereiter is calling a language disability is a question of use. The children he is referring to may perfectly well be able to use if–then logic. Their difficulty comes in applying it to Bereiter's problem concerning the colored squares. Incidentally, his problem strikes us as a fairly demanding test of *any* four-year-old's ability.

When we say that all languages are adequate for communicative systems for the members of the community, we do not necessarily mean that all languages and dialects map experience in the same way. No two languages completely agree in the types of distinctions that are made, because no two cultures completely coincide in their range of experience. Thus, for example, Eskimos may distinguish several dozen different types of snow, whereas a South American Indian tribe may have no word at all for snow, because it is outside their experience. It may be somewhat surprising for middle-class Americans to find out that there are a number of different words in black ghetto culture which refer to different types of verbal activity in the black community. Terms like *signifying, sounding, shucking, rapping, copping a plea, jiving,* and *woofing* all refer to different types of verbal encounters which can only be translated paraphrastically in Standard English. That one language or dialect maps experience differently from another does not, however, mean that a particular language variety does not have the inherent capacity to deal with new experiences. As a dynamic phenomenon, language is always capable of symbolizing new experiences. Thus, for example, an isolated group of South American Indians who have never seen an airplane may not have any linguistic symbol for this object when they see it the first time. But by various means, the language is capable of labeling this new object. It may use a compound word which might be translated as 'bird canoe', or a phrase such as 'canoe that has wings and flies'. And, of course, all languages borrow from other languages so that the Spanish word might simply be integrated into the Indian language. In any case, we must recognize that although different language varieties may segment experiences differently, the dynamic and flexible nature of all languages provides them with the capability of symbolizing new experiences. The fact that the Bible, written originally in the context of Judeo-Christian culture in Hebrew and Greek, has been translated into so many diverse cultures and languages is a testimony to this capability of all languages.

Some linguists, following Chomsky, would assume the communicative adequacy of any language or language variety on the basis of an innate set of universal constraints on what a language can be like (i.e., it is a putative attribute of being human). In a sense, a child is born with a kind of mold which helps to shape the language he learns. This innate language propensity involves the following properties, according to Chomsky:

i. a technique for representing input signals,
ii. a way of representing structural information about these signals,

iii. some initial delimitation of a class of possible hypotheses about language structure,

iv. a method for determining what each hypothesis implies with respect to each sentence,

v. a method for selecting one of the (presumably infinitely many) hypotheses that are allowed by (iii) and are compatible with the given primary linguistic data.   (1965:30)

Other linguists, following the behaviorist tradition explicated by Skinner (1957), insist that the acquisition of language should be attributed to a stimulus-response relationship rather than an innate universal grammar. From this perspective, the adequacy of language systems can be claimed on the basis of cross-cultural comparisons. That is, the postulate about the communicative adequacy of languages is derived inductively, based on the empirical data from a representative sample of world languages. Both approaches, then, would lead to the same claim about the adequacy of language systems, although their reasoning for such a position might differ somewhat. Although the correct interpretation of both approaches arrives at the same conclusion with respect to this issue, there is one important implication that should be brought out. Chomsky's perspective assumes that any normal child will have the equipment to deal with the logical operations underlying language because language is an attribute of the human mind (see Chomsky 1968). But it is possible, given the behaviorist perspective, that a particular type of environment might inhibit the acquisition of the logical properties necessary for an adequate language system.

The question of adequacy of nonstandard dialects as communicative systems brings out a very important matter concerning our views of a nonstandard language variety. In actuality, the viewpoint is much broader than the linguistic situation, reverting to a basic approach to different social groups. One can, for example, view particular cultures or subcultures in American society in terms of two basic models, which Baratz (1968) has called *deficit* or *difference* models. A deficit model treats speech differences in terms of a norm and deviation from that norm, the norm being middle-class white behavior. From a sociological perspective, this means that much of lower-class behavior differing from middle-class behavior is viewed as deviant or pathological behavior. From a linguistic perspective, the speech behavior has been labeled "the pathology of non-organic speech deficiencies." On the other hand, a difference model, which seems to be much more common to anthropology than to sociology and psychology, considers socially subordinate societies and language varieties as self-contained systems, inherently neither deficient nor superior. Language varieties are different but equal.

Although this dichotomy between a deficit and a difference model is somewhat oversimplified, it sets a helpful framework for considering theoretical approaches to nonstandard dialects. But there is also a practical importance in such a distinction. If, for example, one simply considers nonstandard dialects to be corrupt approximations of Standard English, one may miss important structural facts about the nature of these dialects. For example, consider the following interpretation of the finite use of the form *be*, a commonly cited feature of what we shall call Vernacular Black English.[4] Dr. Ruth Golden, who has viewed Vernacular Black English in terms of a descending scale of deviation from Standard English, states:

> Individuals use different levels of language for different situations. These levels vary from the illiterate to the formal and literary. For instance, starting with the illiterate, *He don't be here*, we might progress to the colloquial, *He ain't here*, to the general and informal, *He isn't here*, up to the formal and literary, *He is not present.*   (1963:173)

From the perspective of a deficit model, *be* is simply considered a corrupt approximation of Standard English. The possibility that *be* may have a grammatically different function is precluded. Instead, it is only considered as a "substitution" for the finite forms of Standard English *am, is,* and *are.* The linguist, however, looks at this use of *be* descriptively; that is, he asks about the grammatical function of this form. When such an approach is taken, we find that the form *be* represents a grammatical category that seems to be unique to Vernacular Black English among varieties of American English. Linguists who have studied this construction generally agree that it is used to represent a habitual action of some type. The insistence on language varieties as systems in their own right (with both similarities and differences among related varieties) is the reason that linguists view with suspicion such terms as *substitutions, replacements, omissions, deviations,* and so forth. Such terms used with reference to nonstandard language varieties imply a value judgment about a given variety's relation to the standard variety. Terms like *correspondence* and *alternation* do not have these same implications; they are statements of fact about language relations. Although terminology may seem to be a trivial matter for the linguist to consider, the association of such terms with the deficit type of approach raises a danger signal to the linguist. Viewing nonstandard constructions as simply inaccurate and unworthy approximations of Standard English can lead to an inaccurate description of what is assumed by

---

[4] The term Vernacular Black English refers to the variety most typically spoken by working-class blacks. It is used to refer to the same language variety that is elsewhere identified by the terms Negro Nonstandard English, Negro Dialect, and Black English. We reserve the term Black English for the whole continuum of English varieties used by American blacks, ranging from standard Black English to the Black Vernacular (see Taylor 1969).

the linguist to be a self-contained system that is perfectly adequate for communication.

In terms of sociolinguistic situations, it is quite common for a socially dominant culture to view a socially subordinate one as having an inadequate means of communication. This view is a manifestation of linguistic ethnocentrism of the dominant classes. Thus, Spanish-speaking South Americans often consider the Indian peasants not to have valid language systems—that is, they are considered verbally destitute. The current treatment of socially stigmatized varieties of English is no different, although it may be more subtle because Americans have sometimes denied the sociological facts concerning the subordinate role of some segments of the population in American society.

LANGUAGE PATTERNING

Anyone who looks at language in some detail cannot help but be impressed with the systematic and ordered nature of all language varieties. What at first glance appears to be a maze of confusion in terms of sounds and meanings turns out on closer inspection to be a highly detailed and structured set of patterns. Languages are not thrown together in a haphazard fashion, but reveal an internal coherence that makes the organizational schemata of a computer look retarded by comparison. Subjective impressions of random structuring turn out to be a function of our inadequate or preconceived perceptions rather than empirically based fact. This can be readily illustrated by taking the case of final sounds in some nonstandard dialects, including Vernacular Black English and white nonstandard Appalachian speech. Impressions abound concerning the fact that these dialects "leave things off at the ends of words, anywhere and anytime." But when these characteristics are subjected to close scrutiny, we find that the impressions cannot be justified. That there are certain types of word endings that have no correspondence to "standard" language in some nonstandard dialects is an accurate observation. This lack of correspondence, however, is systematic and ordered rather than random or haphazard. We anticipate our discussion of socially diagnostic phonological features in Chapter Six by noting that the types of clusters which are affected by this phonological rule follow a fairly intricate pattern in which both members of the cluster are either voiced or voiceless. Clusters in which one of the members is voiced and the other voiceless are not affected by this reduction rule, so that items like *jump, belt, junk* do not delete the final stop member of the cluster. The failure to observe this patterned behavior is a function of our inadequate perceptions, not of empirical fact concerning the structure of nonstandard dialects. The same type of patterning could be readily illustrated for the grammatical and semantic components of language organization.

At this point, we should interject that though all linguists will agree that language reveals great organization and systematicity, there is some disagreement over what a linguist is doing when he gives a formal description of a language system. Some linguists assume that there exists theoretically only one correct analysis, and that any failure to arrive at an accurate description is a result of insufficient or faulty procedure. This has sometimes been referred to somewhat facetiously as the "God's truth" position. On the other hand, some linguists assume that theoretically there may be different ways of analyzing the same data and that one solution may be as adequate as another if it accurately accounts for the data. This has sometimes been referred to as the "hocus-pocus" position. The nonlinguist should not, however, be deceived by this disagreement about the representation of a linguistic description. Whatever the position on the description of data, linguists are united in their insistence on the basic systematic nature of language. Structure is not simply imposed as a fanciful artifice of the linguists' imagination; language is inherently systematic. For example, there are a number of different analyses of finite *be* usage in Vernacular Black English and linguists may be quite polemical in defense of the details of a particular description. But this polemic about its grammatical function should not be interpreted to mean that finite *be* can be dismissed as an unsystematic, haphazard, or random approximation of Standard English with no real function in its own right. To say this would unite all linguists who may differ in their grammatical descriptions of this feature in defense of its function as a patterned grammatical unit.

LANGUAGE ACQUISITION

Linguists generally agree that children have a fairly complete language system by the age of four or five, with minor adjustments in language competence occurring sometimes until age eight or nine. This system is acquired from contact with individuals in the child's environment through parent-child relationships or from child peers. All cross-cultural evidence points to the fact that the rate of development is roughly parallel for children of different social groups. Normal Kikuyu children in Kenya, Quechua Indians in Peru, lower-class children in Washington, D.C., and middle-class children in Beverly Hills, California, all appear to learn their indigenous language at approximately the same rate. The difference is, of course, that the Kikuyu child learns Kikuyu, the Quechua child Quechua, the middle-class child in Beverly Hills Standard English, and the lower-class child in Washington, D.C., a variety of Nonstandard English. Slobin's (1967) cross-cultural comparison of language acquisition definitely supports this claim.

Although this may appear to be rather obvious information, a look at some of the current literature in the field of educational psychology on language acquisition of nonstandard-speaking children indicates that this is a matter of considerable controversy. One does not have to search too intensively, therefore, to read statements like the following:

> Disadvantaged children's pronunciation and articulation, vocabulary, sentence length and use of grammatical and syntactic structures resemble the language of privileged children of a younger age level.
>
> (Raph 1967:212)

Linguists usually look at such a conclusion with immediate suspicion. Their suspicions are raised further when the reasons for these language retardations are cited as the lack of verbal interaction in the home between parent and child and a noisy environment which may impair auditory discrimination.

Closer inspection of claims about the retarded linguistic development of lower-class children reveals that the fact that these children do not speak Standard English is taken to mean that they are linguistically retarded, and, in many cases, that they are cognitively deficient. Thus, if a black lower-class child says *He nice,* a correspondence of the present-tense Standard English *He's nice,* it is considered to be an underdeveloped Standard English approximation and equivalent to the absence of copula at a particular stage of Standard English development. The fact that this form is used by lower-class black adult speakers in their community is irrelevant, only meaning that adults may have some stabilized form of language retardation. The linguist, however, suggests that this variety is simply one of many languages and dialects, including Russian, which have a no-copula realization in the present tense. No meaning is lost; an "identity statement" is just as permissible in this dialect as in any other language or dialect. Copula absence is not, by definition, an indication of retarded language development just because it is not found in Standard English.

The linguist, in support of the linguistic equality of nonstandard dialects, considers evidence on relative language proficiency such as that provided by Baratz (1969) to be an empirical justification for his claims. Baratz conducted a bidialectal test in which she compared the proficiency of a group of black ghetto children in repeating Vernacular Black English and Standard English sentences. As might be expected, the black children were considerably more proficient in repeating the Vernacular Black English sentences. When they repeated the Standard English sentences, however, there were predictable differences in their repetitions based on interference from Vernacular Black English. The same test was then administered to a group of white middle-class suburban children, who repeated the Standard English sentences quite adequately but had predictable differences in their repetition of the Vernacular Black English sentences based on interference from Standard English. Which of these groups, then, was linguistically retarded? We must be careful not to confuse social acceptability (and no one would deny the social stigmatization of nonstandard dialects) with language acquisition.

In sum, the relativistic viewpoint of the linguist emphasizes the fully systematic but different nature of nonstandard dialects as linguistic codes. It would be nice if what we have discussed above was self-evident or axiomatic to all those dealing with social dialects in one capacity or another. Unfortunately, our experience has taught us only too well that some of the views with which we have taken issue enjoy current popularity among a number of different disciplines which deal with social dialects. What we are calling for, then, is a basic respect for the linguistic capacity of all language varieties as linguistic codes, whether they be socially stigmatized or prestigious. We are not referring to a paternalistic attitude toward nonstandard speakers because of the social stigmatization of their dialect, but a basic respect for the intrinsic linguistic worth of all languages and dialects as linguistic codes.

Language as Behavior

In the previous section, we limited ourselves to linguistic premises that serve as the basis for for the investigation of the cognitive function of language. But language must also be viewed in terms of its social function: language as behavior. And when we view the role of language in terms of its social function, the linguist, or more properly, the sociolinguist, also operates on the basis of a number of general premises about language in society.

LANGUAGE AND CULTURAL BEHAVIOR

It is axiomatic that language is one form of cultural behavior. If we assume that social differences in culture will be manifested in nonlinguistic behavioral patterns, then we may also expect that behavioral differences may be realized in language. Several anthropological linguists, particularly Hymes (1962, 1964, 1969) and Ervin-Tripp (1964, 1969), have explicated the numerous types of social factors that may affect linguistic differences, including setting (e.g., locale, situation), participants (e.g., sex, age, status), topic (e.g., religion, athletics, politics), and functions (e.g., requests, commands, rituals). Although we are primarily concerned here with language differences that result from the differentiation of social positions, the interrelationship of social class with other social parameters is so intrinsic that it cannot be discussed completely apart from these. It is the intersection of these various social parameters that is basic to the assumption that many language differences result from social differences.

It should be noted that we have deliberately used the term *result from* in describing the relationship of linguistic and social differences, because we wish to imply that this relationship is one of cause and effect. Ultimately, the description of linguistic differences implies a cause-and-effect relationship between linguistic and social differences. Because of this relationship, it may be suggested that the description of linguistic differences is dependent upon an ethnographic description. Hymes observes:

> As the discovery of structure, sociolinguistics can be seen as an extension of usual linguistic description. The extension reaches a point, however, at which its dependence on social description becomes clear and inescapable. As description becomes sociolinguistic, it becomes partly ethnography, for the functions that underlie structure must be empirically determined. They can neither be taken for granted nor merely postulated, and to determine them requires socio-cultural knowledge.
>
> (1969:112–13)

Views on the extent to which ethnographical description must precede the description of language differences within a society vary greatly. Some sociolinguists (e.g., Bickerton 1971) first group speakers solely on the basis of linguistic differences. Having done this, they then proceed to describe some of the social characteristics of this linguistically defined group. Other sociolinguists (e.g., Wolfram 1969) have based the description of linguistic differences solely on predetermined socioeconomic groups. In the former case, it may be argued that the natural division of groups on a linguistic basis is a more reliable indication of sociolinguistic differences than the use of an objective socioeconomic index that can only represent one manifestation of social class. In the latter case, it may be argued that the description of linguistic differences in terms of predetermined social groups takes advantage of what we do know about some of the objective indices of social class, and that it may have implications concerning the validity of social class distinctions. The two approaches are not, of course, mutually exclusive, so that one might manipulate his data to take full advantage of the insights to be derived from both views. We shall have more to say about models for sociolinguistic descriptions in Chapter Five. Although the heuristic procedure and theoretical model for handling the relationship between language and social differences may have important implications for the descriptive adequacy of sociolinguistic data, basic to all sociolinguistic investigations is the cause-and-effect relationship between social and language differences.

Because all societies recognize different types of behavioral roles, we may predict that no society, regardless of its size, will evidence complete homogeneity in speech patterns. A small isolated band or nomadic clan may reflect distinct behavioral roles of males and females in speech characteristics, so that "women talk" cannot be confused with "men talk." (For an example, see Haas 1944.) Adolescents are expected to talk differently from adults, reflecting age-grading in a society. To say that all societies will reveal social differences in speech does not, of course, necessarily mean that relative status roles will be manifested in speech by all societies. We therefore must admit, at least theoretically, that social status differences may not be manifested by societies that do not differentiate clear-cut social classes. By *social class,* we mean a group within a society whose members hold a number of distinctive statuses in common and develop the operation of roles associated with these statuses. In most instances, there is an awareness of like characteristics and interests as opposed to the unlike characteristics and interests of other groups within the society. Other things being equal, the sharper the class lines are, the more clear-cut differences we would expect in the linguistic realization of these class differences. We would, therefore, expect that a caste system would manifest more clear-cut linguistic differences between castes than would a continuum of social class. In reality, of course, this is not always the case, because of the other social factors that intersect with social class to effect speech differences.

Societies that do not admit social class theoretically find it difficult to justify describing speech differences that correlate with social stratification. Realistically, however, social stratification seems to be found to a certain extent in all large societies whether it is overtly acknowledged or not, and we would predict that this stratification will be revealed in speech as one aspect of cultural behavior through which societal roles are carried out.

LANGUAGE NORMS

As an extension of our premise that language differences derive from social differences, we must expect some type of language standardization to take place. In the same sense that certain norms for behavior are set up as "proper" in a culture, norms of linguistic behavior may be set up. It is in this regard that the notion of correctness is used with respect to language. The notion of correctness as traditionally used in linguistics relates to societal norms of appropriate speech behavior. As discussed previously, these norms have nothing to do with inherent linguistic capacity. This can be illustrated by drawing an analogy with societal norms for eating behavior. Whether a person eats his peas with a spoon or a fork is irrelevant in terms of the food value of peas. But it is generally considered bad manners to eat them with a spoon (even if it does seem more efficient). In the same sense, whether a person says *I ain't going* or *I'm not going* is irrelevant in terms of the linguistic code as long as the content is readily understood by both hearer and speaker. But to use *ain't* is considered to be bad or incorrect English because it does not measure up to the norms for appropriate speech behavior in certain contexts.

For various sociocultural reasons, all languages or dialects used in a given society are not considered equal in their social acceptability, so that one of the languages or dialects becomes established as normative when compared with others. Thus, language standardization seems inevitable. Although we might give a general definition of a standard language, such as *a codified set of language norms which are considered socially acceptable to the most prestigious social class in a society,* more specific definition is dependent on the particular language situation. In one case, it may be the language of the high-prestige group that becomes emulated by others. In another case, a dialect or group of dialects may become standardized by default—that is, a dialect *not* spoken by socially stigmatized groups. In another case, it may be defined in terms of sociopolitical dominance.

In many instances, the establishment of a standardized language is formal and is supported by the codification of a norm in prescriptive grammars and codifying agencies like the school. In both Spain and France, there are language academies whose task it is to define such norms. It is also possible, however, for a standard language to be established through informal means. These norms of appropriate speech behavior are effective on two levels. In interlanguage relations, one language may be set up as a standard language for a nation. Thus, Spanish is considered to be the standard language of Peru although there are actually more native speakers of Quechua than Spanish. In terms of an intralanguage framework, one dialect may be set up as a standard as opposed to other varieties of the same language. In Germany, for example, Hochdeutsch is considered the standard dialect as opposed to Schwäbisch or Plattdeutsch, which are spoken in particular regions of Germany.

STANDARD ENGLISH

In working toward a definition of Standard English in America, we will utilize William Stewart's (1968a) distinction between formal and informal language standardization. Formal standardization refers to what is prescribed for a language by grammar and usage books, dictionaries, orthoepical guides, and language academies. Invariably, these formal codes are drawn up so that almost no one speaks the standard language. Formal standardization is based on the written language of established writers, which automatically limits it to the most formal style of older, highly educated people. As we shall show in a later chapter, this is the very last language style to be reached by any changes going on in a language. As a result, the standardized form of a language is nearly always conservative to the point of obsolescence. Because the psycholinguistic forces which account for language change are far more powerful than the influence exerted by the mechanisms of formal standardization, the formal standards are almost universally ignored in spoken usage.

Informal standardization, on the other hand, takes place without the benefit of books and academies and is much more effective. According to Stewart, informal standardization refers to "a certain amount of normalization of language behavior in the direction of some linguistic usage with high social prestige" (1968a:534). That is, people automatically and unconsciously adapt their speech habits in the direction of those they admire.

Stewart's notion must be refined somewhat. Standard American English, in the *informal* sense, or in the informal standard form of any language, must be distinguished not only from substandard forms but also from superstandard forms. There is general agreement about what forms of a language are preferred above others within a language community, even when the preferred forms are not used. It is typical for people to be slightly schizophrenic about their use of language. They acknowledge that some aspects of their use of language are not "correct": they can tell you what the "correct" form is, but they never actually adopt it. At an emotional level, these admittedly correct forms are rejected by some speakers because they are *too* correct. These speakers do not adopt such forms and at unguarded moments will even make negative value judgments about speakers who use them, not because these forms are "bad English" or because the speakers who use them are considered uneducated, but because the forms are "too snooty" and the speakers "too high-falutin'." Of course, the same speakers may smugly reject other vocabulary, grammatical constructions, and pronunciations as "poor English" and tend to consider people who use them as uneducated or stupid. Both the superstandard and substandard speech forms can be considered "nonstandard" (although elsewhere we reserve this term for what we are now calling "substandard"); that is, they are not the standards by which the speaker actually regulates his speech—they are not effective standards. Everything in between substandard and superstandard represents the effective informal standard to which the individual's speech actually conforms.

We have already pointed out that not everyone uses his language like everyone else. It follows that not everyone conforms to the same informal standard as everyone else—the range of forms that constitute the effective informal standard for one individual may be different from the range for another individual. A form that would be included in one individual's range of standard forms may be rejected by someone else as superstandard and part of the latter's standard range of forms may conversely be rejected by the first individual as substandard.

Any individual can test for himself what forms are part of his standard range, but he must be very objective and honest. First, he must put aside the formal rules of grammar he has learned. Then he must imagine what his *emotional* reaction would be to a given sentence, word, or pronunciation. If his reaction to the *form* (not the content) of the utterance is neutral and he can devote full attention to the meaning, then the form is standard for him. If his attention is diverted from the meaning of the utterance because it sounds "snooty," then the utterance is superstandard. If his attention is diverted from the message because the utterance sounds like poor English, then the form is substandard. This test must be applied honestly and the individual must be prepared to face the possibility that some constructions which he has been told are incorrect are actually part of his informal standard language and that some constructions which he has learned are correct are, for him, superstandard.

We will illustrate with Fasold's emotional reactions to some grammatical and pronunciation variations in English.[5]

GRAMMAR:

1. SUPERSTANDARD: Is it not?
   STANDARD: Isn't it?
   SUBSTANDARD: Ain't it?

2. SUPERSTANDARD: I thought them stupid.
   STANDARD: I thought they were stupid.
   SUBSTANDARD: I thought they was stupid.

3. SUPERSTANDARD: He's not so smart as I.
   STANDARD: He's not as smart as me.
   SUBSTANDARD: He not as smart as me.

4. SUPERSTANDARD: He is not to do that.
   STANDARD: He is not supposed to do that.
   SUBSTANDARD: He ain't supposed to do that.
   He does not supposed to do that.

PRONUNCIATION:

1. *Chocolate*
   SUPERSTANDARD: CHOCK oh lit
   CHOCK lit

[5] It is important to emphasize that these are not professional judgments, but only "gut" reactions which reflect Fasold's cultural background (a lower middle-class environment in northern New Jersey). These reactions, in fact, do not even match Wolfram's. As linguists, of course, we would both defend any of these constructions and pronunciations as legitimate variations within the English language as a whole. Other English speakers would reject some of the forms labeled "standard" as substandard and still others would find some of the "standard" forms superstandard.

STANDARD:	CHAWK lit
SUBSTANDARD:	CHEW uck lit

2. *Data*

SUPERSTANDARD:	DAH duh
STANDARD:	DAY duh
SUBSTANDARD:	DEE uh duh

3. *Been*

SUPERSTANDARD:	BEEN (rhymes with *keen*)
STANDARD:	BIN
SUBSTANDARD:	BEN

The definition of informal Standard English given is a highly individualistic one. For each individual it would include all and only those forms after which he actually models his speech; i.e., all those forms of the language which he does not reject as either substandard or superstandard. But this definition of informal Standard English is no more help for our purposes than is the definition of formal Standard English. If formal Standard English is so unrealistically conservative that no one speaks it, then our informal Standard English is so elastically defined that everyone speaks his own Standard English. It is possible, however, to move from our notion of informal Standard English to a definition that does not make every dialect standard but is still more realistic as a working definition than formal Standard English.

In every society, there are people who are in a position to use their judgments about what is good and bad in language in making decisions affecting other people. The most obvious such people in our society are school teachers and employers responsible for placing people in public-contact positions. School teachers consciously judge success and failure in language arts on the basis of the type of language used by students and may unconsciously make judgments about general intelligence on the same basis. Employers and personnel directors make use of judgments about language in their decisions about who gets hired for and advanced to what positions. Because their judgments can really make a difference, our use of the term "Standard American English" will refer to the informal standard language of teachers and employers of people who fill public-contact positions, and of other speakers whose speech resembles the speech of these two groups. This definition is based on the assumption that teachers and employers will not consistently enforce language forms that are superstandard to themselves.[6] Standard American English, then, will be the real spoken language of the educated middle class. Such features of spoken

---

[6] Teachers sporadically attempt to get their students to make distinctions like *shall* versus *will* or to use other linguistic features they do not use themselves, but it is impossible for them to do consistently because they will not always notice departures from rules they do not themselves follow. More importantly, they will not be consistent examples of superstandard features in their own speech.

middle-class English as prepositions at the end of sentences, the use of *who* in some constructions calling for the objective case, and the deletion of *are* in a question like *Where you going?*—features that would be excluded from formal Standard English—all are included when we speak of Standard English. To the extent that the speech of an educated Bostonian differs from that of an educated Atlantan, for example, we can speak of the standard *dialects* of American English. Nevertheless, there are many constructions and pronunciations that would be uniformly rejected as substandard by educated speakers in all parts of the country. These are the features which comprise what we will be calling Nonstandard English.

Perhaps the reason that language standardization seems to be inevitable in American society, as it is in most of the countries of the world, is because these norms appear to serve specific types of behavioral functions. Garvin and Mathiot (1956) have delimited several types of symbolic and objective functions of a standard language which may aid us in understanding why language standardization seems to be so inevitable. A standard language, in the first place, may serve a *unifying function* by linking an individual speaker with a larger community. Whereas the unifying function may unite individual speakers, what is identified as the *separatist function* opposes the standard language to other languages or varieties as a separate entity, thus potentially serving as a symbol of national identity. Weinreich (1953:100) points out that it is in a situation of language contact that people most easily become aware of the peculiarities of their language as against others, and in this situation the standardized language most readily becomes the symbol of group integrity. There is also a *prestige function* associated with a standard language. As Garvin and Mathiot observe,

> . . . one of the ways of achieving equality with an admired high-prestige nationality is to make one's own language "as good as theirs," which in our terms means bringing it closer to the ideal properties of a standard language.   (1956:788)

Whereas the previously mentioned functions are symbolic, an objective function served by a standard language is the *frame-of-reference function.* By providing a codified norm for correctness, speakers can be judged in terms of their conformity to that norm.

Garvin and Mathiot further point out that the functions of a standard language give rise to a set of cultural attitudes toward it. Related to the unifying and separatist functions of a standard language is an attitude of language loyalty; the prestige function produces an attitude of pride, and the frame-of-reference function results in an attitude of awareness of the norm.

Whatever reasons may account for the inevitability of language standardization, this fact must be realistically faced by sociolinguists. Linguists have sometimes objected to the notion of language standardization because of the imposition of prescriptive norms of "correctness"—norms that are opposed to the descriptive framework through which linguists approach language. The basic objection lies in the fact that values of social propriety are misinterpreted as value judgments concerning linguistic adequacy. Despite the philosophical validity of linguists' objections or their ethical preference to eliminate the notion of standard and nonstandard languages, we must realistically concede that the establishment of prescriptive norms for "correct" speech usage is an inevitable by-product of the awareness of behavioral norms of all types.

SUBJECTIVE REACTIONS TO SPEECH

As a concomitant of the premise that language standardization is inevitable, we must also assume that subjective reactions to speech are also unavoidable. Individuals do not respond to speech differences with objective detachment. Rather, they respond evaluatively based on their reactions to the social differences that language differences may imply for them. Thus, Northern middle-class white liberals who have stereotypic notions about segregation in the South may respond to Southern white speech with the same hostility that they feel when they see a rebel flag. And Southerners who have a stereotypic notion of Northern liberals may associate Northern middle-class speech with self-righteous crusaders. Generally, the speech behavior of a socially stigmatized group will be considered stigmatized and the speech behavior of socially prestigious groups will be considered high-prestige. When individuals react subjectively to the speech of a particular group, they are expressing their attitudinal reactions toward the behavioral patterns of that group on the basis of one behavioral manifestation—language. For example, the subjective reactions to lower-class black speech are, in reality, a reflection of a much more pervasive attitude toward the behavioral patterns of lower-class black culture. The rejection of speech must, therefore, be viewed in the wider context of cultural rejection.

The preceding paragraph deals with subjective reactions to speech behavior with respect to the interaction of different social groups on a vertical dimension (i.e., between superordinate and subordinate social groups), but it must also be pointed out that subjective reactions toward different types of speech events are also characteristic within a given social group, which constitutes a horizontal dimension. Within the ethnography of speaking, not only the forms of speech but the uses of speech may be viewed evaluatively. What this means is that within a given social group there will be rules for "good and bad manners" with respect to speech usage. Certain types of speech uses will be valued positively and others negatively. For example, *rapping* as it was originally used in black culture refers to a distinctively fluent and lively way of talking, characterized by a high degree of personal style (see Kochman 1969:27). As a manipulative use of the language, it is positively valued. On the other hand, *loud-mouthing* refers to the use of language in a forceful but non-manipulative way, and generally evokes a pejorative emotive response. In terms of vernacular culture, it is "bad speech manners." We must assume that for each social group there are indigenous values placed on certain uses of speech. It is the realization of a cultural value system with respect to speech that is the basis for subjective reactions to the form, content, and use of speech.

LANGUAGE VARIATION

We previously referred to the fact that everyone is aware that different situations call for different behavioral roles. With respect to language, this means that linguistic variation can be expected in response to different social situations just like nonverbal forms of behavior will vary according to the context. Labov has suggested that one of the fundamental sociolinguistic principles is that "there are no single-style speakers" (1970b:13). By this he means that every speaker will show some variation in phonological and grammatical rules according to the immediate context in which he is speaking.

In the process of enculturation, speakers acquire competence not only in a linguistic code but also in the use of certain variations which are dependent on social context. In contexts determined by some of the factors we mentioned previously, such as the relation of participants, settings, and topic, variations in speech can be expected. To put it another way, we must assume, in the sociolinguistic consideration of language, an "ethnography of speaking" (see Hymes 1962).

To assume that there will be some stylistic range for all individuals does not, however, imply that the same range and competence can be expected from different speakers. Labov notes:

> One must add of course that the stylistic range and competence of the speaker may vary greatly. Children may have a very narrow range in both the choices open to them and the social contexts they respond to. Old men often show a narrow range in that their motivation for style shifting disappears along with their concern for power relationships.
> (1970b:13)

Despite the variations in the range of styles between different speakers, it is most reasonable to assume that all speakers who have acquired a language system have also acquired some flexibility in the use of alternative structures within that system.

One may wonder, at this point, how the notion of stylistic variation relates to the distinction between what Bernstein (1964) has called the *restricted* and the *elaborated* code. Although some have taken this to mean that lower-class speakers are single-style speakers and middle-class speakers multistyle, this interpretation cannot be accepted. A closer look reveals that Bernstein is talking about relative, not absolute, reduction in the alternatives that are open in speech. (This relativity, in fact, is one reason why the notions of restricted and elaborated codes lose their usefulness in any attempt to solidify these concepts.) Bernstein maintains:

> ... with a restricted code, the range of alternatives, syntactic alternatives, is considerably reduced and so it is much more likely that prediction is possible. . . . In the case of elaborated code, the speech system requires a higher level of verbal planning for the preparation of speech than in the case of restricted code.   (1964:57)

That a particular social group may be "limited" to a restricted code does not mean that it has only one style of speech. Whatever criticisms one may make of the theoretical and methodological basis of Bernstein's research, it cannot be argued that restricted code refers to unistyle and elaborated to multistyle speakers. What he does say is that a difference in the range of grammatical alternatives may be related to social class; he is thus attempting to give one explanation to account for the observation that there are differing competencies with respect to stylistic ranges. The verification of this hypothesis, however, is still needed.

In the preceding discussion, we have explicated some of the basic assumptions underlying the behavioral role of language in society. What is essential here is the fact that the valid study of social dialects is based on two sets of premises, one dealing with the structure of the language system and one relating to the structure of society. It is the combination of these premises, which in many ways are interrelated, that is the foundation for sociolinguistic studies as they relate to social dialects.

2

SOCIAL DIALECTS
AS A FIELD OF INQUIRY

A History

Despite the fact that sociolinguistics has only recently been granted recognition as a field of scientific inquiry, awareness of the correlation between linguistic diversity and social status can be documented as far back as our first available records of social interaction. Any student of the classical languages can recall learning the distinction between different varieties of Greek or Latin. References to *koine,* or *common* Greek as opposed to *classical* Greek refer to the fact that different varieties of Greek were used in different eras by different social groups of Greeks. And the distinction between *vulgar* Latin and *classical* Latin refers to the fact that peasants spoke a vernacular variety of Latin while classical Latin persisted in the writings of the scholarly elite.

In the Western hemisphere, the recognition of language differences as one manifestation of social class can be traced back as far as the first recorded impressions of settlement in the New World. Many of the early English settlers were from the middle classes and they brought their linguistic prejudices concerning various British dialects with them. Because the London dialect had been accepted in most parts of England as the literary standard language by the end of the fifteenth century, any peasants who came to the New World were likely to be thought of as crude and without proper manners in the use of the English language. Linguistic manifestations of social differences, therefore, did not arise spontaneously in the United States but developed from a similar situation which existed in the British Isles. In fact, H. L. Mencken's classic description of American English in *The American Language* still recognizes the strong affinity between nonstandard speech in the United States and England.

> The American common speech, of course, is closely related grammatically to the vulgar dialects of the British Isles, and in many ways it is identical with them. In both one encounters the double negative, the use of the adjective as an adverb, the confusion of cases in the pronoun and of tenses in the verb, and various other violations of the polite canon. (1936:416)

The linguistic correlates of social differences were not only limited to British settlers who migrated to the New World; they were also observed with reference to the New World Negro. We thus observe that a British traveler to the American colonies wrote in the July 1746 edition of *The London Magazine:*

> One thing they [the English settlers] are very often faulty in, with regard to their children . . . is when young, they suffer them too much to prowl among the young Negroes, which insensibly causes them to imbibe their manners and broken speech.

It is obvious that throughout the history of the English language in America, the layman has recognized that social differences were often reflected in language differences. Scholars of the English language in America have also been quite aware of these differences. Terms such as *vulgar, uncultivated, common,* or *illiterate* speech all refer to what we now call Nonstandard English. For the most part, English scholars viewed these language varieties as deviations from acceptable usage, reflecting the same linguistic prejudice as the layman. For example, Mencken's lengthy chapter on what he calls common speech views it as undergoing "changes which set off the common speech very sharply from both correct English and correct American" (1936:427). Despite the theoretical and practical limitations of such a viewpoint, a number of these studies resulted in considerable amounts of data on characteristics of English that were considered nonstandard. This is particularly true of those studies, like Mencken's, which sought to study and describe the actual speech of the working classes rather than operate on a formal standard norm that did not coincide with actual usage of English by either the working or the middle classes.

ENGLISH LINGUISTICS

In the first half of the twentieth century, scholars of English who had some background in descriptive linguistics recognized the different levels of English usage without the evaluative connotations concerning its grammar. Thus, Charles Fries in his *American English Grammar* adopts the theoretical viewpoint outlined in Chapter One when he notes:

> This investigation and report assumes as its first principle this scientific point of view with its repudiation of the conventional attitude toward language errors. We shall, therefore, ignore the conventional classification of *mistakes* and *correct forms* and attempt to outline the types of differences that appear in our American language practices.   (1940:5)

From this perspective, Fries describes the use of English taken from the informal correspondence on file with the United States government. In his treatment, three main types of social groups were identified with respect to their use of English: Group I, referred to as *Standard English* users, was composed of subjects who were college graduates from reputable colleges and had professional occupations; Group II, referred to as *Common English* users, was composed of individuals with some formal education in high school who had neither professional occupations on the one hand nor strictly manual or unskilled occupations on the other; Group III, referred to as users of *Vulgar English,* was composed of subjects who had not passed beyond eighth grade and had occupations that were unskilled or manual. In addition to the differentiation of groups on the basis of occupation and education, certain formal matters in the letters themselves were used to determine the group classification. These included matters such as spelling, punctuation, and capitalization.

ENGLISH DIALECTOLOGY

For the most part, the linguistic description of social variation from the 1930s through the 50s was derived from the field of dialectology. American dialectologists recognized that social differences had to be considered even though the primary goal of dialect geography was the correlation of settlement history with regional varieties of English. Hans Kurath, the original director of the *Linguistic Atlas of the United States and Canada* when it began in 1930, was well aware that social differences intersected with settlement history and geographical differences to account for linguistic variation. As reported in the *Handbook of the Linguistic Geography of New England* in 1939, *Linguistic Atlas* fieldworkers divided informants into three main types as follows:

TYPE I   Little formal education, little reading, and restricted social contacts.

TYPE II   Better formal education (usually high school) and/or wider reading and social contacts.

TYPE III   Superior education (usually college), cultured background, wide reading and/or extensive social contacts.
(Kurath 1939:44)

In addition, each of the above types was subdivided as follows:

TYPE A   Aged, and/or regarded by the fieldworker as old-fashioned.

TYPE B   Middle-aged or younger, and/or regarded by the fieldworker as more modern.   (Kurath 1939:44)

As can be seen in these groups, the classification scheme roughly paralleled that of Fries, although certain of the criteria for categorization seemed a bit more vague. The social classifications were dependent on fieldworkers' judgments so that no real objective model for measuring social status was utilized. Education seemed to be primary, but it was only one of the various factors used by social scientists in rating social status. Perhaps more of a problem was the fact that the classification scheme could be applied tautologically. In some cases, the criteria for classifying groups of informants were not based on extraverbal behavior, but on the dependent variable of language itself. An interviewer might, therefore, apply his own subjective judgments about a person's speech to categorize his social group.

Despite some of the reservations regarding the *Linguistic Atlas* that we might have in retrospect, it made available tremendous amounts of material, which made possible other studies of dialect geography. Regional varieties of English were subsequently described not only in terms of their phonological, grammatical, and lexical patterns, but according to the social groups in particular regions. For example, McDavid's list of characteristic regional dialects in Francis's *The Structure of American English* (1958) includes the types of informants who use the forms within each dialect area. Thus, some characteristics of the South and South Midland dialects in the United States are given as follows:

MORPHOLOGY AND SYNTAX

you-all (second-person plural) I, II, III.
I might could I, II. (Also Pennsylvania German area.)
I'm not for sure I, II.
seed 'saw' (preterite of *see*) I.
a apple I, II. Apparently spreading.
I taken 'took' [I], II.
tuck (participle of *take*) I, [II].

holp 'helped' I, [II].
riz 'rose' I. (Also northeastern New England.)
div 'dived' I. (Also northeastern New England.)
mought 'might' I.
/-ɨz, -əz/ in plural ending of *fists, posts, costs* I.
perfective use of *done,* as *I('ve) done told you that* I, II.
bought bread I, II.
use to didn't I, II.   (Francis 1958:526)

In this inventory, the use of Roman numerals I, II, and III following
the form *you-all* refers to the fact that this item is used by South and South
Midland speakers of all social classes; I and II following the item *I might
could* refers to the fact that this item is used by the lowest and middle class,
but not the highest social class; and an item like *seed,* as a preterite form, is
used only by the lowest social class in this region.

Whereas the correlation of social and linguistic differences was of
secondary concern in the work of the *Linguistic Atlas,* later interpretation
of the *Atlas* data gave more direct attention to the importance of social
factors in accounting for linguistic diversity. Dialectologists, for the most
part, however, still seemed to appeal to the social parameter only when
"data proved too complicated to be explained by merely a geographical
statement of settlement history" (McDavid 1948:194). This tradition was
followed in many descriptions of dialects throughout the United States, and
is still the guiding principle for a number of dialectologists.

QUANTITATIVE STUDIES

A small study in the late 1950s on the social stratification of the
participle variants *-in* and *-ing* (e.g., *runnin'* versus *running*) by Professor
John Fischer was, in some ways, quite different from the tradition for
examining the social stratification of language established in dialect geography. Fischer examined variation in the use of *-ing* and *-in* in the speech of
New England children as a matter of "free variation." He noted that practically all of his informants used both of these forms to some extent. A
quantitative tabulation revealed that the relative frequency of these variants
was apparently related to sex, class, personality (aggressive/cooperative),
the formality of the conversation, and the specific verb used. This quantitative study of so-called free variation had not been examined previously.
This is not to say that dialectologists did not recognize optional forms, but
the actual frequency ratios with which optional forms might be used was
not generally tabulated. Fischer's correlation of frequency levels with a
number of social variables also cast a serious shadow on the notion of free
variation. In essence, he was saying that variation was a function of a
number of social constraints on speech.

SOCIAL DIALECTS AS A FIELD OF INQUIRY

It was probably Labov's work in the middle 1960s that provided the major impetus for much of the current sociolinguistic inquiry into social dialects. His study of the social stratification of English in New York City (1966) revealed a number of innovative aspects of the correlation of social class and language. Using a previously existing sociological model, he analyzed the speech of over a hundred randomly selected informants. Five different phonological variables (*oh, eh, r, th,* and *dh*) were correlated with the social stratification of the informants. Labov's first essential contribution was his use of a verifiable sociological model for evaluating social class. As naive as it may sound in retrospect, linguists prior to Labov who looked at the social stratification of English had usually been content to use an impressionistic classification of social class that would be quite unacceptable to a sociologist. Labov's research used a previously established sociological index for the measurement of social status. His use of randomly selected informants was also a departure from the established tradition of linguistics, because traditionally linguists sought out particular types of informants in a nonrandom fashion. In addition to his innovations in sampling procedure, Labov made important changes in the construction of the interview. He attempted to isolate four different contextual styles by giving different tasks in the interview and looking at the use of his phonological variables in each of the styles. First he observed casual style, a type of spontaneous talking style differentiated from more careful conversational style by what he called "channel cues" such as laughter, rhythm or tempo changes, heavy breathing, or conversation with a third party during the interview. Then, by having the informant read a short passage, he observed reading style. Finally, word lists were given in an effort to elicit the most formal style of speech. The end result showed a continuum of styles which ranged from formal to informal speech. Within each of these styles, Labov examined the relative frequency of variants. The notion of quantitative analysis in linguistics was, at this point, still quite exploratory despite Fischer's previous demonstration that the quantitative dimension must be examined in order to accurately assess certain types of language.

Labov's use of tape-recorded spontaneous conversation in his sociolinguistic analysis was another valuable innovation. In the tradition of the *Linguistic Atlas,* single items and any possible variants for these items were elicited, but no study was usually done of the use of these items in a spontaneous conversation. (At the time of the original *Linguistic Atlas* fieldwork, magnetic tape recorders were not available.) The methodological breakthroughs in Labov's study continue to have a significant impact on linguistics in general and sociolinguistics in particular.

Although Labov's methodological innovations have had great impact, his most important contribution was probably the theoretical viewpoint with which he approached the description of language in society. He repudiated the idea that his studies were simply attempts to correlate language differences with social variables. Instead, he saw them as endeavors to look at language in society to solve fundamental linguistic and sociological issues. He thus states in the preface to his dissertation, *The Social Stratification of English in New York City:*

> In the past few years, there has been considerable programmatic discussion of *sociolinguistics* at various meetings and symposia. If this term refers to the use of data from the speech community to solve problems of linguistic theory, then I would agree that it applies to the research described here. But *sociolinguistics* is more frequently used to suggest a new interdisciplinary field—the comprehensive description of the relations of language and society. This seems to me an unfortunate notion, foreshadowing a long series of purely descriptive studies with little bearing on the central theoretical problems of linguistics or of sociology. My own intention was to solve linguistic problems, bearing in mind that these are ultimately problems in the analysis of social behavior: the description of continuous variation, of overlapping and multi-layered phonemic systems; the subjective correlates of linguistic variation; the causes of linguistic differentiation and the mechanism of linguistic change.   (1966:v–vi)

Whereas previous studies of language in society were clearly on the periphery of both linguistics and sociology, the use of sociolinguistic data to solve central issues within these disciplines had significant implications. It meant that linguists could no longer afford the luxury of dismissing such studies as being without significance to fundamental issues in linguistics. The matter of variable rules, which will be discussed in Chapter Five, is one of these issues. Another issue of considerable theoretical significance relates to the dynamics of language change. From studies of linguistic variability, a paradigm has emerged which recognizes the integral function of variation in language change. There are a number of other specific theoretical issues which we might mention here, but there are also problems of a broader theoretical nature for which sociolinguistic research holds important insights. The investigation of "everyday speech" in sociolinguistics came at a time when linguistics was relying more and more on the intuitions of the native speaker as a sole basis for developing adequate grammars. Sociolinguistic studies have demonstrated that there is an important need to counterbalance intuition with empirical data from ordinary speech. At this level, we are dealing with a reaction against an extreme form of rationalism which emerged in some linguistic theories during the 1960s. The philosophical issues of rationalism and empiricism are at the very center of one's view of language. And of course we know that these issues extend much further than language. Although some sociolinguistic studies have not concerned themselves with theoretical issues of the sort mentioned here, it is quite apparent that these investigations hold great potential for solving such central theoretical issues.

Nonstandard Dialects

Although a number of scholars during the 60s investigated language variation across a range of social classes, some researchers concentrated on describing nonstandard varieties of English. A few nonstandard white dialects were included in these studies, but the variety that received the most attention by far was Vernacular Black English. There are several apparent reasons for this concern. In the first place, there was a growing interest in minority-group education during this decade. A number of educational programs funded by federal funds and private foundations set out to develop programs for educating low-income minority-group people. Part of this education process naturally involved language. The language differences between many lower-class black students in these programs and their middle-class counterparts became immediately apparent. This was particularly true in Northern urban areas, where the Southern origin of many blacks resulted in dialect patterns which differed substantially from the Northern varieties spoken in the surrounding white community. Linguistic description, from this standpoint, was considered as a preliminary to the development of adequate education programs in language. Because education in this country is highly sensitive to political pressures, the concern for Vernacular Black English in education must be viewed on a deeper level as the outgrowth of a particular sociopolitical climate.

Apart from the utilitarian motives for such studies, there was a simple descriptive basis for this interest. Some investigators attempted to combine the educational and linguistic concerns, while others were only interested in linguistic description of nonstandard varieties. From the standpoint of linguistic diversity, Vernacular Black English seemed somewhat more divergent from Standard English than most corresponding white nonstandard dialects. In the study of nonstandard dialects, it seemed reasonable to start with the more diverse dialects. This is particularly true given the overlapping nature of various nonstandard dialects of English. Vernacular Black English includes many features also found in corresponding white nonstandards. At the same time it has features that appear unique to this dialect. The overlapping relationship between several nonstandard dialects and Standard English is diagrammed roughly in Figure 2-1.

If we have considerable overlap between various nonstandard dialects, as we obviously do, it is reasonable to start describing these varieties by giving descriptive priority to the more diverse ones. Starting at the furthest point, other nonstandard dialects may then be seen as subsets within the continuum of divergency. In other words, the most efficient way of arriving at a comprehensive catalogue of the characteristics of nonstandard dialects is to begin by describing the variety that overlaps other nonstandard

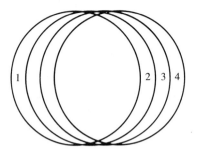

1. Standard English
2. Northern white nonstandard English
3. Southern white nonstandard English
4. Vernacular Black English

Figure 2-1. Relationship among several nonstandard dialects and Standard English.

dialects while diverging most from Standard English. In this respect, Vernacular Black English seemed to be ideal.

Concentration on more divergent nonstandard varieties also may be seen in the light of some of the theoretical issues that have arisen from the study of dialects in social space. For example, the observed fluctuation between forms in Vernacular Black English served as a convenient proving ground for the investigation of linguistic variability in relation to formal grammar rules. From the standpoint of theoretical linguistics, this is the most important issue that arose from the descriptive account of Vernacular Black English by Labov et al. (1968). The description of more divergent dialect varieties also turned out to be of considerable interest to linguists who became concerned with writing language grammars which formally admitted the existence of different dialects within the same grammar. For example, the development of a "panlectal" grammar by Charles-James N. Bailey (1972) relies heavily on these descriptive accounts as a data source for constructing such a grammar.

Finally, the descriptive interest in Vernacular Black English during the past decade must be seen as a consequence of the controversy that arose over its origin. During the 1960s, the traditional position that blacks simply spoke a variety of Southern English identical to that spoken by whites of a comparable socioeconomic class was seriously questioned by a group of scholars who had been studying various creole situations. Although Lorenzo Turner, during the 1930s and 40s, demonstrated that African survivals could be found in Gullah or Geechee, a creole spoken by blacks off the South Carolina and Georgia coasts, this situation was typically considered to be a linguistic anomaly when compared with other varieties of black speech found in the United States. But creolists such as William A. Stewart (1967, 1968b), Beryl Bailey (1965), and J. L. Dillard (1967, 1972), all of whom had been studying creole languages in various parts of the Western hemisphere, noted a number of similarities between some of the features they had found in their previous creole studies and varieties of Vernacular

Black English. On this basis it was suggested that Vernacular Black English was derived from a creole predecessor which, in many ways, was quite similar to those creoles still spoken in the Western hemisphere today. Descriptive accounts of this variety became important to demonstrate the fact that there were still traces of this creole predecessor. The history was important in explaining why this variety was more divergent from white nonstandard varieties of English. During the latter part of the 60s, the controversy over the origin of Vernacular Black English heightened as some dialectologists continued to maintain that Vernacular Black English was simply a Southern variety of English ultimately derived from British dialects. The controversy has still not subsided and it appears that it will be a live issue for some time to come. Whatever the ultimate outcome of this controversy, it must be cited as one of the essential reasons why there has been so much interest in describing Vernacular Black English.

These concerns, sometimes combined and other times isolated, led to some fairly exhaustive descriptions of various aspects of Vernacular Black English. Studies by Labov et al. (1968), Anshen (1969), Wolfram (1969), Mitchell-Kernan (1970), Legum et al. (1971), Fasold (1972), Dillard (1972), and Tarone (1972) all have contributed to our descriptive understanding of different aspects of this variety. Somewhat ironically, the descriptive concern for Vernacular Black English has now placed us in a position where we have more descriptive information about this dialect than we do for a number of the white nonstandard varieties. Our current data on other nonstandard dialects tend to be much more fragmentary and incomplete. There does, however, appear to be a growing concern for different nonstandard varieties, for example, rural white nonstandard varieties, including both the deep South and Appalachia (e.g., Hackenberg 1972; Davis 1971). It is expected that during the 1970s our descriptive knowledge of these varieties will be expanded considerably. Nonstandard dialect varieties which emerge from certain types of language contact situations are also beginning to receive some attention. Ma and Herasimchuk's (in Fishman et al. 1971) description of linguistic variables in a Puerto Rican bilingual community considered this dimension to some extent, while the nonstandard varieties of Puerto Rican English among second-generation males was the concern of Wolfram et al. (1971, 1973). No doubt we will soon have similar studies of nonstandard Indian varieties (see Leap 1973) and Chicano English. Given the current interest in this area, many more comprehensive descriptive studies can be expected to emerge during the current decade.

3

FIELD METHODS IN THE
STUDY OF SOCIAL DIALECTS

In the previous chapters, we have presented a background for the current study of social dialects in the United States. At this point, it may be asked how we collect our data for the analysis of these dialects. How do we obtain accurate and useful sociolinguistic information? This basic question directs our attention to field procedures for investigating social dialects.

In our attempt to collect meaningful data, there are two major areas of concern: (1) the choice of a sample population and (2) the elicitation of adequate speech data.

The Sample

When a sociolinguist decides to describe the speech behavior of a particular population, he is faced with the problem of defining his universe in such a way as to ensure that his observations adequately represent the population. The first decision he must make, therefore, is to delimit the population from which his sample will be drawn. In some cases, it is quite possible to choose a population that is already defined in terms of some arbitrary boundary, such as a geographical one. For example, we may decide that we are going to study the speech of a given locale, such as Detroit, Michigan, Rochester, New York, or Meadville, Mississippi. For a population of this type, the boundaries of our universe have already been established for us, so that our only task is to select a representative sample from that population. In other cases, we may want to describe the speech behavior of a population defined socially rather than geographically, such as a lower-class inner-city group. If this is our universe, then we need to establish the boundary on the basis of criteria such as social class, age, and so forth. Once we have established who qualifies according to our social criteria, we can decide how to obtain a representative sample of this population.

In some types of sociological studies, *random sampling* is used, in which each person in the total population has an equal chance of being selected for the sample. Random sampling, however, should not be equated with haphazard or casual selection. It is an organized procedure for choosing the informants in such a way as to eliminate selection bias. One of the traditional ways of obtaining an authentic random sample is through the use of a table of random numbers. This procedure relies on the assignment of a number to each individual in the population. The investigator can then use a table of random numbers, simply following the numbers in consecutive order. (Tables of random numbers can be found in most basic statistics textbooks.) Each individual with an assigned number corresponding to the one selected in the list of random numbers is then chosen for the sample, until the researcher arrives at the number of informants he desires for his study.

Although a list of random numbers is often used in random sampling, this is not the only procedure that can be utilized. The researcher can simply designate every *n*th unit in his population for study; for example, every fifth, tenth, twentieth, hundredth, or other *n,* depending on the ratio of the total population that he chooses for his sample.

Strict random samples, though advantageous for some reasons, have limitations for the investigation of social dialects. They often include numbers of subjects whose speech cannot be considered because they are recent immigrants from another section of the United States or from another country. Labov notes the various types of problems faced by the sociolinguist when dependent on a strict random sample:

> A trial random sample of my own involved counting every tenth building in a block, and calling on every seventh apartment. This method seemed to be free from bias, but did not enable me to choose my informants randomly within the family, nor could I predict how large an area I would be able to cover by this method before available resources were expended. Most importantly, any sampling on this basis would be unable to discriminate between native speakers and foreign language speakers, and a great deal of effort would be spent on fruitless calls on the latter type of resident.   (1966:201)

A strict random sample should also result in the representation of population proportionately with respect to the various social groups. For example, if there are large numbers of middle-class whites in a particular area but few working-class whites, this should be represented in the sample. In some cases, this may result in excessive numbers of subjects representing one group while another group is underrepresented for the sake of a sociolinguistic analysis.

As an alternative to strict random sampling, it is often more efficient to obtain a representative sample for predetermined social categories. In this procedure, the social composition of the sample is first determined, then informants are chosen to represent these categories, which are sometimes referred to as *cells* of the sample. Informants can be chosen randomly until an adequate number is obtained to represent each cell. This procedure avoids the problem of over- and underrepresentation for particular social categories, because the investigator stops selecting informants for given cells when a quota is reached. To illustrate, we might set up a hypothetical study in which we decide to investigate the variables of social class, sex, age, and ethnicity. We choose to have a sample representing four social classes, both sexes, three age groups, and both black and white subjects. If we want each of the logically possible social categories represented in our sample, we will have a sample distribution as in Figure 3-1.

In our sample, we want to make sure that all cells (e.g., upper middle-class white 10 to 12-year-old females or lower working-class black 25 to 35-year-old males) are adequately represented, so we choose only a given

	White						Black					
	Male			Female			Male			Female		
	10–12	14–17	25–35	10–12	14–17	25–35	10–12	14–17	25–35	10–12	14–17	25–35
Upper Mid. Class												
Lower Mid. Class												
Upper Work. Class												
Lower Work. Class												

Figure 3-1. Sample distribution of logically possible social categories in a hypothetical field project design.

number of informants for each. The total number of cells in the sample is the number of categories of each social variable multiplied by each other. There are four social classes multiplied by two races, two sexes, and three age groups, and so the total number of cells is 48, $4 \times 2 \times 2 \times 3 = 48$. When speaking of a sample of this type, it is more crucial to speak of the number of informants in each cell than of the total number of informants. For example, if we just had 5 informants in each of the cells in our sample, we would have a sample of 240 subjects. But if we were conducting a study of sex differences in the speech of lower-class whites, we would have only one variable. In this case, a total of 100 subjects would be divided equally into categories of 50 males and 50 females. Thus the total sample in this instance would be considerably smaller, but the representation in each of the two cells much greater. If we have a large number of cells, it may be possible to collapse some of them for some types of analysis, but an analysis of the effect of all the intersecting variables on each other will require adequate representation of all of our cells.

The question of optimal sample size for the study of social dialects is still undertermined. On the one hand, there is the tradition of linguistics which generally relies on very small samples. In some cases, one or just a few individuals serve as informants, and sometimes the linguist acts as his own informant. On the other hand, the tradition of sociological surveys is to have rather substantial numbers of subjects, often in the hundreds or thousands. The investigation of social dialects must rely on samples that are somewhere in between these two traditions. It is, however, difficult to even approximate what might be a reasonable number of informants in each cell. There are both theoretical and practical considerations. To a certain extent, the size of the sample is dependent upon how homogeneous behavior can be expected to be. The more homogeneous the behavior, the smaller the sample may be. It appears that linguistic behavior is considerably more homogeneous that some other types of behavior, so that we might obtain a reliable sample by using a smaller sample than some types of sociological surveys. Linguists have a tradition of assuming that the speech of a few informants may be sufficient to represent a language system, but exactly how many informants is sufficient in each cell is still difficult to predict for a given study. In part, the size depends on the type of socio-linguistic problem with which we are dealing. If, for example, we are dealing with subjective reactions to speech through a formal questionnaire, there is no reason why we cannot use samples that are rather large in size. A requirement of 10 to 20 subjects in each cell would appear to be a minimum in such a case if we expect to arrive at statistically significant results. On the other hand, if we are doing a quantitative analysis of linguistic variables of the type undertaken by Labov et al. (1968), Wolfram (1969, 1973), or Fasold (1972), the sample must be limited in size for quite practical reasons. As we shall see in Chapter Four, this type of analysis requires detailed extraction of speech data. The simple procedure of extraction may take several days for each informant, so that a comprehensive analysis of hundreds of tapes is precluded if we are to complete our analysis within a reasonable amount of time. The larger the sample, of course, the more social variables we can examine and the more confidence we can have in our conclusions, but there are sometimes practical limitations of time. It appears, however, that if we have fewer than five informants in each cell for this type of analysis, we run the risk of getting quite skewed results.

So far we have referred only to samples dependent on some type of random selection procedure. But there are studies in social dialects for which we may wish to abandon randomness completely in favor of some structured pattern of informant selection based on other criteria. For example, Labov and his associates' most insightful linguistic data on black adolescent speech in Harlem came not from his random sample, but from his study of selected peer groups. The selection of peer-group informants is described by him as follows:

> The next step in approaching the NNE peer group and its use of the basic vernacular was to study a particular recreation center in detail. . . . In the initial series of discussions and interviews, we located one major peer group at the Stephen Foster Center, and began to study it using the "S-G-S" [Sociogram Scale] paradigm. . . . When we speak of "members" of the group, we mean the peer-group structure formed by the daily activities of the boys, and most clearly by the hang-out patterns. (1968:31)

The sociogram technique mentioned by Labov involves the objective presentation of relationships within groups. It is a diagram showing the informal group structure, including such elements as friendship patterns and the position of each individual among individuals in the group. The actual questions used in sociogram analysis may vary from study to study, but typical types of questions concern friendship and leadership choices within the group. (See Broom and Selznick 1963 for a more complete description of the technique.) If we are interested in peer-group speech patterns, this type of informant selection is obviously preferred over a random sample.

The crucial consideration in selecting a sample is the goal of the research. If our goal is to describe peer-group adolescent black speech in Harlem, for example, our essential goal is to define the sample in terms of criteria related to the establishment of peer groups. But if we desire to describe the various social parameters of social stratification in the speech of several classes of adult New Yorkers, we want quite a different type of sample. Our sample cannot be selected without prior consideration of what social parameters of speech we want to examine.

SOCIAL STATUS

Any study that attempts to correlate linguistic behavior with social stratification must have not only a clear-cut delimitation of the linguistic data, but valid delimitation of social strata as well. We need to know what the various social levels in a community are, and how we can measure a given individual's status in terms of these levels. In some cases, we may desire to delimit the various social levels before we begin our linguistic analysis, so that we can correlate our linguistic variables with predetermined social levels (see Wolfram 1969). In other cases, it may be advantageous to first delimit the population on the basis of linguistic differences, then examine the social characteristics of the various linguistic groups (see Bickerton 1971). Or we may use a combination, starting with a finely stratified group of informants but combining and manipulating the social groups in such a way as to most clearly reveal patterns of correlation between linguistic phenomena and social stratification (see Labov 1966).

Whatever procedure we choose for the delimitation of social levels, we need a reliable method for assessing social stratification. The essential question is, how do we assess the relative social rank of individuals in the community? There are two main types of procedures for doing this—those dependent on the objective measurement of an outside investigator and those dependent upon the subjective evaluations of the community participants themselves.

OBJECTIVE MEASUREMENTS. The objective approach to the study of social stratification is based on the detailed observation of the various strata that exist in a community, regardless of whether or not the strata are recognized by the members. The researcher "stands outside" the community and attempts to determine the criteria that will divide it into the strata most significantly affecting social behavior. One of the most common types of objective evaluation involves the use of what Warner (1960) has called the Index of Status Characteristics (ISC). The ISC is primarily an index of certain socioeconomic factors. Most typically, the criteria used for evaluating subjects are occupation, education, income, house type, and dwelling area. For each of these criteria arbitrary divisions are set up so that a ranking is given in each area. For example, occupations may be divided into seven categories, described roughly as follows:

CLASS	OCCUPATION
1	Major professionals Executives of large concerns
2	Lesser professionals Executives of medium-sized concerns
3	Semi-professionals Administrators of small businesses

CLASS	OCCUPATION
4	Technicians
	Owners of petty businesses
5	Skilled workmen
6	Semi-skilled workmen
7	Unskilled workers (Shuy, Wolfram, and Riley 1968:12)

A fairly typical delimitation of educational rank is given in the following list:

CLASS	LEVEL OF EDUCATION
1	Any graduate degree (professional)
2	College graduation (four-year)
3	One year or more of college
4	High school graduation
5	Some high school (tenth grade up)
6	Junior high school (seventh through ninth)
7	Less than seven years of school
	(Shuy, Wolfram, and Riley 1968:12)

Two types of income indices are commonly used in ISC evaluations—those which delimit actual salary levels (e.g., above $30,000, $20,000–$30,000, etc.) and those which delimit the source of the income (e.g., inherited income, profits and fees, etc.). The source of the income is often more reliable than the actual income levels because income levels can become outdated quite rapidly and actual income is not always commensurate with status.

Two types of residency scales are also used, one relating to the individual house type and one to the more general dwelling area. With reference to house type, characteristics such as size, condition, number of inhabitants per room, and plumbing are considered. Dwelling area refers to overall neighborhood conditions (such as nondeteriorating single homes with spacious yards or deteriorating block homes with no yards). Although this type of evaluation may appear to be dependent on the personal impressions of the evaluators, quite objective measures can be set up on the basis of various census tract data.

All ISC evaluation measures do not use the same criteria, so that one study may use the scales of occupation, education, and residency whereas another may use occupation, house type, and dwelling area. It is also possible to assign different values to the various scales used in assessing an overall status ranking. Occupation, for example, may be weighted more heavily than education and residency in computing an overall ISC score. In the Detroit Dialect Study, which used the criteria of occupation, education, and residency to evaluate social status, the following procedure was employed to obtain an ISC rank:

> At this point, each informant had three rating numbers: (a) a rating from one to seven on education; (b) a rating from one to seven on occupation; and (c) a rating from one to six on residence. These numbers were then multiplied by factors of 5, 9, and 6, respectively, the sum of these numbers being the informant's position on the scale. For instance, a lawyer who lived in a Class I neighborhood would receive a 1 for education, a 1 for occupation, and a 1 for residence. Multiplied by 5, 9, and 6 respectively, these give a combined score of 20. For a person rated 7 on both education and occupation (a laborer with a third grade education, for example), with a house in a Class VI neighborhood, the score is 134. Obviously, the lower the number the higher the prestige, and vice versa.
> (Shuy, Wolfram, and Riley 1968:15)

Once overall scores are computed, it is possible to divide the population into discrete social levels. In the Detroit study cited above, subjects who had status scores between 20 and 48 were classified as upper middle class, those with scores between 49 and 77 lower middle class, those with scores between 78 and 106 upper working class, and those between 107 and 134 lower working class. Subjects whose scores fall at the lower or upper ranges of an individual level are generally considered marginal, so that an individual with a status index score of 76 would be considered as marginally between upper working and lower middle class.

The use of ISC for the measurement of social status is based on two propositions: (1) that certain economic factors are closely correlated with social status, and (2) that these social and economic factors are translated into social-class behavior acceptable to the members of any given level of the community (Warner 1960:39). ISC presumes a set of values and behavioral patterns. Because it is an indirect method for assessing social class, we must expect that some discrepancies will, of course, occur—some individuals who are given a particular status ranking on an ISC may reflect behavioral characteristics more typical of individuals of a different socioeconomic level.

The fact that ISC is an indirect way of getting at social class is one of the weaknesses of the procedure. It is actual behavioral patterns that are the basis of social class, not an objective ranking on selected socioeconomic indices. The general applicability of objective socioeconomic measures may also vary considerably from community to community. This is particularly true with respect to applicability for various ethnic groups. For example, how important should occupation be considered in the black community, given the history of discrimination which has kept blacks from job opportunities commensurate with their abilities? Even if such scales are applicable to the black community, their weighting may be considerably different from that for the white community. For example, education (not only the amount, but where it was obtained) appears to be more heavily weighted than occupation for some black communities. Various adjustments must be made in ISC weighing from region to region for any group, but quite substantial adjustments may be necessary for its application to various ethnic groups.

Although the ISC method is the most commonly used objective measurement of social stratification, there are other objective approaches not exclusively dependent on socioeconomic ranking. It is quite possible to examine certain types of institutional membership and differential social roles in a community, for example. An investigator may look at such things as church membership, leisure-time activities, or community organizations. In these cases the total configuration of institutional membership is considered, because various affiliations will often imply each other. On the basis of these configurations, different social groupings can be established. On a large scale, this type of objective measurement is not as simple as ISC and is not used nearly as frequently, despite the fact that it is probably more directly related to social class than the simple measurement of economic factors.

SUBJECTIVE EVALUATION. One of the major criticisms of an exclusively objective approach to the measurement of social status is the fact that the differentiation of social strata is determined on the basis of an outsider's criteria. Ultimately, however, the real discriminators of social class are the members of the community themselves. From one perspective, social classes exist because the members of the community believe that they exist. If the community members are the real determiners of social class, then it stands to reason that their judgments about social class might be the primary basis for class delimitation. The method of subjective evaluation referred to by Warner as Evaluated Participation (EP) is based on this proposition. It assumes that the members are implicitly or explicitly aware of the social rank of those around them and can evaluate their social participation into social-class ratings. The investigator asks the community members how they rate each other (and, in some instances, themselves) in terms of social-class categories recognized within the community. This can be done in a number of ways. (For specific details consult Warner 1960.) For example, it is possible to rate informants on the basis of status reputation. Using this technique, community members are asked to evaluate personal acquaintances on the basis of certain imputed character traits. One person may be thought to be "from the wrong side of the tracks" whereas another may be thought of as "upper crust." A community member may be asked to designate his own social categories and then rank other community members. Individuals can also be asked to rate themselves and other community members above or below them in the social hierarchy. This not only gives an indication of how they view other people in terms of social class but also shows how they view themselves. Class is a concept that is generally recognized throughout American society, and a valid picture of social rank would appear to take into account the perceptions of class from the participants within the community class structure.

Although the use of EP techniques seems to avoid some of the pitfalls of the objective approaches, there are both theoretical and practical questions that can be raised concerning their use. We may, for example, receive quite different pictures of social class itself from the various classes—the lower classes may perceive social class quite differently from the upper classes. Which of these reflects an accurate picture, or are there as many structures as there are classes looking at them? We must also recognize that we may not receive a consistent picture of the divisions of social class. One community member may believe there are five social classes and another, three. Are we justified in assuming that the majority opinion of social-class divisions is necessarily the authentic one? These are the kinds of questions that researchers who use an EP procedure must deal with on a theoretical level.

On a practical level, the sociolinguist who wants to use EP as the basis for differentiating social class must recognize that it assumes a certain knowledge of the community beforehand. He must also know the community members who are ranked by a given member. It is difficult to use an EP procedure on a large scale because of the ethnographic knowledge that it presumes.

Ideally, an accurate assessment of social class should combine subjective and objective measurements of many types of behavioral roles and values. For sociolinguistic studies, this is often precluded because of the enormous task this is in itself. Where convenient, it appears reasonable to utilize sociological or anthropological studies that have previously delimited various social strata. This is the procedure, for example, that Labov (1966) adopted in his study of social stratification of English in New York City and that Shuy, Wolfram, and Riley (1966) followed in their study of Detroit speech. Not only does it provide a more practical solution to what may be a very time-consuming problem, but it provides a base for examining the validity of social-class distinctions as reflected in the linguistic data.

Elicitation of Data

Once we decide *who* we want to interview, the next step in research on social dialects is to elicit the data that we want. No study of social dialects can hope to succeed without having adequate data for analysis. As we shall see later, there are a number of different types of data and methods for collecting this data at the disposal of the fieldworker. Before discussing these methods, however, it is appropriate to consider the ethics of fieldwork in sociolinguistics.

FIELDWORK ETHICS

In recent years, the question of fieldwork ethics has become increasingly important to social scientists and the communities in which they carry out their research. Unfortunately, suspicions have been aroused because some social scientists have misrepresented their intentions to the community or obtained their data through devious means. Understandably, some communities have thus become reticent about cooperating in research projects in which they feel they may be exploited. As a result, an increasing number of professional organizations have come to realize that it is their responsibility to set ethical guidelines concerning data collection.

The first question that arises with respect to an investigator is the role that he assumes in the community. Samarin notes:

> There are obviously questions of ethics when one assumes a role and states a purpose in a community. The first one concerns the ethics of role-playing itself. Is it deceitful to assume a role which is in conformity to the local role expectations even when these are far removed from the explicit purpose of the research? The answer to this question will be decided in part by the amount of disparity there is between the role and the purpose. It will be decided also by the expectations of the community. It is not unethical to act in harmony with these expectations.
>
> (1967:61)

To assume a natural role in a community as a means of establishing rapport appears to be quite appropriate, but it is possible for the portrayal of a role for the exclusive purpose of obtaining information to be deceptive and unethical. Much depends on the role one is fulfilling. For example, when one of the authors was investigating the sociolinguistics of glossolalia ("speaking in tongues") among some New England church groups, it would have been possible for him to assume a role as a participant. The productive skill in glossolalia, however, had no religious significance for him. To assume a role as a glossolalist would, no doubt, have helped in the acquisition of data, but this role would have been out of harmony with his own religious beliefs and would have offended the group had they discovered the fraud. It was, therefore, considered inappropriate role-playing.

On the other hand, the same author has participated in "pick-up" basketball games with informants he wanted to interview during the course of research on social dialects of English. This activity, however, is a natural one for him to engage in, because he still actively plays pick-up basketball games in his leisure time. His participation helped establish rapport with informants and set a casual atmosphere for an interview situation. To adopt this sort of role was not seen as inappropriate, because it was an extension of a natural role, used to alleviate suspicion and create an informal setting.

It should be mentioned that *natural* membership within a group (such as an ethnic group, for example) no more justifies deceit in obtaining data than does pretended membership—in fact, it may be even more pretentious.

Once we have assumed a role in the community, we may ask how we should represent our research to the informants specifically and to the community in general. To what extent is a social scientist responsible for telling his informants exactly what he is doing? One option, of course, is to simply deceive the informants and tell them that we are interviewing for another purpose. This is a practice that social scientists have used in the past, and it is one of the reasons that some communities are suspicious of researchers. Unless we actually intend to investigate the information that we tell the informant we are interested in, this procedure seems unwarranted. On the other hand, there is no need to relate all the precise details of our research. Many of these are irrelevant to the informant. We should be able to reach a compromise without a boring account of all the details. In our recent study of the English of second-generation Puerto Ricans in Harlem, we typically represented our research in the following manner:

> We're interested in what teenagers in different parts of the country are interested in. For example, I'm from Philadelphia and we don't fly pigeons from the top of buildings there so I'm interested in how you do it. We're also interested in how teenagers think about some things, because they look at things differently. For example, teenagers use different words and stuff when they're talking so that we're interested in how teenagers talk and think about some things. We're going to tape record it because we can't remember all the things you might say. . . .
>
> (Wolfram et al. 1971:14)

In this explanation, we did not attempt to disguise our interest in language or culture, but we were nonspecific in talking about the type of language diversity in which we were interested. In most cases, we found that this type of explanation was satisfactory, but any questions were answered by honest but nondetailed comments.

Our representation of interests to informants is often more problematic once the interview has started. We sometimes project interest in the subject matter when what we are really interested in is how the person talks. Are we being dishonest with the informant? In order to elicit speech, we must project personal empathy concerning the informant's interests, and more often than not we do find ourselves quite engrossed in the subject matter, whether it is our central purpose or not. A necessary qualification of a good researcher and interviewer is an honest and sincere interest in his subject and in those who aid him in his study of it.

Another matter that must be considered by fieldworkers is the recording of interviews. Current types of analysis in the study of social dialects make it virtually impossible to operate without tape-recording speech. Are we obligated to tell the informant that he is being tape-recorded? Even though it may present obstacles in obtaining speech samples, we are invading a person's right of privacy unless we do so. Although we may argue that we are not going to use the speech we obtain via a hidden tape recorder or video camera for any exploitative purposes, we still do not have the right to record a person's speech if for some reason he is against it. In some cases, it may be appropriate to "bug" a room after the informants have been forewarned that this is planned, but all those who are being tape-recorded should be so informed before the fact. Constraints that may arise from the presence of a tape recorder must be neutralized by means other than the deception of informants.

Finally, we must mention the matter of confidence. It is surprising how much privileged information some people will share with an empathetic fieldworker; however, this is given in confidence and should not be used in any way to exploit the informant. Our task is to analyze speech and we should keep in mind that this is why the informant has consented to the interview. What happens if we obtain certain types of information concerning illegal activity (e.g., narcotics, delinquency, etc.) during the course of the interview? In these cases, it seems appropriate to view our role as that of the priest in a confessional, unless there are some very extenuating circumstances to warrant otherwise. Social scientists have an obligation to keep privileged information in the confidence that the informant assumed when he disclosed it.

Obligations to informants also include obtaining proper permission to conduct interviews. If we are conducting research within a school system, we must follow the specified procedures for obtaining this permission. And, in the case of minors, this often involves getting written consent from parents or guardians before conducting our interviews.

At this point, having discussed the very important area of ethics in fieldwork, we return to discussion of the actual strategies used in eliciting meaningful data in investigations of social dialects.

SPONTANEOUS INTERVIEWS

The spontaneous or free conversation interview is basic to current sociolinguistic research for a reasonable approximation of how language is actually used. Obtaining data from relatively casual contexts is crucial for current types of sociolinguistic analysis. It serves, for example, as the basis for much of the quantitative tabulation which some types of sociolinguistic analysis call for. Unfortunately, the very fact that a person is being interviewed and tape-recorded is a formidable obstacle to obtaining casual speech. Labov refers to this problem as *the observer's paradox:* "To obtain the data most important for linguistic theory, we have to observe how people speak when they are not being observed" (1972:113). By using various techniques, it is possible to neutralize the natural obstacles inherent in any interview situation. The goal of spontaneous interviewing is quite straightforward and simple: the interviewer wants to get as much free conversation as possible. He wants the informant to focus on the topic of his conversation so that he pays minimal attention to the way he is speaking. The less attention paid to his speech, the more informal and natural we can expect his speech to be. In most cases, this means that what informants talk about is less important than the fact that they talk. Therefore, lengthy narratives are tolerated, and in fact encouraged, even though they may be tangential to the specific questions asked.

INDIVIDUAL INTERVIEWS. Although fieldworkers must realize the limitations in recording a free conversation with an informant in a one-to-one situation, the effectiveness of this technique should not be underestimated. People like to talk about themselves, and if they are not threatened by the situation many people can become interesting conversationalists even in this type of interview. The fieldworker is a captive audience and if the informant feels him respond to his interests, he will usually give more than adequate amounts of conversation. There are, of course, informants who are reticent about talking because of either the artificial situation or their personal inhibitions, but even the most skilled interviewers will have difficulty obtaining adequate free conversation from these individuals. For the most part, they constitute a small minority of interviews.

A spontaneous conversation calls for considerable flexibility in what the informant talks about, but this should not be interpreted to mean that no general outline is followed for eliciting conversation. Certain types of questions (not always the ones we might predict beforehand) tend to naturally elicit conversation more readily than others. It is possible to informally direct an interview in such a way as to get specific types of sociological information about such things as the informant's peer associations, social status, and general patterning of social interactions, as well as to obtain a natural representation of certain types of linguistic structures. Suppose we wanted to ensure that there was an adequate representation of past-tense constructions in our interview. This could be accomplished by asking the informant to relate an incident from the past. On the other hand, if we wanted to get a representation of present-tense forms, we would have to make sure that we had adequate conversation about present-time activities. In our analysis of the use of invariant *be* in Black English, we observed that its occurrence was often concentrated in stories about the way in which children's games were played (e.g., *We run and hide and the last person that get to base, they be it*). This observation was a cue to the type of conversations from which we might hope to elicit its usage. Our informal direction of spontaneous conversation, then, can elicit both sociological and linguistic data.

There is obviously no certain guarantee for success in the elicitation of free conversation. The observation of certain general common-sense principles, however, may help us to get a maximum amount of conversation. Following are some of the principles that can help obtain free conversation.

1. The use of questions that must be answered by conversation rather than yes–no answers. For obvious reasons, questions that can be answered by yes or no replies are not the most efficient means of getting adequate samples of free conversation. Questions that elicit narratives or descriptive accounts must be used. For example, if we want to discuss children's leisure-time games, we would not ask questions such as "Did you play hide and seek?" or "Did you play kick the can?" Rather, we would make requests like "Describe the types of games you played as a child" or "Tell me how you played hide and seek, because there are different ways of playing it."

2. The use of questions to which informants can relate. General sets of questions must be adapted according to a number of informant variables, including a person's class, sex, age, ethnicity, and personal interests. Flexibility in this regard is the earmark of the successful interviewer. The use of questions to which informants can easily relate assumes that we have a certain pre-knowledge of the community in which we are interviewing. An interviewer in an inner-city, suburban, or rural area must be aware of the different types of indigenous activities and interests of the respective groups. For example, in inner-city New York, some of our most elegant descriptions of recreational activities involve the hobby of breeding, raising, and training homing pigeons. This activity requires specialized knowledge; it can sometimes elicit long and animated accounts from involved informants. Following is an excerpt from one of our interviews conducted in the study of English used by second-generation Puerto Ricans in East Harlem, New York.

> O yeah, I got a birdcage. You go like, you go up on the roof, you know, and you get like some boxes or some wood and some nail on stuff and you start building a bird coop. And then you go to the store and you buy round two birds and keep them in the bird coop for a long time so they can get used to it and make like a certain whistle, you know, make a certain whistle for them, and then, you know, you keep on whistling that and

they get use to it and you let them fly out one day and they start flying around in circles over the roof; and you whistle to them and they come right back in, and then after that, you let them go one day and they come back with some more birds and you lock those up in there. Yeah, you lock those birds up in there and they'll get used to call and they fly out and come back again and you lock them up again and you let them go, they'll go out, and they will find some more like that, you know, 'cause most of the kind of bird they got is one kind of bird, you know, nobody like to pick him because he is called the "Clinker," that's the disease bird, you know he be flying around, eating this, eating that, putting him nose in this drink and that, they got like a, a "Baldie" and a "Clinker" and a "Homer" and a "Black Bird." . . . I got a "Homer" and a "Black Bird." . . . I got a "Homer" and a "Black Bird," those are the only kinds I got, I got round three of those. . . . Yeah, and then, I let, I tried, you know, I tried to train those, but, you know, I let them out and they ain't come back, the only thing come back was my two birds, I believe they were black ones. . . . Yeah, you get them at a pet shop mostly a whole lot of, see, one thing about it, you got to be careful what you doing because, you know, it's like, I say right now it's round thousands of people in Harlem, they got a lot of bird cages and they go up on they's roofs and they take they bird, they take, you know, other people birds and put them on they arms and they pockets and stuff and walk out and take them to they coop and you know, they get use to it. . . . No, yeah, cats get up there, but, you know, we build them high off the ground real high off the roof so you know the cat won't, you know, you can't reach them we put barb wire around the entrance.   (Wolfram et al. 1971:258)

An interviewer who is not aware of some of the indigenous interests and activities of the community is at a serious disadvantage in obtaining relatively natural speech data.

3. Cues of informants' interests should be pursued. To a certain extent, a lack of knowledge concerning the community can be compensated for by sensitivity to the interests of the informant as expressed in the interview. Alert fieldworkers should be able to pick up cues concerning subjects for discussion in the interview. For example, Shuy, Wolfram, and Riley cite the following interchange as an example of alertness to the interests of the informant:

Fieldworker: Do you play marbles?
Informant: Yes, I have 197 marbles right now.
Fieldworker: Oh, tell me about them. How'd you get them? What are
              the different ones called?   (1968:117)

Skill in marble-shooting is something some adolescents can be quite proud of, and naturally would be a matter that a good marble-shooter could describe in some detail. In the above instance, the fieldworker's sensitivity to this fact resulted in a detailed description of the activity. This alertness can be contrasted with the opposite extreme, also illustrated in Shuy, Wolfram, and Riley:

> Fieldworker: Did you ever play hide and seek?
> Informant: Yes, I played that a lot.
> Fieldworker: What other games did you play?   (1968:118)

In this instance, the fieldworker missed an opportunity to discuss an activity that was quite familiar to the informant. The informant was apparently quite willing to discuss a favorite game, but the fieldworker missed the chance to elicit a detailed account of it.

4. Questions should help alleviate the informant's consciousness of his own speech. Although a tape-recorded interview, by its very nature, is an artificial situation, our goal is to get speech as natural as possible. This can be structured in the interview by asking questions that will focus the informant's attention more on what he is saying than on how he is saying it. Direct questions about speech, though valuable for some purposes, often make a person very aware of how he is talking. Therefore, if we want to ask questions about speech as part of the interview, they should probably be asked after we ask questions that will make him forget about the way he is talking and concentrate on the subject matter. Certain types of topics apparently are more apt to have this effect than others. For example, Labov has noted that when informants are asked if they have ever been in a situation in which they thought they were going to die, many informants will answer in the affirmative. If they are then asked to describe the situation, they will often become so involved in convincing the interviewer that this was an authentic rather than an imagined experience that they will forget about how they are talking in their effort to convince him. We cannot guarantee the types of topics that will have this sort of effect, but the informant's emotional involvement in a conversation is a fairly reliable indicator that he is more engrossed in his subject matter than in his style of speaking.

The style of speech by the interviewer can also help direct the focus away from the speech itself. Interviewers should use a casual style in their own speech repertoire. This does not mean that they should talk exactly like the informant or talk in a manner in which they would not normally talk—this can appear pretentious and insulting to the informant. It would be pretentious for a white middle-class interviewer to try to use Vernacular Black English when interviewing a black informant, but if he can naturally adopt a nonstandard variety of white speech, it may help in setting an informal atmosphere for the interview.

5. Questions should not arouse suspicions about any hidden intentions in interviewing. Even if we represent our purpose for interviewing in a straightforward and honest manner, we must realize that informants can easily become suspicious of our motives. It is sometimes difficult for informants to believe that we are simply interested in speech. We have, on occasion, been suspected of being everything from tape-recorder salesmen to FBI agents. It is, therefore, necessary to be sensitive to these potential suspicions and not pursue topics that will unnecessarily arouse the informants. This observation was forcefully brought home to one of the authors when he was interviewing a working-class adult male in Detroit. In a parenthetical remark, the informant mentioned some of the racial tensions that existed in the city at the time. The interviewer, out of curiosity, pursued the subject. The informant immediately became suspicious of some underlying motive for the interview and became very reticent about discussing anything at length after that point. Thus the elicitation of extended conversation was sacrificed because the interviewer had aroused the informant's suspicions about the true purpose of the interview.

To say that we should not unnecessarily arouse an informant's suspicions does not mean that we can only ask trivial questions. As we mentioned previously, many interviews are used to obtain valuable sociological as well as linguistic data. Our general procedure in eliciting this type of information, however, is to structure it well after we have gotten into the course of the interview. The initial questions are generally quite innocuous, involving such topics as childhood games, leisure-time activity, movies, TV, and the like.

Following is a rough outline of spontaneous interviewing that we conducted in our recent study of the English of second-generation Puerto Rican males in East Harlem. The general outline used here was not completely unique for this research project, but represents a modification of other types of questionnaires that were used for Labov's study of the social stratification of English in New York City, Shuy, Wolfram, and Riley's study of Detroit speech, and Fasold's study of Vernacular Black English in Washington, D.C. Specific items are included for the specific population, but a number of questions were simply adopted from previous spontaneous interview outlines.

A. *Games and Leisure*

What kinds of games do you play around the neighborhood (stickball, games with bottle caps, marbles, handball, flying pigeons, etc.)?

How do you play these games (rules for the games, deciding who's IT, etc.)?

Do you follow any of the NY sports teams? What do you think of the Mets this year? How about the Knicks for next year (or Joe Namath and the Jets)?

What are your favorite TV programs? Describe a recent program.

What is your favorite movie of all time? What happens? (If you can elicit movies without trouble, ask about *West Side Story* and an opinion of how life in Harlem is portrayed in this movie.)

B. *Peer Group*

How about the guys you hang around with? In this group is there one guy that everybody listens to? How come?

What makes for a leader in the group (tough, hip with girls, good sounder, etc.)?

Do the guys in the group sound on each other? How does this work?

What do you sound on? Can it be true, etc.? (If rapport right, get some sounds.)

What makes a good sounder?

Say a new kid moves into the tenement. Any way he can get into your group?

Who are some of the guys you're tight with? Name some.

Of the guys you named, are there any Negroes? Puerto Ricans in the group? How about Whites?

Any of these guys speak Spanish? How about their parents?

C. *Aspirations*

How about when you're through with school? Any idea of what you might do? What does a ———— do?

If someone came up to you and said, "Here's all the money in the world," what would you do with it?

What is a successful man (if informant responds, have him define unsuccessful, good, bad, smart man)?

D. *Fighting and Accidents*

What kinds of things do fights usually start about on the street?

Any rules for a fair fight? (How about if someone was kicking somebody or hitting them with a chain or lead pipe, what would you do?)

Ever see anybody get beat up real bad? What happened?

Do the kids around here still fight in gangs? How do these start? (If answer negatively, pursue why gang fights have stopped.)

Ever been in a hospital, or automobile accident? Describe.

How about a situation where you thought, "Man, this is it, I'm gonna die for sure now"? What happened? (Wolfram et al. 1971:438–39)

As with all previous questionnaires we have used, the success of particular topics in eliciting conversation varies considerably from informant to informant. And, of course, the actual interview sometimes strays considerably from the structured topics of discussion.

In the final analysis, success in individual interviews is largely dependent on the personalities involved. The qualities of rapport and empathy may be discussed at length, but ultimately they cannot be programmed.

GROUP INTERVIEWS. Probably the closest we can come to getting completely natural speech in an interview situation is by interviewing groups of peers. In the group interview, a set of informants is tape-recorded in conversation with each other. The topic for discussion is generally up to the participants rather than the fieldworker. It is expected that natural leaders of the group will direct the conversation, so that the fieldworker, if he is present, will not have to actively participate in the conversation. The greatest advantage of the group interview is that it is the context most conducive to obtaining casual speech. The constraints of the interview either from the tape-recording, the artificial situation, or the presence of an outsider are most readily overcome in this setting. It is also the most natural setting for the elicitation of indigenous themes. Certain types of indigenous verbal activities (e.g., ritualistic insults and singing among black inner-city males), in fact, can only be obtained from a group interview situation.

The group interview has probably been used to its greatest advantage by Labov and his colleagues (1968) in their study of adolescent peer speech in Harlem. First, the fieldworkers conducted some exploratory face-to-face interviews, including some of the peer leaders. Then acquaintance was made with peer groups in various social outings. Finally, group sessions were conducted in which multitrack recordings were made. Much of the interviewing was conducted by a participant observer who used his knowledge of the indigenous community to elicit verbal activity appropriate for peer interactions among members. This procedure resulted in some of the most detailed structural and functional data now available on the speech of this group.

Once the organizer of a group session has arranged for the details of the interview, there is often little that he has to do in terms of participation in the verbal interaction, unless there is some specific topic he wants discussed by the group. In most cases, a natural peer group will follow its own structural procedure for verbal interaction. Leaders should assume their natural roles in directing the session.

In setting up a group interview, researchers should be aware of the technical problems that can arise. Each speaker must be recorded on a different track in a group interview. A single recording for a group interview will often result in data that is unusable for the detailed analysis that is necessary for some types of sociolinguistic analysis. Phonological details, in particular, are almost impossible to transcribe reliably when an entire group is being recorded on one track. Furthermore, it can be extremely difficult to identify speakers on the tape if just one track is used. Even the group members themselves may have difficulty in identifying various speakers. We must also recognize that some speakers will dominate group sessions while others will have very little to say, due to the patterns of social interaction that exist in the group. For some speakers, adequate linguistic data may not be derived from the group session, so that this will have to be compensated for in later individual sessions.

Although a well-defined peer group gives the most authentic type of speech, it is not always necessary to have complete groups. Group interviews can also be conducted with smaller friendship groups or even dyads. In some cases, the selection of just two peer informants may result in quite casual speech. The essential matter in all group interviews is to involve the participating members primarily in conversation with one another rather than having individual responses to interviewer questions.

DIRECT QUESTIONING

At one end of the continuum of linguistic interviewing we have the spontaneous conversation, in which we get speech in its most normal setting. But even in quite extended interview situations, we may not get all the linguistic data for which we are looking. Some of the features we are looking for may occur potentially so infrequently that we cannot depend on our chances of observing them during the course of the conversation. And, in some cases, the particular features that we are looking for are crucial for a descriptively adequate linguistic statement.

In current linguistic theory, particularly in transformational-generative grammar, native speaker judgments of grammatical acceptability have become an essential procedure for determining the grammatical boundaries of the native speaker's linguistic competence. Direct questioning on grammatical acceptability is considered appropriate evidence for arriving at particular analyses. For example, suppose we want to write a rule that governs the linear order of adverbial particles in verb-particle constructions (so-called separable verbs) like *look up, put out,* and *beat up.* We observe that the particle may precede or follow the noun phrase after the verb so that we may get *He looked up the number.* But we notice that our data do not reveal any sentences in which the particle precedes a following noun phrase when it is a pronoun. We have sentences like *He looked it up* but not *He looked up it.* In order to determine if this is an accidental or systematic gap, we may contrive sentences like *He looked up it, He put out it,* or *He beat up it* and ask native speakers if these are grammatically acceptable utterances. We can also use personal intuition, if we qualify as native speakers. On the basis of this acceptance or rejection, we formulate the specific nature of our rules for the permutation of verbal particles. One needs only to survey most current linguistic journals to discover the widespread use of this direct type of questioning. There are, however, special problems that arise when one considers the use of this technique for the investigation of social dialects—in particular, nonstandard ones.[1]

The basic problem involves getting the informant to respond purely on the basis of linguistic data. Even with explicit instructions to ignore the content of the sentence or to overlook the fact that it is socially stigmatized, it is difficult for informants to respond solely on the basis of grammatical form. The authors recall many such instances of this difficulty when the grammatical function of habitual *be* as it is used by Vernacular Black English speakers was being analyzed. In one instance, a ten-year-old boy was asked to give a judgment on the grammaticalness of the sentence *He be at school more often than he be home.* In our recorded data, we happened to lack examples of *be* with adverbs like *often* and we wanted to find out if this was a systematic or an accidental gap. The informant would not accept the sentence. When asked why, he replied, *"Because he don't be at school more often than he be home. He be at home more often than he be at school."* In this case, the sentence was rejected because it did not match the speaker's conception of the real-world situation. Perhaps more important when dealing with social dialects is the fact that social norms for acceptable speech are transferred to matters of pure linguistic acceptability. We can recall numerous cases in which we drilled informants to react on the basis of linguistic rather than social norms, only to be frustrated with the comment that a sentence was unacceptable because it wasn't "good English." In most instances, speakers of a subordinate dialect will shift in an irregular way toward the superordinate dialect when asked direct questions about their language. Labov (1972:111) refers to this as the *principle of subordinate shift.* It is very difficult for informants to divorce linguistic acceptability from social acceptability. A level of linguistic expertise is required which most nonstandard speakers simply do not have. There may be exceptions, but for the most part, this technique is generally of limited reliability in examining social dialects.

Even though we have dismissed direct questioning as an elicitation technique appropriate for the investigation of social dialects, there are methods more direct than spontaneous interviewing which may be utilized for getting at certain types of linguistic competence. Many of the techniques that have been used in psycholinguistic studies, particularly those dealing with language acquisition, can be of great usefulness in eliciting data for the analysis of social dialects.

[1] In the current investigation of standard dialects, the use of direct speaker judgments is becoming more suspect. Thus, Quirk and Svartvik, after extensive research in the area of acceptability testing, assert: "In most of our own tentative sorties in this field over the past few years, however, we have taken it as axiomatic that direct questioning is the least reliable technique and that the informant's focus of attention should be systematically shifted away from the investigator's problem, as a necessary condition of achieving a controlled and natural (if not naive) reaction." (1966:13)

REPETITION

The repetition, imitation, or shadowing test is a technique that has been used in many instances for assessing the grammatical competence of young children. The results of many studies of this type indicate that children's reproduction is limited by the rules they have in their grammar at the time, because they often reproduce the sentences on the basis of the structural description that they have in their productive capability rather than on the basis of the stimulus sentence (see Menyuk 1971:154). Structural descriptions of the sentences they produce often appear to be quite accurate representations of their grammatical competence. When children are able to reproduce an adult sentence in an appropriate translation on the basis of their grammar, we also have an indirect indication of receptive competence of the adult grammar on the part of the child (even though he may not indicate productive competence). Although the majority of research utilizing this technique has been conducted with respect to language learning, one can readily see the applicability for the study of various social dialects. We can hypothesize that certain features that are not part of the dialect speaker's competence will be translated into an appropriate dialect structural description. We might further hypothesize that nonstandard accurate "translations" of Standard English stimuli indicate a receptive competence in Standard English. Indirect evidence of this type is one of our strongest arguments for maintaining that Standard English is generally comprehended by Nonstandard English speakers.

Repetition tests have been used in a number of social dialect studies, including research by Labov et al. (1968), Baratz (1969), and Natalicio and Williams (1971). Labov et al. describe the type of sentence structures included in their repetition test among black indigenous peer groups as follows:

a. Sentences with SE patterns which differed from NNE patterns we knew to be strongly entrenched, or even categorical. Example: *Nobody ever took an airplane, and none of us took a bus, either.*

b. Sentences with syntactic patterns which did not occur frequently, where we were not sure of the NNE rule, such as *William is a stupid fool and I know that's what he is.*

c. Long sentences which seemed to pose no grammatical problem, such as *John told Boo and Boo told Roger and then Roger told Ricky.*

d. Tongue twisters, such as *Bugs' black blood.*

e. Sentences of natural interest, containing taboo words, general insults, such as *She sits and shits by the seashore; Money, who is 11, can't spit as far as Boo can; The more he farts, the worse it smells.*   (311–12)

Quite useful data can sometimes emerge from these repetition tests:

> *Results.* Our expectations were fulfilled by the results of this first memory test: categorical NNE patterns were imposed upon the SE sentences, whereas variable SE patterns were not. There was no problem of length: long, unproblematical sentences were repeated back easily. What was most impressive was the way in which certain SE sentences were understood and repeated back instantly in SE form—a process of considerable significance for linguistic theory. . . . in many cases, actual quotations from the responses will yield the clearest view of what is taking place beneath the surface productions.   (Labov et al. 1968:312)

Baratz (1969) has used a repetition test to demonstrate that there is dialect interference when a Vernacular Black English-speaking child attempts to speak Standard English or a Standard English-speaking child attempts to speak Vernacular Black English. In her test, thirty sentences, half in Standard English and half in Vernacular Black English, were given to a group of white middle socioeconomic-class suburban children and lower socioeconomic-class inner-city black children. These sentences included many of the characteristic differences between the dialects. For example, at one point the children were given the sentence, *Do Deborah like to play wid da girl that sit next to her at school?* while at another point they were given the Standard English counterpart, *Does Deborah like to play with the girl that sits next to her in school?* A sentence pair such as this focuses on the difference in the use of third-person, singular, present-tense -Z forms. On the basis of this test, Baratz concluded that the nonfamiliar dialect stimuli resulted in predictable structural differences for both groups and that many of the children were *not* bidialectal.

Although sentence repetition tasks may be useful for studying some aspects of social dialect studies, their limitations should be kept in mind. They do bring a person's awareness of speech to a very conscious level; in some cases, this will have considerable effect on his speech, particularly if he is somewhat adept at style or dialect shifting. We must also realize the limitations they impose because of their basis in mimicry. If an utterance is short enough, an informant may be capable of mimicking it whether it is part of his competence or not, thus making the results of the test useless. Finally, there is the matter of interpreting data. Many of the features of nonstandard dialects are variable rather than categorical phenomena, as we shall see in Chapter Five. Therefore, we cannot jump to conclusions on the basis of a few isolated instances that occur in a response on a memory test. In summary, then, although we should keep these limitations of repetition tests clearly in mind when interpreting results, they can be useful corroborative evidence along with more natural types of speech.

STRUCTURAL ELICITATION

In the direct methods of data elicitation discussed above, the constructions in focus were part of the stimuli given to the informant. Although useful for some purposes, this can also be the cause of considerable bias in the informant's response. It is, therefore, advantageous to consider methods that set up specific frames to elicit data without exposing the informants to the data in focus in the interviewer's stimulus. This particular technique has traditionally been used for many decades now in dialectology. In the method most frequently used, particular items are defined and the informant simply "guesses" the item the interviewer is defining. Thus, if we want to elicit particular pronunciations of *pen,* we might elicit the form by saying, "The thing that you write letters with is called a _____." The informant then simply fills in the blank with the appropriate form. This type of frame can also be used to elicit certain types of grammatical forms. We may, for example, elicit the present perfect form of *drink* by setting up a frame like, "If I drink some coffee today, I have _____ it." In this case, the informant responds with the appropriate form, either *drank, drunk,* or *drinked.* Setting up frames of this type can often produce data quite helpful in evaluating certain types of phonological and grammatical structures. In our own research we have elicited items for the analysis of word-final consonant clusters by employing a technique originally used by Berko (1958) for the analysis of morphological forms in language acquisition. In this exercise, we wanted to find out how certain plurals were formed depending on the form of the final consonant. Pairs of illustrative cards were designed; one of the cards had a single item illustrated and the other several of the same item. Some of the words were real English forms while others were nonsense words. For example, we may use a word like *desk* and its plural counterpart, illustrated in two cards as in Figure 3-2a. Similarly, we may illustrate a fictitious form and label it with a nonsense word such as *wust* (Figure 3-2b). The informants are given the single item and told, "This is a *wust.*" Then the plural card is shown and the informant is told, "If this is a *wust,* then a whole bunch of them would be called _____." On the basis of the informant's responses (e.g. [wusəz] or [wus:]), we can gather essential information about the pluralization of certain types of consonantal endings.

Similarly, we can set up certain types of verbal frames in which we train the informant to respond in terms of a prescribed pattern. For example, at one point in our analysis of consonant clusters in Vernuclar Black English we wanted to observe what happened when the suffix *-ing* was attached to items which ended in a cluster in Standard English. A simple frame was therefore devised in order to elicit these items. Informants were taught the response pattern on the basis of items that do not end in con

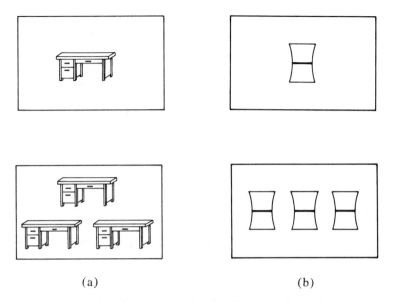

(a)   (b)

Figure 3-2. Sample cards for the elicitation of plurals.

sonant clusters, then asked to use the same pattern for the items that do. The specific task was taught using three examples which the fieldworker produced for the informant.

STIMULUS	RESPONSE
A. They eat	They eat
	They are eating
B. They play	They play
	They are playing
C. They buy things	They buy things
	They are buying things

The informants were then asked to produce the same pattern for the following items, all of which end in consonant clusters in Standard English:

1. They rest
2. They ask
3. They paste it
4. They bust it
5. They lift it
6. They test it

On the basis of these responses we came to important conclusions about the status of consonant clusters in the underlying phonological representation of Vernacular Black English (see Wolfram 1970). Before eliciting the data, we were unsure of the underlying status of certain consonant clusters in this variety of English.

All types of constructions are not as easy to elicit as were the above phonological realizations—some require more sophisticated elicitation frames. The type of stimulus used in eliciting can vary considerably, depending on the construction that we desire to obtain. The different types of stimulus frames that must be used for specific grammatical constructions are probably better illustrated than described.

One of the elicitation experiments we have utilized involves a procedure for getting at the different sources for the use of *be* as a finite form in Vernacular Black English (e.g., *Sometime he be busy and sometime he don't;* see Chapter Seven). We wanted to elicit a particular type of abbreviated sentence in which *will* or *would* could not be contracted. The sentence type we used was a short affirmative answer of the type, *I know* + *pronoun* + *auxiliary.* For example, the short affirmation of a sentence such as *I know he should do his homework* is *I know he should.* When there is no overt auxiliary preceding the verb, a form of *do* is used, as in *He shines his shoes; I know he does.* We had previously hypothesized that there were three functions of finite *be* as used in Vernacular Black English: one in which *be* was used as a correspondence of Standard English *will be,* one in which it was used as a correspondence of *would be* in Standard English, and one in which it occurred with the auxiliary *do,* having a distinct grammatical category that indicated a habitual type of activity.

The experiment that we conducted to elicit these forms involved interaction between the informant and a tape recorder, in which the informant was asked to respond to stimulus sentences on tape. The sentences had actually been spoken by informants in spontaneous conversations. To begin the elicitation of the diagnostic items, sample sentences with the answers provided were played for the informant. Each stimulus sentence was recorded by a male voice, the answer by a female. In this way the informant was instructed that he would have to respond in the same way the woman did. The following sample sentences were given:

> (M) He can drive a motorcycle. (F) I know he can. (M) Can what? (F) Drive a motorcycle.
> (M) The teacher could be wrong. (F) I know she could. (M) Could what? (F) Be wrong.
> (M) Darryl hit his brother. (F) I know he did. (M) Did what? (F) Hit his brother.
> (M) Them boys over there, they can beat up anybody. (F) I know they can. (M) Can what? (F) Beat up anybody.
> (M) My cousin should do his work. (F) I know he should. (M) Should what? (F) Do his work.

Sample sentences are necessary in order to ensure that the informant understands the task. Once it is clear that the task is understood, the diagnostic sentences can be given. In this case, four diagnostic sentences were interspersed in a test consisting of eleven sentences. These included:

1. If he got a walkie-talkie, he be happy.
2. Sometimes Joseph be up there.
3. He be in in a few minutes.
4. Sometime my ears be itching.

The working hypothesis was that *would* should appear in the response to sentence (1), *will* for (3), and *do* for (2) and (4).

A typical response was as follows:

Tape:	He be in in a few minutes.
Informant:	I know he will.
Fieldworker:	Will what?
Informant:	Be in in a few minutes.

The success of this technique is illustrated in the tabulation of responses given by thirty-one black working-class informants.

	do	will	would	TRANS-LATION TO SE	OTHER MODALS	NO RESPONSE
1. ... be happy	0	1	21	1	1	7
2. ... be up there	11	2	8	4	2	4
3. ... be in	0	25	2	0	2	2
4. ... be itching	14	0	2	11	0	4

(Fasold 1969:771)

Although there are some instances in which the informant apparently did not complete the task for one reason or another, the results tend strongly to confirm the hypothesis.

Structural elicitation of this type can obviously be done for a number of different items. As we mentioned previously, quite different structural stimuli have to be planned in accordance with the particular things we seek to elicit. Thus, the technique described above varies considerably from the technique we used to elicit embedded questions. In Standard English, embedded questions are often realized by using the items *if* or *whether* while retaining the linear ordering used in declarative sentences. Thus, in a sentence such as *He asked me if I could come,* the order of the auxiliary and subject is not inverted as it would be in a direct question such as *Can I come?* In some nonstandard dialects, we observed that *if* or *whether* was not found in the surface form of the embedded question. Instead, inverted word order was retained, giving us *He asked could he come?* In order to elicit this construction from our informants, we needed to devise a frame which would force the informant to form embedded questions.

The following exercise thus was constructed:

> You're going to hear the man on the tape say two sentences. The lady is going to put them together. After you hear some examples, you will hear some sentences and we'll see if you can put them together in the same way.

STIMULUS	RESPONSE
A. John told me this. Roy was going home.	John told me that Roy was going home.
B. John thinks this. Mary is cute.	John thinks that Mary is cute.
C. John told me this. Go home.	John told me to go home.
D. John remembers this. Peter hit his brother.	John remembers that Peter hit his brother.
E. John told Peter this. Bring a pencil.	John told Peter to bring a pencil.

(Now you try it.)

1. John thinks this.
    Peter is stupid.
2. John told Raymond this.
    Go home.
3. John asked me this.
    Did the mail come yet?
4. John knows this.
    Gary has a bike.
5. John wonders this.
    Is there water on the moon?
6. John thinks this.
    The job is too hard.
7. John wants to know this.
    Can the boys come over?
8. John asked him this.
    Where did they go?

In the above exercises, sentences 3, 5, 7, and 8 are the diagnostic sentences in which the informant can either give the inverted question order or the noninverted order with surface forms *if* or *whether*. The other sentences are inserted in order to assure that the informant understands the task. This sort of task gave us important information that corroborated evidence on embedded questions obtained from spontaneous conversation.

Although there are important insights that we can gain through structural elicitation of this sort, we must be aware of its limitations. For one, we are setting up a context in which speech is a primary focus of the informant. We, therefore, may expect more formal responses than in spontaneous conversation. For example, it is not uncommon for informants to pluralize nouns ending in *s* + stop clusters with [-əz] forms in informal conversation ([tɛsəz] "tests"), yet when we focus on plural terms in the structural elicitation, we may elicit Standard English plurals ([tes:] or [tɛsts]). Or we may be forcing informants into options that are a function only of the task rather than of the way that they actually *use* language, leading to distorted data. Direct structural elicitation should only proceed from an adequate base taken from our knowledge of how particular social dialects are used in a natural setting.

READING

In order to get a range in the continuum of informal to formal speech, reading passages are sometimes included in sociolinguistic fieldwork. This represents a context in which one is quite aware of the way he is talking. Data from reading passages do not usually yield essential information in themselves, but when compared with other contextual styles of speech, can provide an important basis for stylistic analysis.

There are several different types of reading that might be included as part of an interview. One might construct a reading passage in which a number of linguistic variables are purposely included for analysis of the realizations of these variables. Following is a sample passage from Labov's work in 1966, in which he investigated the parameters of five phonological variables in several styles of speech in New York City. The particular phonological variables he was analyzing are underlined.

TEXT FOR CONCENTRATING FIVE PHONOLOGICAL VARIABLES.
[Underlining added to indicate concentration of the variables.]

Zero
When I was nine or ten, I had a lot of friends who used to come over to my house to play. I remember a kid named Henry who had very big feet, and I remember a boy named Billy who had no neck, or at least none to look at. He was a funny kid, all right.

(oh)
We always had chocolate milk and coffee cake around four o'clock. My dog used to give us an awful lot of trouble: he jumped all over us when he saw the coffee cake. We called him Hungry Sam.

      We used to play *Kick-the-can*. One ma̲n is "IT": you run
pa̲st him as fa̲st as you can, and you kick a tin ca̲n so he ca̲n't tag
you. Sammy used to gra̲b the ca̲n and da̲sh down the street—we'd

(eh)   chase him with a baseball bat, and yell, "Ba̲d boy! Ba̲d! Ba̲d!" But
he was too fa̲st. Only my a̲unt could catch him. She had him do
tricks, too: she even made him a̲sk for a glass of milk, and jump
into a paper ba̲g.

      I remembe̲r whe̲re he was run ove̲r, not fa̲r from ou̲r co̲rne̲r.

(r)   He da̲rted out about fou̲r feet before a ca̲r, and he got hit ha̲rd.
We didn't have the hea̲rt to play ball o̲r ca̲rds all mo̲rning. We
didn't know we ca̲red so much fo̲r him until he was hu̲rt.

      The̲re's some̲thing strange about tha̲t—how I can remember
every̲thing he did: thi̲s thi̲ng, tha̲t thi̲ng, and the othe̲r thi̲ng. He

(th)   used to carry thre̲e newspapers in his mou̲th at the̲ same time. I
(dh) suppose it's the same thi̲ng wi̲th most of us: your first dog is like
your first girl. She's more trouble tha̲n she's wor̲th, but you can't
seem to forget her.   (Labov 1966:597)

As illustrated in this passage, it is essential to have an adequate representation of the variables to allow for their quantitative measurement. As an
added incentive such passages should deal with topics of common interest.

    In addition to entire story passages like Labov's, some investigators
have used isolated sentences as a basis for focusing on single items. Levine
and Crockett describe their use of diagnostic words in sentences.

      First, each word was embedded in a sentence. Each sentence con-
tained from one to four of the words chosen, with no rhymes permitted
in any sentence. Further, each sentence contained a blank, to be filled in
by the respondents. This device was used to distract respondents from
their pronunciation; the blanks were also the vehicles for the collection of
data on grammar (e.g., preterite-participle choice, adjective-adverb choice)
and on idioms and choices of words (e.g., *sick to-, at-,* or *in my stomach;
pail* or *bucket,* etc.). The sentences, themselves pretested, were listed in
an order which distributed word-types throughout the test instrument.
                           (1967:80)

    Finally, it is possible to give simple word lists that focus on some of
the crucial phonological realizations of items when one is most aware of
speech. Another type of word list is the minimal pair list, in which two
items are read and the informant then decides whether these items sound
the same or not. In many cases, the words are distinct in one dialect but
potentially homophonous in another dialect (i.e., interdialectal homophony). As illustration, we can consider the following list used in our
study of Puerto Rican English in Harlem:

SAME/DIFFERENT WORDS

rows	rose	side	sód
run	rum	shoe	chew
hut	hot	mass	mask
sold	soul	deaf	death
boat	vote	yellow	jello
sin	sing	time	Tom
rain	reign	pin	pen
west	Wes	watch	wash
bet	bat	boil	ball

(Wolfram et al. 1971:443)

In the above minimal word-pair list, there are some items that are homophonous in all dialects of English and therefore nondiagnostic. Items like *rows* and *rose* and *rain* and *reign* represent this category. These items are included in order to ensure that the informant understands the task and is responding accordingly. There are also some items we would expect to be homophonous in certain varieties of Spanish-influenced English, including *bet* and *bat* and *shoe* and *chew*. These items give us an indication of the extent of Spanish influence on English in formal style. There are also items we would expect to be homophonous on the basis of the surrounding Black English dialect, such as *deaf* and *death* and *pin* and *pen*. Two main aspects of minimal word lists must be recorded: (1) whether the informant actually pronounces the items the same or differently and (2) whether he says that they sound alike or not. The first qualification gives us objective data while the second gives us an intuitive judgment about the speaker's sound system. Although intuitive reactions may appear to be quite important for an analysis of a phonological system, researchers cannot always take the informant's reactions at face value. In some cases there may be stated differences even though careful analysis (including acoustic analysis) shows the words to be produced similarly, while in other cases the converse may be true.

THE ELICITATION OF
SUBJECTIVE REACTIONS

Up to this point, we have discussed primarily the elicitation of objective speech data for sociolinguistic analysis. Little mention has been made of the subjective reactions of informants toward either their own or other people's speech. Yet it is the perception of dialect differences and the social evaluation of these differences by participating members of the society which is the real basis for the existence of social dialects. A complete description of social dialects should therefore include examination of the subjective reaction to distinct speech varieties.

There are several different ways in which we can elicit subjective evaluations of speech differences. The most traditional method is through the use of an interview questionnaire. In some cases, it may be useful to ask open-ended questions, in which informants are simply asked to give their opinions on certain speech varieties. For example, in our study of the English spoken by second-generation Puerto Ricans in Harlem, we wanted to ascertain their perception of the way they talked as compared with the speech of the surrounding black community. Informants were simply asked, "Do you think that Puerto Rican and black teenagers talk alike? In what way do they talk the same or differently?" The informant was to answer this question, being allowed to state whatever reasons he felt were relevant. Similarly, Labov's study of English in New York City included questions designed to elicit how New Yorkers felt about New York speech. These questions allowed the informant to express his reaction toward New York speech and explain why he felt the way he did. Although open-ended questions concerning subjective reactions allow us to gather data we might not anticipate in a nondiscursive questionnaire, it can become difficult to taxonomize and quantify results on this basis. For this reason, many questionnaires are designed to elicit responses in terms of predetermined categories. In some cases, informants may be asked to make a forced choice between a positive and a negative evaluative response. A questionnaire may simply require a subject to respond Yes or No to a statement such as, "I think nonstandard dialects are as logical as standard dialects of English." Or we may ask an informant to pick out what he considers the most socially stigmatized and most prestigious dialect, given a list of American English dialects that includes Southern White speech, Black English, New England speech, and Midwestern speech. There are, of course, a number of variations in the types of questions that can be asked in this way. For example, we may ask an informant to place each of the given dialects in rank order in terms of relative prestige rather than make a single choice.

One technique that has become relatively popular in recent subjective reaction questionnaires is that of the semantic differential. This procedure, originally developed by Charles Osgood and his colleagues at Indiana University, attempts to investigate the connotative aspects of a subject's reactions. In the typical semantic-differential task, the subject is asked to judge entities or concepts by means of a series of bipolar, seven-step scales defined in terms of descriptive opposites. The concept is given at the top of the sheet and the subject responds by putting a check mark in the appropriate position on the scale for each of the bipolar opposites. For example, a study of speech identification in Detroit by Shuy, Baratz, and Wolfram (1968) included the following semantic polar adjectives in the attempt to elicit the connotative aspects that several different speech varieties evoke.

WHITE SOUTHERN SPEECH

worthless	—:—:—:—:—:—:—	valuable
dull	—:—:—:—:—:—:—	sharp
difficult	—:—:—:—:—:—:—	easy
positive	—:—:—:—:—:—:—	negative
rough	—:—:—:—:—:—:—	smooth
weak	—:—:—:—:—:—:—	strong
fast	—:—:—:—:—:—:—	slow
sloppy	—:—:—:—:—:—:—	careful
complex	—:—:—:—:—:—:—	simple
thick	—:—:—:—:—:—:—	thin
bad	—:—:—:—:—:—:—	good
smart	—:—:—:—:—:—:—	dumb

The closer one checks to one of the poles in the scale, the more heavily weighted is his response in terms of the particular extreme. A particular numerical value is assigned on this basis for computation of the results. For example, starting with 0 as the midpoint, each scale may have a value of $+1$, $+2$, and $+3$ (immediately contiguous to the positive side of the adjectival pole), or -1, -2, and -3 (immediately contiguous to the negative side of the pole). Using the technique of factor analysis, researchers have found evidence indicating that the judgments tend to cluster into three main domains of connotative meaning, including the dimension of *evaluation* (e.g., good–bad, positive–negative), *potency* (strong–weak, dull–sharp), and *activity* (fast–slow, difficult–easy). By employing the semantic-differential technique, it is possible to compare reactions to different concepts on a positive–negative continuum rather than by means of binary choice. Used properly, the semantic differential can be a useful tool for getting at subjective reactions to speech and speech concepts.

The typical problem with questionnaires used to elicit subjective reactions involves the disparity between expressed attitudes and overt behavior. In an effort to look at the responses between these two poles, Fishman has designed an instrument labeled the *Commitment Measure*. His study, carried out with respect to bilingualism, sought to determine "whether commitment items show any greater relationship to pertinent language behavior criteria than do more traditional dispositional or role playing language use and language attitude items" (1969:5). In addition to the traditional types of attitudinal responses asked on his questionnaire, Fishman included a ten-item commitment scale in which a person's willingness or commitment to respond or perform a particular type of activity with respect to language was measured. The type of questions Fishman asked were calculated to measure a person's willingness to maintain and strengthen the use of Spanish on a personal and community level in New York City, and ranged from willingness to participate in a small-group discussion on the topic of improving the person's command of Spanish to willingness to contribute money to help finance the activities of an association for building up the use of Spanish in New York. When the commitment questions were correlated with the previously given noncommitment attitude scale, a significant difference arose. Commitment measures as a data-gathering technique are more useful than traditional attitude questionnaires because they can more directly get at behavioral tendencies rather than eliciting simple cognitive or evaluative responses.

So far, we have only referred to subjective reactions made on the basis of a fieldworker's questioning or a written questionnaire. But we can also use other types of stimuli in eliciting subjective reactions to speech. The elicitation of responses from tape-recorded samples of speech is one of the current techniques used to considerable extent in the study of social dialects. One such method, originally developed by Lambert and his colleagues at McGill University for evaluating personality traits of bilinguals, has been labeled the *Matched Guise Technique*. In this procedure, a select group of subjects evaluates the personality traits of speakers' voices played to them on the tape recorder. The recording is made by a speaker who has considerable ability in producing different language or dialect varieties. The subjects are not told that the different varieties heard on the tape belong to one speaker, but are simply asked to judge certain traits of the speaker. This is the technique that Baratz employed in the bidialectal task we described earlier in this chapter (see p. 59). The major advantage of this technique is that it controls a number of variables such as the voice quality and personality of the speaker. One of the disadvantages is that it is sometimes difficult to find speakers who have acquired nativelike control of the various social dialects we might require to produce such a tape.

Rather than use one speaker, some researchers have had speakers from different social groups simply read the same passage. This is the technique that Bryden (1968) used in his study of the identification of social class and race in Charlottesville, Virginia. The use of a tape-recording in this case sets up an artificial situation, however, because most speakers are unable to read in a natural speaking manner. For this reason, other investigators have simply extracted topically comparable passages (e.g., TV programs, games, etc.) from tape-recorded spontaneous interviews rather than using identical passages that have been read. Although variables such as content and voice quality are much more difficult to control, this has the advantage of authenticity. This is the type of stimuli that was used by Shuy, Baratz, and Wolfram in their study of speech identification in Detroit and Washington. In this study 20 to 30-second portions were excerpted for the interviews of four socioeconomic classes of whites and blacks in Detroit. At the conclusion of the main passages, a number of short portions (one sentence of from 3 to 5 seconds) were included in order to determine reactions on the basis of much shorter stimuli. For each of the longer passages, subjects were asked to identify the race of the speaker, as well as the relative socioeconomic class, and to make some attitudinal judgments on a semantic differential. This was presented as follows:

a. What is the race of this speaker? Black ( ) White ( )

b. What is the educational/occupational level of this speaker?

    ( ) 1. College graduate usually with graduate training.
Dentist, mechanical engineer, personnel manager.

    ( ) 2. High school graduate, probably some college or technical school. Printer, post office clerk, small business owner or manager.

    ( ) 3. Some high school or high school graduate.
Bus driver, carpenter, telephone lineman.

    ( ) 4. Not beyond 8th grade.
Dishwasher, night watchman, construction laborer.

c. Rate the speech sample on each of the following scales:

awkward	____:____:____:____:____:____:____	graceful
relaxed	____:____:____:____:____:____:____	tense
formal	____:____:____:____:____:____:____	informal
thin	____:____:____:____:____:____:____	thick
correct	____:____:____:____:____:____:____	incorrect

In most cases, repeated passages of from 20 to 30 seconds were more than adequate for making judgments of the type we asked above. In fact, fairly accurate identification (over 70 percent) of race and social class was often made just on the basis of the 3 to 5-second sentence. It should be noted that questions concerning a wide range of reactions may be asked on the basis of tape-recorded passages. For example, we have used tape-recorded passages as the basis for obtaining data on language and employability. Labov asked questions about masculine virtues such as toughness on the basis of tape-recorded passages and concluded on this basis that the use of nonstandard dialects has a positive effect for conducting some societal roles that call for expressed toughness. The types of reactions that we may have subjects make on the basis of recorded speech samples are almost limitless.

Recent studies of language attitudes have also utilized videotapes to some advantage (e.g., Williams, Whitehead, and Miller 1971; Williams 1973). In the study of language attitudes and stereotyping reported by Williams (1973), stereotyping was investigated by using videotapes from three different ethnic groups: black, white, and Chicano. In one of the exercises, the respondents were shown side views of children speaking. The respondent could observe the person speaking, but was unable to lip-read what he was saying. Audiotapes of Standard English were then dubbed onto the videotapes of the children from the three different groups to create a type of *ethnic guise*. Stereotyping was measured by looking at the extent to which the visual picture determined a particular reaction despite the constancy of the Standard English. Modern technology affords the creative researcher a great deal of variety in designing ways of "teasing out" various dimensions of subjective reactions to language differences.

4

THE SOCIAL VARIABLE

The correlation of linguistic variables with social variables is at the foundation of the study of social dialects. In this chapter we turn our attention to the social variable, and in the following chapter we will look at the linguistic variable. When we speak of the *social variable,* we are referring to the behavioral factor(s) that may be isolated to correlate with linguistic diversity. Obviously, there are a large number of these. In the following discussion, we will look at how some of these main variables operate, including the factors of region, status, style, age, sex, and ethnicity. Others could certainly be added to this list, but our discussion will be limited to a representation of some of the major variables. Although the various factors are discussed independently, it should be understood that this is an artifice of our description. In reality, it is an interaction of the various social factors that accounts for linguistic diversity.

Region

Although it is our main purpose to deal with the interaction of social forces with language variation, we must always bear in mind that social dialects exist in the context of regional variation. Our intention here is not to give a comprehensive treatment of regional varieties of English, but simply to put social variables in a proper perspective. More concentrated studies from the traditional viewpoint of dialect geography can be found in the works of Kurath (1949), McDavid (1958), Atwood (1962), and Allen and Underwood (1971); recent work by Bailey (1972, 1973) provides an exciting new framework for looking at regional variation. Quite clearly, regional variation is integrally related to a number of social variables.

Three essential reasons are often cited for the emergence of regional dialects within the United States (see Shuy 1967:33–41). First, we have different patterns of settlement history. Dialect areas in the United States often indicate the migration of the early settlers. In some cases, these dialects reflect the fact that many settlers came from different parts of England. In others, there is evidence that the colonists developed their own regional varieties which were extended westward with the spread of the settlers to the western part of the country. German influence may be found in regions such as southeastern Pennsylvania, where there were heavy early settlements of German immigrants. Dutch influence on dialect is seen in Holland, Michigan, for example; and Irish influence in Beaver Island, Michigan. We have already mentioned the direct influence of Africanisms on Gullah and the possible indirect influence on other varieties of Vernacular Black English in the United States.

The second factor affecting regional varieties of English is the general pattern of population movement. The major drift of the white population of America has been from east to west. It is, therefore, not coincidence that major white dialect boundaries are more apt to run horizontally than vertically. The boundaries of dialect areas can be expected to outline the major migration trends that have taken place throughout the history of the United States.

Finally, there is the matter of physical geography. Although transportation obstacles are not generally considered to be a serious handicap with our modern technological advances, separation of areas by rivers, mountains, and other natural barriers has inhibited the spread of language in the past because it has inhibited physical mobility. Mountain ranges, islands, and other isolated areas as a result often become *relic areas*—areas in which the older forms of a language are preserved. For example, parts of the Appalachian Mountain range, isolated by a natural boundary, reveal a number of older English forms that have been replaced in other parts of the United States. Geographical isolation cannot, of course, be separated from social isolation. The two often go hand in hand since there are often important social reasons why a particular group has been assigned to a given geographical area.

In opposition to relic areas, we have what are commonly called *focal areas*—dialect areas that serve as centers for linguistic spread. This spread often emigrates from important cultural and regional centers. Prestigious urban centers often serve as focal areas, so that a city like Boston may show the spread of dialect features outward from that area. Obviously, not all dialect areas qualify as being either relic or focal areas. In between, there are a number of varieties related to the extreme points and to each other in a continuumlike relationship.

When we examine the nature of regional variation, we find that it is the result of the spread of language changes through geographical space over time. As a hypothetical case, let us assume that there are four rules in the process of change in some language. Each one starts later temporally than the other so that R1 is the earliest, R2 the next, R3 third, and R4 the last. We will assume further that all four begin at the same geographical point. Another factor we will need to consider is the extent to which the output of the rule is complete. A rule that has not yet appeared obviously has no output. A rule that is in the process of change has a variable output —that is, it does not operate every time the situation in which it could operate arises. There is, instead, fluctuation between the previously existent form and the new one. A rule that has completely moved into the language has a categorical output—that is, it operates every time the situation in which it could operate arises. To illustrate this principle, let us imagine that English is gaining a rule that inserts *a* between two consonants at the beginning of a word. Before the rule begins, it has no output and words like *stop* and *please* are pronounced much as they are spelled. When the new rule begins to emerge, speakers sometimes say *satop* and *palease* and at other times *stop* and *please*. When the rule has completed its integration into the language, speakers say only *satop* and *palease*. The geographical location and the output status of the four rules at successive points in time would be as in Figure 4-1. In the figure, R1 is the leftmost in each series, R2 next, and so on. The 0 indicates no output, x variable output, and 1 categorical output.

At Time vii, all four rules have reached the fourth area away from the point of origin and all four have become categorical at the point of origin. Unless something happens to stop the change, the four rules will eventually become categorical in all four regions. This example is the simplest version of the new *wave model* proposed by Bailey (1973).[1] If there were several points of origin, or if one or more of the rules stopped spreading, the picture would be more complicated. There are a number of factors that would complicate the picture considerably.

Occasionally, a barrier of some kind (physical, social, or some com-

[1] The traditional concept of *wave model* is discussed in Bloomfield (1933:328–31, 340–45).

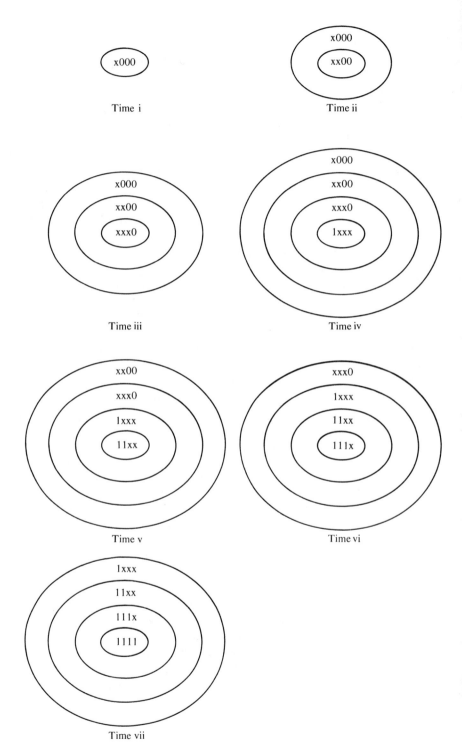

Figure 4-1. Wave spread in time and space.

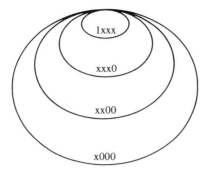

Figure 4-2. Wave with spread
arrested in one direction.

bination thereof) can interrupt the spread of change in one direction. In such a case, the situation at Time iv in Figure 4-1 would have the appearance shown in Figure 4-2.

In this situation, at the top of the figure it would be possible to find a line on one side of which all four rules are present and on the other side of which none are present. The study of dialect geography attaches considerable significance to such situations. The line that marks the limits of a certain rule or feature is called an *isogloss;* the lines in our figures are examples. If several of these isoglosses collect at the same point, as in Figure 4-2, they are referred to as a *bundle of isoglosses,* and are used in dialect geography to establish dialect boundaries. Although it is easy to see that the situation at Time iv in Figure 4-1 is linguistically identical to the situation in Figure 4-2, and there is no particular linguistic significance attached to the fact that the isoglosses bundle in Figure 4-2, it is nonetheless interesting to see how varieties of English may be distributed geographically. One such distribution can be seen in the map in Figure 4-3, taken from Bailey (1972). Care must be used in interpreting any geographical language variety because regional variation interacts with social variation so that class, age, and other variables must be artificially held constant in order for a map to have any real validity. Even when social factors are held constant, isoglosses still tend not to bundle very well. Dialect geography has sometimes been forced to accept "bundles" of isoglosses which are separated by more than one hundred miles. To construct a map such as Figure 4-3, it is necessary not only to hold social factors constant, but to draw lines based on estimates of which isoglosses are more important than others to avoid the problem of poor bundling. Bailey has used the isoglosses based on *r*-lessness, the syllabications of liquids and glides, and the vowel quality in words like *wife* and *about* as his estimates of the most significant isoglosses.

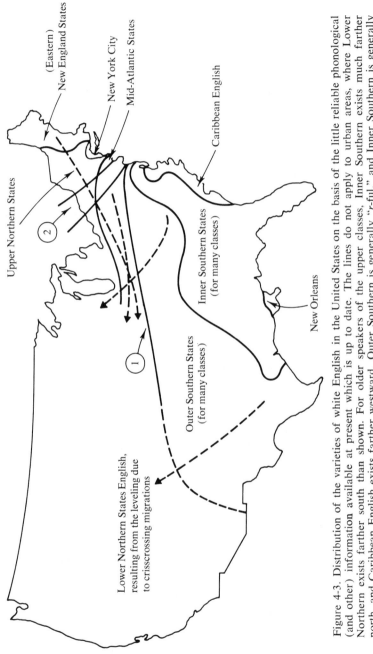

Figure 4-3. Distribution of the varieties of white English in the United States on the basis of the little reliable phonological (and other) information available at present which is up to date. The lines do not apply to urban areas, where Lower Northern exists farther south than shown. For older speakers of the upper classes, Inner Southern exists much farther north, and Caribbean English exists farther westward. Outer Southern is generally "r-ful," and Inner Southern is generally "r-less." Caribbean and Southern States English have been influenced by Black English. The dotted lines on this map (those having arrow heads) indicate migrations. (1) designates the isogloss separating the marked and unmarked syllabications of intervocalic liquids and glides, (2) is the corridor in which the diphthongal peak in *wife* and *about* is a central vowel in Northern States English. New York City and New Orleans are special urban areas, Mid-Atlantic English (Lower Northern States) mainly derives from the North of Britain, in contrast with Eastern New England States English.

Upper Northern States

(Eastern)
New England States

New York City

Mid-Atlantic States

Caribbean English

Inner Southern States
(for many classes)

New Orleans

Outer Southern States
(for many classes)

Lower Northern States English,
resulting from the leveling due
to crisscrossing migrations

Social Status

Any linguistic variable whose distribution differs on the basis of social class is called *socially diagnostic*. All of the phonological and grammatical features we shall describe in Chapters Six and Seven, for at least some populations in the United States, have been determined as socially diagnostic. That is to say, the incidence of variants correlates with different social status groups. As we have alluded to above, not all socially diagnostic variables are relevant for every region within the United States. Some variables may be socially diagnostic only in certain locales while others appear to be diagnostic regardless of region.

Many large Northern urban areas have been drastically restructured within the last fifty years because of the immigration of Southern blacks. Because of the extent of the intersectional migration and the segregation patterns established in the North, the dialect of many blacks living in the North has not been adapted completely to a Northern dialect of English. In Northern locales, some features quite acceptable in Southern speech have been transformed into class and ethnic patterns. Thus, in a city such as Detroit or Chicago, postvocalic *r*-lessness, the neutralization of the contrast between *I* and *ɛ* before nasals (e.g., *pin* and *pen* pronounced identically), and the monophthongization of upgliding vowels (e.g., *time* as /tahm/) have taken on social significance even though they are quite acceptable pronunciations in certain parts of the South. On the other hand, there are a number of variables which have social significance regardless of the regional locale where they are found. For example, the absence of third-person singular *-Z* forms (e.g., *he go*), the uses of invariant *be,* and multiple negation appear to be socially diagnostic in all regions of the United States. The distinction between these two types of socially diagnostic items has sometimes been referred to as *specific* and *general* significance. Region is only one of the factors that may be cited to account for the distinction between general and specific social significance. As we shall see later, certain variables are only diagnostic for certain age levels or for particular ethnic groups.

All socially diagnostic variables for a given population do not correlate with social status in the same way. Differences in the discreteness of the correlation have led us to distinguish between what we have labeled *sharp* and *gradient* stratification.[2] Gradient stratification refers to a pro-

---

[2] Labov has used the terms *sharp* and *fine* stratification in a way somewhat similar to our terms. Sharp stratification is defined as "a wide separation of a few discrete layers (necessarily by comparison with at least one pair of narrowly separated layers); fine stratification is a correlation of two continuous or near-continuous variables into an indefinitely large number of narrowly separated layers" (1966:581).

gressive increase in the frequency of occurrence of a variant when compared for various social groups. As an illustration of gradient stratification, we can look at the incidence of postvocalic *r* absence in the black community in Detroit in Figure 4-4. Four social groups are distinguished, upper mid-

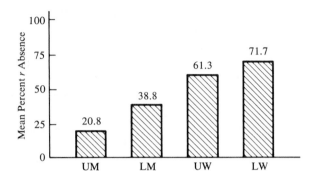

Figure 4-4. Postvocalic *r* absence: an example of gradient stratification (adapted from Wolfram 1969:110).

dle (UM), lower middle (LM), upper working (UW), and lower working (LW) class. The figures are based on *r* absence in spontaneous conversation between the fieldworker and the informant.

In Figure 4-4 it is observed that there is a progressive increase in the absence of postvocalic *r* between the four social groups; none of the groups shows a significantly greater frequency discrepancy than the others. But there are other variables which indicate a sharp demarcation between contiguous social classes. The case of -*Z* third-person present-tense singular forms shows this type of distribution for the same community. This is illustrated in Figure 4-5. In contrast to postvocalic *r*-lessness, we find that the

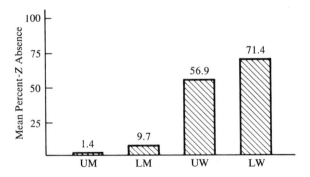

Figure 4-5. Third-person singular -*Z* absence: an example of sharp stratification (adapted from Wolfram 1969:136).

two middle-class groups (UM and LM) are sharply contrasted to the two working-class groups (UW and LW). In the case of sharp stratification, we find clear-cut patterns of correlation in terms of major social classes, whereas gradient stratification does not show the same discrete distribution. The most clear-cut linguistic boundary is found between the lower middle class and upper working class. This represents a typical pattern of distribution. There is usually less clear-cut distinction between the two middle-class groups and two working-class groups with respect to sharp stratification.

In the illustrations of sharp and gradient stratification given above, we may note that the *r* variable is phonological and the *-Z* variable grammatical. Grammatical variables more typically show sharp stratification than phonological ones. Gradient stratification is more characteristic of phonological variables although there are, of course, exceptions. In the sense that grammatical variables more discretely divide the population than phonological ones, we may conclude that they are generally more socially diagnostic.

The relative social diagnosticity of a particular feature may vary not only from linguistic variable to variable but also within a given variable, based on independent linguistic constraints such as environment, constituent type, and so forth. Take, for example, the absence of the final member of a consonant cluster in word-final position (e.g., /dɛs/ for Standard English 'desk'). This type of pattern affects items in which both members of the cluster are part of the same lexical item (i.e., monomorphemic, as /gɛs/ for Standard English /gɛst/ 'guest') and also clusters that result from the addition of the grammatical suffix *-ed* (i.e., bimorphemic clusters such as Black English /gɛs/ for Standard English /gɛs-t/ 'guessed'). The social significance of these two types is not equal, however. The former type, monomorphemic clusters, reveals a gradient stratification whereas the latter, the bimorphemic clusters, reveals sharp stratification. Likewise, the analysis of copula absence for several classes of blacks in Detroit reveals that there are certain types of constructions in which the absence of a copula is much less socially significant than others. The absence of a copula with the intentive future *gonna* (e.g., *They gonna go now*) is commonly used by middle-class speakers, although they typically do not reveal copula absence in other types of constructions such as predicative nominals, adjectives, and locatives (e.g., *He a nice man*).

In terms of the social significance of the variants of a variable, we may distinguish between socially *prestigious* and *stigmatized* variants. Socially prestigious variants are those features adopted by a high-status group as linguistic indications of social status, whereas stigmatized variants are those features associated with low-status groups. In some varieties of American English, such as those spoken in Midwestern cities, a slight raising quality in the vowel height of *æ*, in words such as *ban, pass,* and *rack,* appears to be a prestige pronunciation. On the other hand, the pronunciation of the interdental fricative ð as a stop *d* in words such as *that, the,* and *then* is a socially stigmatized variant. The absence of a prestige variant does not necessarily imply that the alternative variant is stigmatized, or vice versa. For example, the pronunciation of the vowel in *bat* and *rack* without a raised quality is not necessarily socially stigmatized, nor is the consistent pronunciation of the interdental fricative in *that* and *the* necessarily prestigious.

It is also important to note that the relationship between prestige and stigmatized variants is not always a stable one. Just as language constantly undergoes change, the social significance of language varieties is in a constant state of change. Thus, it is quite possible for the prestige value of vowel raising in *æ* to be eventually lost, so that it is simply adopted as a particular regional pronunciation with little or no prestige value. This is, in fact, what appears to be taking place with respect to this feature in some parts of the United States. High-status groups are a constant source of emulation in what Fischer has called "the protracted pursuit of an elite by an envious mass and consequent 'flight' of the elite" (1958:52). Although Fischer's characterization now seems too simplistic to account for the complexities of linguistic change in society, it is nonetheless to be expected that prestige variants often are assimilated by the lower classes, in which case they lose their prestige value. At this point, the middle class may simply introduce new prestige variants. Innovations can also begin in the lower classes, but unless they win acceptance by the middle classes they do not become characteristic of the language as a whole.

In New York City, Labov (1966:342–49) has shown that the prestige value of postvocalic *r* presence has changed from generation to generation. For the older generation, the presence of the *r* is of little or no prestige value, because there is very little differentiation between social classes of older informants. But for younger informants, the presence of *r* is quite clearly correlated with class, having a clear-cut prestige value.

Likewise, stigmatized features undergo constant change. We mentioned in Chapter One that multiple negation of the type *He didn't do nothing* has not always been stigmatized. There are periods in the earlier development of the English language when this form was commonly used by all speakers and not associated with low-status groups. Although it may be the high-status groups in positions of sociopolitical power who are originally responsible for setting social values with respect to speech, this does not mean that their judgments of speech differ drastically from the values of other classes. The study of subjective evaluations of speech by Shuy, Baratz, and Wolfram (1968) indicates that the low-status groups are quite aware of socially stigmatized and prestigious speech. Even though low-status groups may use a stigmatized variety, their overt assessment of it tends to match that of the high-status group.

Perhaps more important than the objective stratification of features in terms of socially diagnostic features are the types of subjective reactions to them. The subjective evaluation of socially diagnostic linguistic features can be classified into three basic types (Labov 1964b:102). First, there are *social indicators*. These features can be correlated with social class but have little effect on a listener's judgment of the social status of speakers. One of the most important clues for social indicators is the lack of variation in different styles. If speakers show a conscious or unconscious awareness of a socially diagnostic feature they will generally vary its frequency in more formal styles. Thus, a prestigious variant would become more frequent in more formal styles of speech and a stigmatized one less frequent. In the case of social indicators, this does not generally take place because of relative unawareness of the socially diagnostic variable. There are other features that show both social and stylistic variation and have regular effects on a listener's judgment of a speaker's social status. These have been referred to as *social markers*. It is not necessary for social markers to be recognized on a conscious level; in many cases, they may evoke an unconscious effect in a listener. The third type is the *social stereotype*. In the case of social stereotypes, particular linguistic features become the overt topics of social comment in the speech community. Features such as the use of *ain't* or *dese, dem,* and *dose* would probably be classified as stereotypes. These particular features often become topics for social comment in the speech community. Because there are a number of stereotyped items that do not correspond to actual sociolinguistic behavior, we should caution that we are only referring to those stereotyped features which relate to actual speech. In many cases, stereotyped features also refer to single vocabulary items rather than patterned grammatical or phonological processes. The pronunciations of *vase, either,* and *aunt* are more often the objects of social comment than regularly occurring phonological patterns.

Style

It does not take any particular sociolinguistic expertise to realize that speakers may show considerable flexibility in their use of the language. Most of us do not need to be told that we talk to a casual peer acquaintance in a manner different from the way we talk to a respected authority. Similarly, we are quite aware that writing style is expected to be different from spoken style. Stylistic variation has for some time now been considered the proper domain of a number of different disciplines and has been described from a number of different perspectives.

Within linguistics, one popular attempt to define style was formulated in Martin Joos's entertaining monograph entitled *The Five Clocks* (1962). In his description, five styles are delimited on the basis of both linguistic and nonlinguistic criteria. *Frozen* style is essentially written material for people who are total strangers. It therefore lacks participation and intonation. *Formal* style is determined by personal detachment and overall cohesion of content. In formal style, the primary consideration is to inform. *Consultative* style involves the continuous participation of the addressee and the speaker's supplying of background information. In *casual* style we have frequent ellipses and the use of slang. The formal features characterizing *intimate* style are extraction (i.e., "the speaker extracts a minimum pattern from some conceivable casual situation" [1962:23]) and jargon. Joos does not directly relate his styles to social class, but presumably there is a range of at least the more informal styles for all classes.

Although a classification such as Joos's is taxonomically appealing, it is quite difficult to rigorously delimit some styles on the basis of his characteristics. Much of the evidence is anecdotal and is impractical to use for careful descriptive studies. The view of qualitative rather than quantitative differences between various styles is also quite untenable when we look closely at actual speech behavior. In the description of style as it relates to social dialects, we need to look at a framework that rests upon a detailed empirical base.

Although there are obviously a number of ways in which we might approach style, the essential dimension of stylistic variation in social dialectology relates to the amount of attention that is paid to speech—the more attention paid, the more formal the style. Formal styles are defined as those situations within an interview where speech is in primary focus, whereas the informal styles are defined in terms of those contexts where there is the least amount of audio-monitoring of speech.

Ideally, we might delimit a vast number of styles along a continuum which intersects with situation, interlocutors, function of communication, and so forth. Although authentic contexts are obviously preferable, it is possible to structure a single interview in such a way as to elicit different styles of speech. Labov has shown that it is possible to structure the context so as to get discrete points in a continuum of formal to informal speech (see Chapter Three for the actual elicitation techniques). A possible continuum of styles ranging from informal to formal may include the following points:

Spontaneous Conversation
Reading Passages
Word Lists
Minimal Word Pairs

Presumably, each of these points indicates a different level of awareness with respect to speech.

In Labov's original delimitation of styles, he also distinguished between what he called "careful" and "casual" speech in spontaneous conversation. According to Labov (1966:100–111), casual speech in the interview situation is defined by specialized contexts (e.g., discussion not in direct answer to a question, speech directed to a third person) and paralinguistic channel cues such as changes in tempo, pitch, laughter, or heavy breathing. Our own attempts to distinguish different styles in spontaneous conversation on this basis were largely futile. Labov's later work does not depend on this technique but uses group interviews as a basis for the investigation of casual speech in conversation. It is difficult to be dependent on paralinguistic cues when these same cues may be interpreted in several different ways. For example, laughter or pitch changes may be indications of the informant's increased awareness of the artificiality of the interview situation. Can nervous laughter reliably be distinguished from relaxed or casual laughter? Also, subjective interpretation of the paralinguistic cues tends to bias the interpretation of casual speech even though the channel cues are theoretically supposed to be independent of the measurement of linguistic variables. To what extent must there be a change of rhythm or pitch and how close to the actual feature being tabulated must it occur? Such calculations may vary considerably between investigators. Without formally changing the task, it is difficult to assess style changes within a single interview with consistent reliability.

Linguistic features that bear social significance will show parallel behavior along a social-class continuum and style continuum from less formal to more formal styles. In particular, if a feature is more common in the lower social classes than in the upper classes, it will also be more common in less formal styles than in more formal styles for all speakers. Figure 4-6 is a hypothetical illustration of the typical pattern for a stigmatized feature, assuming two social classes and two styles.

We naturally would expect that a stigmatized variant will show decreased frequencies and a prestigious variant increased frequencies as one moves from informal to formal styles. This sort of patterning is quite

SOCIAL CLASSES	STYLES	
	Informal	*Formal*
Middle	Intermediate Frequency	Low Frequency
Working	High Frequency	Intermediate Frequency

Figure 4-6. Hypothetical frequency pattern for stigmatized variant.

apparent and is generally quite predictable for all social groups, as can be
seen in Figure 4-7, taken from Labov's study of the *th* variable in New
York City (1964a:109). Because the use of a stop [d] rather than the
interdental fricative [ð] is stigmatized, we expect the frequency of [d] to be
reduced in the more formal styles.

The most revealing aspect of stylistic variation occurs when we compare the different social groups with each other. Labov has demonstrated
that this comparison may reveal quite interesting arrays of relations for
some prestige variants. Consider, for example, the presence of postvocalic
r in New York City (Figure 4-8), where the presence of *r* in items such
as *beard* and *four* has a prestige value. As expected, there is a general
tendency to increase the use of *r* for all classes as one goes from informal
to formal in the continuum of styles. The most interesting phenomenon,
however, is the nontrivial (i.e., it is not an artifice produced by an inadequate research design) crossover pattern shown for the lower middle class
when compared with the upper middle class. In the less formal styles, the
lower middle class uses less *r* than the upper middle class, but in the more
formal styles, the frequency of *r* presence is greater for the lower middle

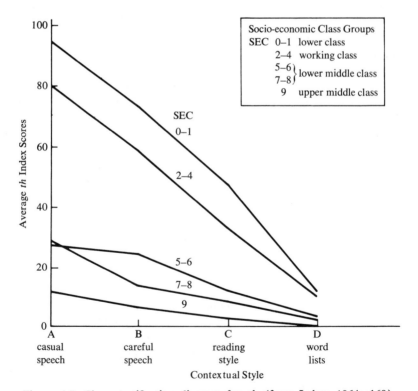

Figure 4-7. Class stratification diagram for *th* (from Labov 1964a:169).

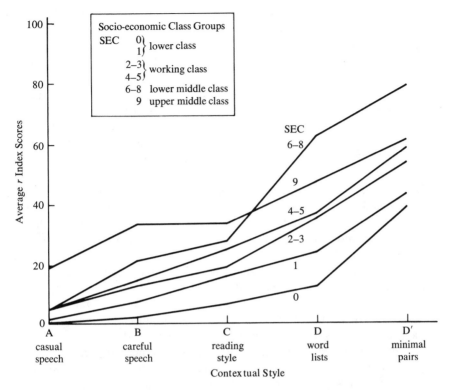

Figure 4-8. Class stratification diagram for *r* (from Labov 1964a:171).

class than the upper middle class. This is what may be called *statistical hypercorrection.* In statistical hypercorrection, the structural placement of forms follows that of the more prestigious groups, but the relative frequency of the forms exceeds the norms of the more prestigious social group. In order to understand the dynamics of this hypercorrection, we must note that the lower middle class is typically quite desirous of attaining upper middle-class status. The upper middle class already "has it made," and therefore can afford to be linguistically secure in more formal contexts. The lower middle class, however, constantly strives to emulate the upper middle class and attain equal status. This striving makes it very conscious of the external reference group with which it has contact but by which it is not completely accepted. The linguistic insecurity of this position is reflected in the fact that this group uses frequency levels higher than the more secure upper middle class when speech is in primary focus.

Statistical hypercorrection is not the only consequence of the conflict that speakers may experience between their overt opinions about which speech features are preferred and what features social realism demands they actually use. *Structural hypercorrection* is another. Structural hypercorrection results when an overtly favored feature is not thoroughly under the control of the speaker. He realizes that the feature is highly valued in the speech community, but he is not aware of all the linguistic constraints on its use. For example, the *y* sound between a consonant and an *oo* sound has high prestige in English. In some words, this *y* sound is always present, regardless of the social dialect of the speaker. The word *few* is always pronounced *fyoo*, never *foo*. In other items, the *y* sound is present for some speakers but not others. For example, *dyoo* is a more prestigious pronunciation of *due* than *doo*, but many speakers say the latter. In still other words, the *y* sound is never used by native speakers of the prestige dialect. However, a speaker who normally pronounces *due* as *doo* realizes that the pronunciation with *y* has prestige and may try to introduce this pronunciation into his speech in formal situations. It is entirely possible, though, that he does not know exactly which words take the *y* pronunciation and which do not. As a result, he may introduce the *y* into words that would not have this sound in the prestige dialect. He may not only use the *dyoo* pronunciation for *due* but also introduce the *y* into *goon*, giving *gyoon*. A frequently cited example of this is the news broadcaster who announced "the news [pronounced *nyooz*] at noon [pronounced *nyoon*]." Although the word *news* has the *y* pronunciation in the prestige dialect, the word *noon* does not. The overextension of the *y* pronunciation to words like *noon* due to the fact that the speaker does not know precisely which words actually take this pronunciation in the prestige dialect is an example of structural hypercorrection.

Another example involves the *-s* suffix with present-tense verbs. There are varieties of English in which the *-s* suffix is not required by the grammatical rules of those varieties. Yet speakers of such dialects realize that the suffix is preferred usage. In formal situations they may introduce the use of verbal *-s* but not control the restriction that *-s* is only used with present-tense verbs when the subject is third-person singular. The result is the utterance of sentences like *We goes to school* or *Those kids lives on our block,* in which the *-s* suffix is used with present-tense verbs but with subjects other than the third-person singular.[3] In general, structural hypercorrection is characterized by the overextension of a favored feature to linguistic environments in which the feature is never used by native users of the favored feature involved. This situation typically occurs because of constraints of formality which make the speaker aware of a need to use preferred forms.

---

[3] It is not correct to infer that all speakers who use sentences like *Those kids lives on our block* are displaying hypercorrection. Further discussion is found in Chapter Seven.

Age

The variable of age must be viewed in terms of two different parameters. First, there are age differences that relate to generation differences— older generations have often not undergone linguistic changes that have affected the younger generations. But there are also differences that relate to *age-grading;* there are characteristic linguistic behaviors appropriate for different stages in the life history of an individual. Although these two types of age variables can only be observed in combination, they are best understood by being discussed separately.

GENERATION DIFFERENCES

Most of us are well aware of the fact that this generation does not speak precisely like the preceding one. It is these changes from generation to generation which account for the gradual change of the English language. Each generation retains, to some extent, the language patterns that were originally learned early in life. Thus, we find that older residents may use the term *ice-box* even though ice-boxes have not been in use for many years. Likewise, the older generation may retain phonological and grammatical patterns they learned in their youth while the new generation may use different forms. Even though there are age-grade differences for every generation, a group born in 1930 will be different from a group born in the 1960s at each stage of life. The teenage expressions of the 1940s differ from those of the adults of that period, but they also differ from the teenage expressions of our time. And we expect that the teenagers of the next generation will not use the same expressions teenagers today use. More importantly, phonological and grammatical changes take place as generations adopt different speech patterns. The farther apart generations are, the more apparent differences in language structure become. The difference between Elizabethan English and current English is, in one sense, a summation of the changes that have taken place between the generations over a period of time.

Although we may not always have access to detailed accounts of specific language behavior of various generations at different time periods, it is possible to observe language changes that take place in *apparent time.* From this perspective, we view different generations within a population as a reflection of different time levels. Thus, the speech of a contemporary group in the age range of 60 to 69 may represent one period in the history of the language while a younger group, say 30 to 39, represents another time period. We can observe linguistic change in progress by noting the linguistic behavior of these groups. Using this framework for his study of New York City speech, Labov (1965) has made important observations of language change as it relates to social stratification. In some cases, we observe considerable stability when we look at the social stratification of language over several generations. For example, we witness little change in the stigmatization of *d* for ð when we look at its distribution over several generations. In other cases, social significance of linguistic variables can be quite flexible. We find that postvocalic *r* absence has changed its social significance for New Yorkers over succeeding generations. For speakers over forty, there is little or no social significance attached to *r* presence or absence; it is simply a regional characteristic. But for the under-forty generation it has assumed considerable social diagnosticity.[4]

AGE-GRADING

Within the life history of an individual, there are behavioral patterns that are considered appropriate for various stages. We often make assessments of a person's dress according to his age, so that we consider the style of dress appropriate for "teeny-boppers" quite inappropriate for middle-aged persons. The term "teeny-bopper" itself indicates our awareness of age-grading in our society because it refers to a particular adolescent stage of life and its associated behavior. In some cultures age-grading is quite definitive and there are elaborate initiation rites that mark a person's transition from one stage into another. Our society, however, reveals more gradual transitions and does not usually demark age grades through formal *rites de passage.* Speech is but one of the behavioral means through which age-grading is revealed.

In some instances, the differences between age groups may be on a superficial level, as shown, for example, in the use of vocabulary terms by adolescents. We may hear a teenager say to a friend, *I'm going to lay some heavy sounds on you* ('I'm going to play some nice music for you'). The use of the same expression at a party attended by middle-aged people would be considered quite inappropriate and evoke a negative reaction. For the most part, these vocabulary items have a rapid life cycle, so that adolescent slang expressions such as *heavy* for 'nice', *lay* for 'play', and *sounds* for 'music' will no doubt be obsolete within a few years, if they are not already.

Of a more substantial nature is the fact that there is a correlation between age and the use of certain socially stigmatized phonological and grammatical variants. During the first stage of a child's life, up to approximately the age of five or six, the main rules of language are learned in order for a child to participate in basic communication. During the pre-adoles-

---

[4] For a more extensive discussion of the stages of linguistic change as they relate to social factors, see Labov 1965.

cent and adolescent years, a child learns a local dialect that is primarily that of his immediate peers. The emphasis on peer influence on speech cannot be underestimated. There is clear-cut evidence that adolescents desire to talk like their peers and there is considerable peer pressure to do so. During this period, the influence of peers can readily negate any potential influence from the norms of parents. Our study of the English used by second-generation Puerto Rican teenagers in East Harlem clearly revealed that their speech can be understood only in terms of their peer contacts. Those with extensive contacts with blacks will speak authentic Vernacular Black English, despite pressure from parental adult norms not to do so. How the parents speak has little or no effect on their English, because adolescent norms are determined usually by the peer reference group.

During the adolescent years, the use of socially stigmatized forms may be expected to be at a maximum. Our comparison of different age levels for the black community in Detroit plainly indicates the greater incidence of stigmatized forms by adolescents. In Figure 4-9, the incidence of multiple negation of the type *He didn't do nothing* is tabulated for three age levels and four social groups in Detroit. The numbers represent mean percentages in terms of how frequently multiple negation is actualized in relation to the potential occurrences of this type of construction.

This figure demonstrates that there is an age-level difference that generally obtains regardless of social class. Adults typically use fewer stigmatized forms than either the 10 to 12-year-old or the 14 to 17-year-old informants. A similar distribution could be indicated for any number of phonological or grammatical features. There is, however, no clear-cut pattern of differentiation between the 10 to 12- and 14 to 17-year-old infor-

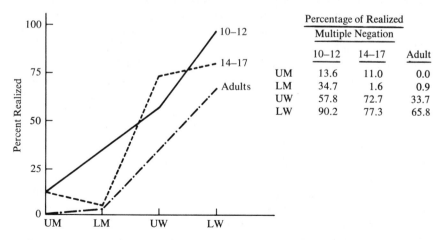

		Percentage of Realized Multiple Negation		
		10–12	14–17	Adult
	UM	13.6	11.0	0.0
	LM	34.7	1.6	0.9
	UW	57.8	72.7	33.7
	LW	90.2	77.3	65.8

Figure 4-9. Percentage of realized multiple negation: by social class and age (adapted from Wolfram 1969:163).

mants. If we could follow the informants in a longitudinal study, we would probably find that in latter adolescence, the usage of stigmatized forms will begin to match the adult norms more closely as they depart somewhat from the vernacular patterns. Contact with a wider range of social classes and exposure to the language of the upper middle class usually will have some effect in the movement from the vernacular pattern toward a more prestigious form of speech.

The variable of age cannot be considered independent of the previously discussed variables of class and style. Those who show upward social mobility can be expected to change their speech in conformity with the norms of the social class to which they are moving. As young adults begin to achieve their social status independent of their parents, through education, occupation, and social class associations, their speech will conform to their own status groups.

Although even young children are sometimes aware that they are expected to talk differently in different situations, stylistic variation is acquired in various stages. In pre-adolescence there is generally little stylistic variation. In early adolescence the social significance of indigenous dialects becomes apparent through exposure to other speech forms. At this point, a child may still be close to a monostylistic speaker of his local vernacular. His perceptions of social dialect differences is the impetus for modifying his speech in the direction of the prestige dialect, particularly in formal situations, but it may also be reflected in casual speech to a certain extent. Labov observes that "the great turning point seems to be exposure to a group larger than the neighborhood group in the first year of high school" (1964b:91). During this period, subjective reactions to speech also begin to match those of the adult pattern. At this point, a pattern of stylistic variation becomes an essential part of the speaker's linguistic repertoire.

Throughout the early adult years, a considerable amount of stylistic variation is quite typical. This is particularly true of those years during which an individual is primarily responsible for achieving his status. In the later years, as a person's status becomes relatively fixed, stylistic variation may tend to diminish. This is particularly true of the upper middle class and the lower working class. For the upper middle class this is due to relative linguistic security and the fact that the prestige norm has been incorporated into casual speech. By the time he has graduated from college, the upper middle-class speaker has had maximum exposure to the prestige dialect, and it is unlikely that he will undergo much shifting later in life. For the lower working-class speaker, the tendency to reduce stylistic shifting in later life may be due to his realization of the reality of social distance between the prestige norms of the upper classes and his own social position. At the point in life where he realizes that upward social mobility is "out of reach," he may assume a passive acceptance that it is too late to change his social position or a negative attitude toward upward mobility. This will be reflected in a reduced stylistic variation as he advances in years.

Sex

In some cultures, there are important differences between men's and women's speech. Entire systems of grammatical categories may vary, based on the sex of the speaker and/or the sex of the addressee. In the United States there is no dramatic differentiation of this sort. This is not to say, however, that sex does not interact with other variables to account for some aspects of dialect differentiation.

As sex differences relate to social dialects, we find that females tend to use stigmatized forms less frequently than males. For example, if we look at multiple negation as it is distributed by sex in the Detroit population, we find the frequency distribution for four social classes as shown in Figure 4-10. In this distribution, it is observed that in all four social classes the stigmatized variant is used more frequently by males than females. Females show more awareness of prestige norms in both their actual speech and their attitudes toward speech. Female sensitivity to speech is particularly characteristic of lower middle-class and upper working-class speech, although it is generally characteristic for all social classes. If we look further at Figure 4-10, we note that the greatest difference between males and females is found for the lower middle and upper working classes. This general pattern could be duplicated for a number of different socially significant variables. As we have mentioned previously, the lower middle-

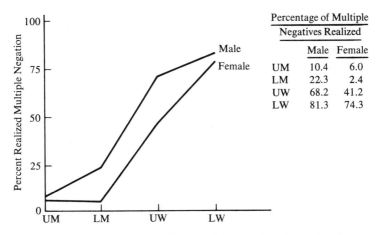

Figure 4-10. Percentage of realized multiple negation: by social class and sex (adapted from Wolfram 1969:162).

class population is linguistically quite insecure, constantly striving to emulate the linguistic behavior of the higher status group. This linguistic insecurity is reflected in the fact that the greatest stylistic shifts among the prestige variables are recorded for this group. Statistical hypercorrection, as we have defined it, is often the result of this tendency to show extreme stylistic variation among females. In more formal styles, lower middle-class women are much more apt to show substantial increases in the frequency levels of prestige variants, so that they use them more often than their middle-class counterparts. Younger female adults in the process of social mobility are particularly susceptible to this tendency.

The sensitivity to prestige norms demonstrated by women makes them prime candidates for linguistic change. The study of speech variation in a Piedmont community by Levine and Crockett led them to the conclusion that "the community's march toward the national norm was spearheaded by women, young people, short-termed residents of the community, and by those who are near but not quite at the top of the 'white collar' class" (1967:98). Studies of linguistic change occurring across the United States indicate that females are often responsible for the initial adoption of new prestige variants in a given locale.

Females are also credited with the primary responsibility for perpetuating the prestige norms of language to the next generation. It is generally considered a mother's role to spend a great amount of energy trying to speed up the normal process of language acquisition and warning children against the pitfalls of socially stigmatized speech. It is also interesting to note that occupations dealing with speech, such as speech therapy and language arts, tend to attract many more females than males.

The tendency of males to use more stigmatized variants in their speech than females must be seen in terms of the possible positive value that non-standard speech can have for a male. Nonstandard speaking may indicate virtues of masculinity and toughness for a male. It is no accident that our stereotypic notions of masculine heroes such as boxers and football players often include nonstandard speech. Tough men are supposed to talk in a masculine way, and this includes the use of stigmatized features. For females, there do not appear to be positive values associated with working-class speech which are analogous to those operating for males.

Ethnicity

The extent to which ethnicity correlates with linguistic diversity is a function of the distance between particular ethnic groups. Where there is assimilation of ethnic members into the larger culture, we may expect the factor of ethnicity to be of minimal significance, but where there is ethnic isolation of one type or another we may expect this variable to be of major significance. In reality, of course, ethnic isolation occurs in various degrees depending on the social role of various ethnic groups in our society. We may expect, for example, that a relatively homogenous Jewish community will reveal some linguistic differences from other groups, but we would predict that the difference will not be nearly as striking as that shown for the black community because of the relative social roles of these ethnic groups.

Just as ethnic correlates of speech differences must be viewed in terms of a continuum of isolation, members of a particular ethnic group will demonstrate different degrees of ethnic identification. It is, therefore, necessary to look at the particular types of contacts revealed by the individual members of an ethnic group. Our study of speech differences among the Detroit black population (Wolfram 1969), for example, indicated that it was necessary to distinguish between those black informants who had extensive and those who had limited contacts with whites. As it turned out, the variable of *racial isolation* was only relevant for middle-class black preadolescents and adolescents. Those blacks who had extensive contacts with whites, based on the criteria of peer contacts and residential and school integration, tended to use considerably fewer stigmatized variants than those with extensive black contacts. It is interesting to note that this difference was observed despite the fact that the parents of both the middle-class groups of informants did not characteristically use stigmatized variants in their speech.

Our study of the English used by second-generation Puerto Ricans in East Harlem (Wolfram et al. 1971, 1973) has further demonstrated the importance of distinguishing ethnic groups on the basis of the types of contact. The second-generation Puerto Rican in Harlem may be subjected to several different pressures in terms of language usage. In the home, and until he is of school age, a variety of Puerto Rican Spanish is typically the predominant language. As the child enters school and some of his contacts are expanded outside the immediate community, however, English becomes a competing language. And by the time he is a teenager, English and Spanish fill specialized roles of communication depending on a number of different variables such as participant, topic, location, and so forth (see Fishman et al. 1971 for a detailed account of these variables).

On the one hand, we observe that there is a concentrated adult Puerto Rican community that maintains Puerto Rican Spanish to a considerable extent. The predominant language of these first-generation Puerto Ricans is Spanish. On the other hand, however, second-generation Puerto Ricans may extend their associations beyond the Puerto Rican community through peer contacts, residency, and school. In most cases the extension of peer contacts outside of the Puerto Rican community involves the surrounding black community in Harlem. This means that these Puerto Ricans are going to be exposed to Vernacular Black English as the major source of English outside the Puerto Rican community. It is at this point that we must distinguish between those Puerto Ricans with extensive and restricted black contacts. If we take a typical Vernacular Black English feature such as the use of morpheme-final [f] as a correspondence of Standard English [θ], we can see the extent of linguistic assimilation to the surrounding phonological system. Figures for the [f] realization in items such as *tooth, Ruth,* and *both* are compared for two groups of Puerto Ricans and a control group of black speakers in Table 4-1.

No. Informants	Occ. *f*	Occ. θ	% *f*
Black (10)	36	8	81.8
PR with Extensive Black Contacts (6)	20	3	87.0
PR with Limited Black Contacts (23)	53	44	54.6

Table 4-1. Comparison of *f* realization morpheme-final position for blacks, Puerto Ricans with extensive black contacts, and Puerto Ricans with limited black contacts.

The results of this tabulation are quite straightforward. Puerto Ricans with extensive black contacts use the Black English variants much more frequently than do those with restricted contacts. It is interesting to note, however, that even those Puerto Rican teenagers with restricted black contacts have assimilated Black English phonological forms to a certain degree, so that the difference is quantitative, not qualitative. The black influence on both groups of Puerto Rican teenagers may be due to the fact that it is virtually impossible for a Puerto Rican teenager in Harlem to avoid some contact with blacks, despite the fact that he may not include them in his peer group. It may be that this restricted contact is sufficient for the assimilation of Black English features to a limited extent. But even if Puerto Ricans with restricted black contacts do not assimilate phonological features from the sporadic contact that they have with Blacks, it is quite reasonable to suggest that some assimilation may have taken place indirectly. That is, Puerto Rican adolescents with restricted black contacts may be assimilating phonological features of Vernacular Black English from Puerto Ricans with more extensive black contacts rather than the blacks themselves.

Although interference from a foreign language may be quite obvious in the speech of first-generation immigrants, straightforward interference from another language is of little or no significance for the second- and third-generation immigrant. In fact, the occurrences of this interference are so rare that we have referred to them as matters of *vestigial interference.* The lack of straightforward interference does not, however, rule out the possibility of a more subtle substratal effect on language. For example, Labov observes that the vowel patterns for the Jewish and Italian communities do not coincide with that of other New Yorkers, and reasons that this may be because of a *substratum language* effect from the languages spoken by previous generations. With reference to the vowel systems of these two groups, Labov concludes that "ethnic differentiation is seen to be a more powerful factor than social class, though both exist in addition to marked stylistic variation" (1966:306).

The extent to which ethnic membership is a factor in accounting for linguistic diversity may, of course, vary according to the linguistic variable. Whereas the Italian and Jewish groups do not participate in the general vowel pattern found elsewhere in New York City, these groups participate fully with respect to the pattern of postvocalic *r* absence. Similarly, our study of the use of English by second-generation Puerto Rican teenagers revealed that Vernacular Black English has exerted some influence on both the Puerto Ricans with extensive and those with restricted black contacts for phonological features (the differences being largely quantitative), but that grammatical patterns in Vernacular Black English are typically revealed only in the speech of those with extensive black contacts.

Before concluding our discussion of the effect of ethnic membership on linguistic behavior, we should mention the possible effect of the race of the interviewer on speech variation. Anshen (1969), in his sociolinguistic study of a small North Carolinian community, has shown that the race of the interviewer may affect variability. Anshen's study indicated that the younger age groups of blacks, for whom postvocalic *r* absence was socially diagnostic, revealed more *r* absence when interviewed by a black rather than a white interviewer. The results were consistent for three types of elicitation styles. The speech of older black residents, for whom *r* absence was not socially diagnostic, did not show a consistent correlation with the race of the interviewer.

The study of the Washington, D.C., black community also revealed that there is a tendency to use more stigmatized variants when talking with black interviewers, although the results were not as clear-cut as Anshen's. The effect of interviewer race on three socially diagnostic variables is given in Figure 4-11. The variables include word-final *d* deletion (e.g., [ga] for 'God'), word-final consonant cluster deletion (e.g., [wes] for 'west'), and third-person, singular, present-tense -*Z* deletion (e.g., *go* for 'goes').

Although all three variables show an increase in the stigmatized form when the interview was conducted by a black interviewer, the only really significant contrast (in terms of statistical tests of significance) is found

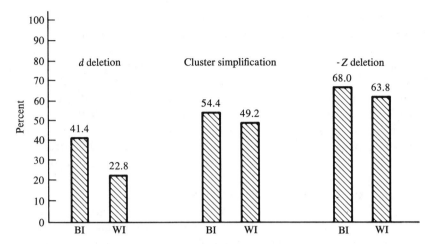

Figure 4-11. Covariation with race of interviewer for d deletion, final consonant cluster simplification, and verb concord $-Z$ deletion (from Fasold 1972:215).

for d deletion. For other variables investigated in the Washington study, there was no correlation with the race of the interviewer. In some instances, the effect of race is minimized by particular interviewing styles of field-workers. A white nonstandard speaker who can establish rapport may elicit as many or more stigmatized variants from a black speaker than a middle-class Standard English-speaking black with a fairly formal inter-viewing style.

In the preceding description we have discussed a number of different aspects of ethnic correlations with speech diversity, including the ethnic group's social position, the contact situation between ethnic groups, and the ethnicity of the interviewer. All of these aspects can potentially affect language variation. The matter of ethnic correlates with language vari-ability can indeed present a very complex picture based on the intersection of these subvariables.

5

THE LINGUISTIC VARIABLE

In Chapter Four we discussed social status, style, age, sex, and ethnicity as influences on patterns of variability. We have seen that social dialects are typically differentiated by variations in the frequency of occurrence of various features. In this chapter, we wish to show how aspects of the language itself interact with each other to influence variability and how to incorporate these linguistic influences on variability into a formal theory of language. To do this, we will need to make explicit a theoretical framework for looking at language. The framework to be used will be a version of generative-transformational grammar modified to handle variation. It will not be necessary for us to go into all the formal details of rule-writing for this theory; essential formal conventions will be introduced as we go along.

Optional Rules

A basic notion which is found in generative-transformational theory and all other linguistic theories is that of *obligatory* and *optional* rules. If a rule is obligatory it applies every time the appropriate conditions are present (except, of course, for slips of the tongue). An example of an obligatory pronunciation in English is the slight puff of air (called *aspiration*) that occurs with certain consonants in English at the beginning of accented syllables. One consonant of this type is *p*. In the word *pit,* for example, the *p* has aspiration (if the aspiration were not present the word would sound like *bit* to an English speaker).[1] Because the aspiration is virtually never absent, a phonology of English will contain an *obligatory* rule for the insertion of aspiration with consonants like *p* in syllable-initial position. At the end of the word, the aspiration may or may not occur. The word *tip,* then, is sometimes pronounced with the lips parting from the *p* position to emit the puff of air and sometimes with the lip-parting substantially delayed or the lips being parted without emitting aspiration. In a typical analysis, this would be expressed by means of an *optional* rule for the insertion of the aspiration feature.

An optional rule simply states that the effect designated by the rule may or may not take place even when the conditions are appropriate. But it has been shown for many optional rules that the surrounding linguistic environment has a definite effect on *how often* the rule can be expected to apply. The optionality of the aspiration of the *p* in *tip* may well be affected by the surrounding sounds. Although apparently no one has investigated this, it is quite possible that the aspiration will occur more often if the words like *tip* are not immediately followed by other words than if they are. It is quite conceivable, for example, that if we were to observe 100 examples of sentences like "Thanks for the tip," perhaps about 25 would have aspiration on the *p* of *tip.* Taking 100 examples of phrases like "tip of the iceberg," spoken by the same speaker or speakers in the same style, it might be that only 10 examples would have an aspirated *p* in *tip.* Aspiration would sometimes occur even when other words followed and would sometimes not occur when no other words followed, but the absence of following words would favor aspiration.

The above hypothetical example can readily be replaced by real examples. Labov has pointed out that many linguists working with theories that allow for only obligatory and optional phenomena have nonetheless informally stated that there are influences on frequency. For example, from a linguistic description of Walapai:

> The dental and glottal fricatives are usually voiceless except that /θ/ is very often voiced intervocally and between a voiced consonant and a vowel.   (Redden 1966:10, quoted in Labov 1971:435)

In other words, the consonant symbolized by θ may or may not be voiced (ð) in any position in the word, but it is "very often" voiced between vowels and between voiced consonants and vowels, but "usually voiceless" elsewhere.

---

[1] There is no such aspiration rule in Spanish and in many other languages. For this reason, together with differences in vowel pronunciation, a Spanish speaker saying *pit* will make the word sound vaguely like *beet* to an English speaker.

Variable Constraints [2]

When linguists have actually looked for the influences on frequency, they have discovered that not only are there many influences which favor the operation of certain rules, but some of these will affect the rule to a greater degree than others.[3] For example, the frequency of final stop deletion in English, in addition to being affected by the kinds of social constraints isolated in Chapter Four, is affected by a number of linguistic factors. These factors include whether or not the deletable stop is followed by a word beginning with a vowel and the kind of consonant that precedes it (when a consonant actually does precede). Considering the cases in which consonants precede final stops, we find that final stops are deleted in collocations like *wild elephant* and *east end* (where words beginning with vowels follow) 28.7 percent of the time, and in examples like *wild horse* and *east precincts* (where words beginning with vowels do not follow) 75.6 percent of the time.[4] Similarly, the deletion rule is favored if

[2] The word *constraint,* when applied to variable rules, refers to factors that *promote* operation of a rule. Other linguists (e.g., Ross 1967) use the word for factors that *prevent* the operation of certain rules.

[3] At first glance, the reader may think that counting variants is a rather simple procedure. Those who have engaged in this type of research, however, can readily testify to the fact that there are a number of subtle problems in actually tabulating such data. Determining what to count is only approached through a long series of exploratory procedures which, in many cases, actually involves the final solution to the problem at hand. Although we shall not go into detail here (see Wolfram 1969 for more detail), several procedural guidelines may be helpful for the reader interested in carrying out such types of quantitative studies. In the first place, it is essential to identify the total population of utterances in which an item may "potentially" vary. This involves the systematic exclusion of those environments where one item may occur categorically and thus skew overall figures. It is also crucial to get sufficient numbers of examples so that the quantitative data will not be distorted for a particular environment. It is further necessary to be very careful in delimiting the number of variants that can be reliably identified. With grammatical variants, this may not be much of a problem, but with some types of phonological data, the gradient nature of the data makes it difficult to delimit discrete categories of variants in some instances. Finally, care must be taken so that different environments and items are adequately represented. Without keeping *type-token* relations in mind, frequency levels may be misleading. The researcher who attempts to tabulate data unaware of these potential problems may end up with quite unmanageable data.

[4] These figures are based on data from Washington, D. C., working-class black speech (Fasold 1972:67–70). Actually the data examined is on bimorphemic consonant clusters (i.e., where the deletable stop is *t* or *d* representing the *-ed* suffix). More accurate examples, perhaps, would be *killed* (pronounced *killd*) *an elephant* and *missed* (pronounced *mist*) *his bus.* If we had data on both monomorphemic (like *wild* and *east*) and bimorphemic (like *killed* and *missed*) consonant clusters, the percentages would be somewhat higher, but the difference would be in the same direction and of comparable magnitude. Similarly, if our data were on higher or lower social classes, or on speakers of different ethnic backgrounds, the percentages would differ accordingly, but the differences between the *linguistic* influences under discussion

the preceding consonant is a sonorant (a nasal consonant or *l*) compared to cases in which it is a nonsonorant (a stop or fricative). Examples like *wild elephant* or *sand castle* were pronounced with the final stop deleted 63.3 percent of the time while only 43.0 percent of the examples like *lift it* or *fast car* turned up with the final stop missing. It is clear from these figures and figures on other similar data that the deletion rule is favored by not having a vowel immediately following and by having a sonorant consonant rather than an obstruent (nonsonorant) consonant preceding. What is less clear is which of these two influences outranks the other. One way to determine this is to examine first the cases in which one factor favors the rule and the other does not, and then the cases in which the favoring and inhibiting factors are reversed. This is done in Table 5-1.

Environment		Example	Percent Deleted
Following vowel	Preceding obstruent	lif(t) it	25.2
Following vowel	Preceding sonorant	wil(d) elephant	34.9
Following nonvowel	Preceding obstruent	fas(t) car	68.8
Following nonvowel	Preceding sonorant	san(d) castle	83.3

Table 5-1. Ranking of two linguistic factors favoring final stop deletion (from Fasold 1972).

The lowest percentage is found, predictably, where neither feature favors deletion. The highest, equally predictably, occurs where both features favor deletion. But of the two situations in which the two features conflict, the higher percentage occurs where the following nonvowel, favoring deletion, occurs and the preceding consonant is an obstruent, which does not favor deletion. Thus it appears that the effect of the following nonvowel exceeds the effect of the preceding sonorant. A following nonvowel will be called the *first-order constraint* in a situation like this, while the preceding sonorant is the *second-order constraint*.

The relationship between first- and second-order constraints is readily seen by placing them in a hierarchical display such as the one in Figure 5-1. In this type of hierarchy, the correct ranking of orders should reveal that the percentages of the final branching progress from high to low (or low to high). If we hypothesize that the preceding sonorant was the first-order

would be just as apparent as in our figures. For more detailed discussion of the final stop deletion feature, see Chapter Six.

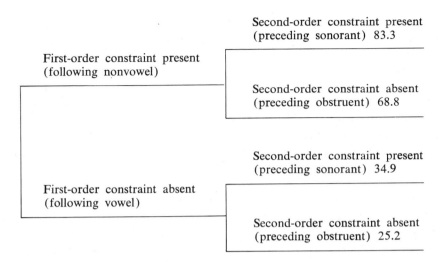

Figure 5-1. Correct hierarchy of constraints.

constraint and the following nonvowel the second-order, the expected progression would not obtain. Thus, Figure 5-2 does not represent the correct ranking, while Figure 5-1 does. In the incorrect hierarchy (Figure 5-2), the low branching in the upper bracket and the high branching in the lower bracket, called "cross products" by Labov (1969), are reversed. It is precisely these cross products which are crucial for determining constraint orders.

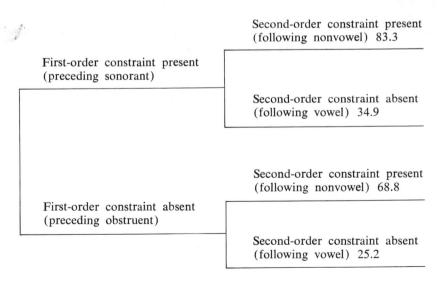

Figure 5-2. Incorrect hierarchy of constraints.

It may be that a demonstration based on only two variables is not totally convincing. It simply stands to reason that the lowest percentages would correspond to the case in which neither favoring feature is present and that the highest would occur when both are present. The other two cases naturally have to occur in one order or the other. If the percentages had appeared in the reverse order, we would say that the type of preceding consonant outranks the following nonvowel as a constraint, so that our claim that the linguistic effects on frequency are ranked is not really proved. But there are two further kinds of demonstrations which show that constraints are, in fact, ranked. One is that when two constraints on the same linguistic phenomenon are investigated for more than one population, they are ranked in the same way. Our example of the final stop deletion rule is a case of this type; the same ranking can be seen for Detroit black speech in the data in Wolfram (1969) for four social classes. Because the speakers in the different social classes were interviewed separately and were not acquainted with each other, each of Wolfram's social classes can be considered a separate population, even though all are black and all live in Detroit. As a result, the four populations of Detroit speakers and one population of Washington speakers comprise five data sets, all of which show the same ranking for the two constraining features.

Another demonstration of systematic regularity involves forms in which there are three or more constraints. In such a case, the data must fit a table with not four, but at least eight lines. This means that between the presence of all constraints, which has to appear on the top, and the absence of all, which has to appear on the bottom, there have to be six or more lines in precisely the right order for the claim about constraint hierarchy to be validated. When there are three constraints, it must be possible to assign one as the first-order constraint, another as the second-order constraint, and the last as the third-order constraint so that when they are arranged as below, the frequency of deletion goes from high to progressively lower values, with no value lower than the one below it.

Constraints present	Percent deletion
1. First-order, second-order, third-order	Highest
2. First-order, second-order	Lower
3. First-order, third-order	Lower
4. First-order	Lower
5. Second-order, third-order	Lower
6. Second-order	Lower
7. Third-order	Lower
8. None	Lowest

Such that $1 > 2 > 3 > 4 > 5 > 6 > 7 > 8$

Unlike the case of a rule with two constraints, it seems highly unlikely that a rule with three constraints would emerge with the constraints correctly ordered by chance. But data do exist in which three constraints are ordered in just this way. To illustrate this pattern, we will use other data on the final stop deletion rule, this time taken from a study of black and Puerto Rican male adolescents from New York City (Wolfram et al. 1971). This time the examples under investigation are cases in which the final stop is not preceded by another consonant.[5] The three constraints which emerged from the analysis were again the absence of a word beginning with a vowel following the final stop, the accent of the syllable which ends in the stop, and whether or not the stop in question represents a grammatical suffix. Because the only postvocalic final stop in English that represents a suffix is *d* (representing the *-ed* suffix), *d* is the only stop tabulated. The ranking that was discovered has the following nonvowel again as the first-order constraint, the accent of the syllable as the second-order constraint, and the grammatical status of the *d* as the third. In Table 5-2, the actual data are presented. With one very minor exception, all the required relationships appear in the predicted order. The lone exception is a deviation of 0.1 percent at the bottom of the chart. Data that turn out as neatly as this are not rare, but have come to be the expected pattern.

ENVIRONMENT		EXAMPLE		PERCENT DELETED
Following vowel	strong accent	{ ed	tried it	17.1
Following vowel	strong accent	{ not ed	side angle	18.6
Following vowel	weak accent	{ ed	borrowed everything	26.3
Following vowel	weak accent	{ not ed	rapid increase	39.3
Following nonvowel	strong accent	{ ed	tried hard	41.2
Following nonvowel	strong accent	{ not ed	side street	66.6
Following nonvowel	weak accent	{ ed	borrowed money	70.4
Following nonvowel	weak accent	{ not ed	rapid stream	70.3

Table 5-2. Ranking of three linguistic factors favoring final stop deletion.

[5] It would no doubt be possible to study the final stop deletion rule with respect to *all* the constraints that affect it, at one time. Although the rule has been studied by several linguists, none have actually assembled data on all the constraints from the same population at the same time.

Variable Constraints and Linguistic Theory

It is now important to consider how linguistic theory is to capture such facts about language variation. To develop a theory that accounts for a certain language phenomenon is to do much more than to state a given linguist's preferences. Linguistic theory, if studied seriously, has as its goal accounting for exactly the capabilities people have in using their language—no more and no less. Linguistic theory, then, can be viewed as a special kind of study in psychology. Taken seriously, every capability built into a linguistic theory constitutes a claim that the same capability is built into the language control parts of the human brain and speech mechanism. The theory should not include such aspects of language use that may be derivable from general probabilities on events in the world, or even those derivable from general (not language-specific) human capabilities. On the other hand, the theory should not fail to include capabilities which human beings actually have in their ability to control language. Ultimately, then, linguistic theory will only be shown to be correct or incorrect when much more is understood about the operation of human brain neurology. To the extent that there are neurological analogues for theoretical constructs, the linguistic constructs will be validated. In the meantime, we must rely on careful observation of language data analyzed with all the intelligence and scientific rigor that can be brought to bear.

In the area of optionality, it is important to decide just how much capability our theory is to claim for the human language user as far as influence on variability is concerned. We will discuss six degrees of control over variability, each making stronger claims for the human language user than the last and each stronger capability including less strong ones. We shall attempt to determine which claim actually accounts for what speakers can be observed to do without making excessive claims for what they can do. The first claim, and the weakest, is that human beings are capable only of discriminating which rules are optional and which are obligatory. For example, a person who speaks English knows that a syllable-initial p must be pronounced with aspiration, but that aspiration is optional for final p. Proponents of this view, which has had a long history in linguistic theory and has not been challenged until very recently, would say that this is the full extent of the language user's capability. The influences on degree of optionality are either ignored or taken to be derived from general principles not language-specific and therefore not to be included in linguistic theory. This is the traditional position in linguistics and the one probably accepted by most linguists today.

Another conceivable claim would be that a speaker knows which rules are optional and furthermore what the factors are that favor the operation of the rule. To go back to our example of the final stop deletion rule when another consonant precedes, this would mean that the theory would have to have the power to identify the final stop deletion rule as a variable rule and also account for the fact that its operation is favored if a nonvowel follows or if the final stop is preceded by a sonorant. No claim would be made for the relative strengths of the two influences, however. This intermediate position, though a reasonable one, has never to our knowledge actually been adopted by any linguist.[6] Most linguists willing to make a claim as strong as this one are willing to go further.

The next stronger position—which actually *does* have adherents—is that the language user recognizes that some rules are variable, can identify the factors that favor the operation of the rule, and knows the hierarchical order of constraints. If this claim is correct, language users have the capability, derived from their ability to control language, of identifying a following nonvowel as a stronger influence favoring final stop deletion than a preceding sonorant. This position is the one taken in Labov's 1969 article in *Language* proposing the variable rule as a theoretical construct, and by several scholars who have followed him.[7]

A further suggestion would be that the user of a language knows which features favor variability, what the hierarchy of constraint strength is, and also *how much* stronger a higher-order constraint is than a lower-order one. Given the hypothetical ordering in Figure 5-3, it is possible to state that the first-order constraint exceeds the second-order constraint in strength by a wider margin than the second-order constraint exceeds the third-order one.

In the case in which the first-order constraint is present and the second-order constraint is absent, the rule operates 62.5 percent of the time. When the second-order constraint is present but the first-order constraint is absent, the output is only 37.5 percent, a difference of 25.0 percent in favor of the first-order constraint. There are two cases in which the second- and third-order constraints conflict. In the one case, the presence of the second-order constraint without the third-order constraint produces an output of 77.3 percent, while the presence of the third-order constraint

---

[6] It is possible to interpret the theory of Cedergren and D. Sankoff (1972) and G. Sankoff (1972), to be discussed later, as being of this type. Their rules consist of a rule proper, which includes all the linguistic constraints on the rule's operation, and a "key," giving the probabilities of operation of the rule contributed by each linguistic constraint and also by social constraints. If the "key" is to be taken as separate from the rule, then the rule proper is of exactly this type.

[7] We will explain the formal mechanism for writing variable rules later in this chapter.

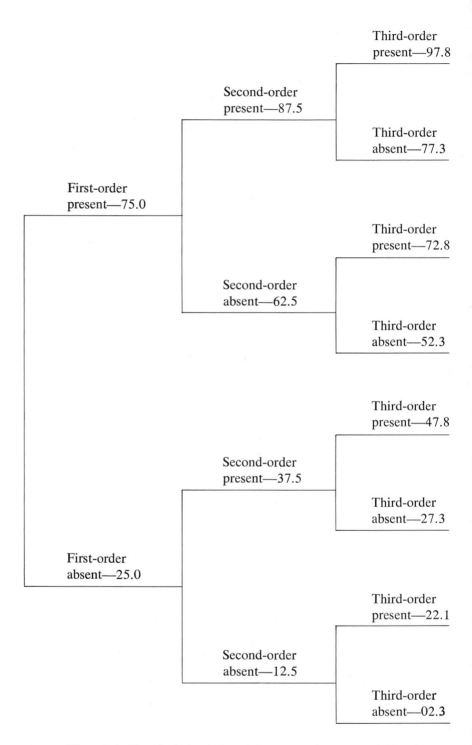

Figure 5–3. Hypothetical ordering of three constraints on a variable rule.

in the absence of the second-order constraint results in a 72.8 percent output. In the other case, the second-order constraint exceeds the third-order constraint by 27.3 percent to 22.1 percent. In both cases, the difference between the two is about 5 percent. Therefore we can say that the first-order constraint exceeds the second-order constraint by a margin five times greater than the margin by which the second-order constraint exceeds the third-order constraint. It may be conceivable that human users of language have precisely this capability, but to state it formally in a rule is extremely difficult. At this point no one has proposed that rules be constructed to include relative margins of difference between constraints.[8]

(5) A further claim would be that the language user knows the probabilities which each of the constraints contributes to the frequency output of the rule. Such a theory has been proposed by Henrietta Cedergren and David Sankoff (1972) and developed by Gillian Sankoff (1972). The constraints on each rule are listed and a probability figure is associated with each constraint. It is clear that if such figures are known to the language user, he also knows the hierarchy (which can be derived simply by ranking the probabilities from highest to lowest). It is also true that the relative strength of each constraint can be derived by subtracting the probability of a lower-order constraint from the probability of a higher one. To illustrate how the system works, consider the formula for calculation of the probability of application of a variable rule. The formula, modified in noncrucial ways from the one in Cedergren and Sankoff (1972), is:

$$\varphi = 1 - (1 - \text{1st-order}) \times (1 - \text{2nd-order}) \times \ldots$$
$$\times (1 - n\text{th-order})$$

This is to be interpreted as φ (the probability of application) is equal to 1 minus the product of 1 minus the probability of the first-order constraint times 1 minus the probability of the second-order constraint and so on times 1 minus the probability of the nth-order constraint. Each of the probabilities reflects the likelihood that the rule *will* apply. Subtracting each from 1 gives the probability that the rule *won't* apply contributed by each constraint. The product of these is the aggregate probability that the rule won't apply, given these constraints. Subtracting this figure from 1 gives the probability that the rule *will* apply. Assume a hypothetical rule with three constraints such that the probability contributed by the first-order constraint is .89, by the second-order constraint .57, and by the third-order constraint .16. Substituting in the formula, we get the probability of application in cases where all three constraints are present.

---

[8] Although there are no proponents of this position at this point, there do appear to be some important implications of constraint strength (Wolfram 1973b).

$$1 - (1 - .89) \times (1 - .57) \times (1 - .16)$$
$$= 1 - (.11) \times (.43) \times (.84)$$
$$= 1 - (.04)$$
$$= .96$$

That is, the probability is that the rule will apply in 96 out of every hundred cases in which all three constraints are present. It is to be emphasized that a figure such as .96 is a *probability*, not a fixed frequency of prediction. Observations of representative examples should result in observed frequencies clustering around 96 percent, not reaching exactly 96 percent in every observation.[9]

Finally, it could be proposed that the theory must include all the factors that predict precisely the percentage frequency with which a rule will operate in every case. Associated with each rule would be all the information necessary to determine for a speaker the exact frequency of operation of that rule. No one has actually proposed a theory with this capability, although Labov (1969) has been widely misunderstood to have proposed just this.

To recapitulate, we list the increasingly powerful theories about control of variability:

SPEAKER CAPABILITIES	PROPOSED BY
Speaker can identify optional (variable) rules.	Traditional view
Speaker can identify variable rules and which linguistic factors favor rule operation.	Cedergren and D. Sankoff (1972) (rule proper) (?)
Speaker can identify variable rules, which linguistic factors favor rule operation, and the hierarchical order in which they are ranked.	Labov (1969)
Speaker can identify variable rules, which linguistic factors favor rule operation, the hierarchical order in which they are ranked, and the extent to which higher-order constraints are stronger than lower-order ones.	No one, implied in Wolfram (1973b)
Speaker can identify variable rules, which linguistic factors favor rule operation, the hierarchical order in which they are ranked, the extent to which higher-order constraints are stronger than lower-order ones, and the probabilities toward rule operation contributed by each.	Cedergren and D. Sankoff (1972) (rule proper and "key")

[9] In Cedergren and Sankoff's formulation, not only linguistic constraints (like the presence or absence of a vowel, strength of accent, etc.) but also social constraints (sex, social class, ethnicity) are taken into account by the same mechanism.

SPEAKER CAPABILITIES	PROPOSED BY
Speaker can identify variable rules, which linguistic factors favor rule operation, the hierarchical order in which they are ranked, the extent to which higher-order constraints are stronger than lower-order ones, and not just the probability contributed by each, but an exact determination of the force of each in any given situation.	No one, common misunderstanding of Labov (1969)

For our purposes it is assumed that the issue is not yet settled but that the two weakest theories (optional rules and variable rules with unhierarchized constraints) and the strongest (variable rules that purport to determine precise frequencies of application) can be safely ruled out. We will assume that the correct theory will at least be capable of handling hierarchized constraints in general as proposed by Labov in 1969, and may be powerful enough to predict the probabilities contributed by each constraint. (This capability, as we have pointed out, presupposes the hierarchized constraint capability.) The theories we find plausible are bracketed in the above list.

Implicational Arrays

Given a theory capable of expressing linguistic constraints in this way, it is possible to see how linguistic constraints can interact with the sorts of social factors discussed in the previous chapter. Comparing linguistic constraints with social class, we observe patterns like that in Table 5-3.

	Orders of Constraints Present			
CLASS	NONE	2ND	1ST	1ST, 2ND
Upper Middle	.07	.28	.49	.79
Lower Middle	.13	.43	.62	.87
Upper Working	.24	.65	.73	.94
Lower Working	.34	.72	.76	.97

Table 5-3. Interaction of linguistic constraints and social class for a stigmatized feature: final stop deletion in Detroit black speech (adapted from Wolfram 1969:59–69).

It is clear from this table that both lower-class membership and the presence of the most and strongest linguistic constraints tend to raise the output of the rule.

A display like Table 5-3 based on different frequency levels is not the only systematic way in which the data may be viewed. The data may also be seen as representing a type of patterning which Guttman (1944) originally referred to as a *scalogram*. The scalogram is a specialized technique which is intended to produce an ordinal scale with a built-in logical structure. In this procedure, structural relations are seen to be related in implicational sets. That is, item X implies item Y and Y implies Z, but the converse is not true. The columns and rows in a table can be set up to summarize rather elaborate implicational arrays.[10] Some linguists have adopted this framework (in some cases arrived at independently) for displaying sociolinguistic variation, referring to it as *implicational patterning* (DeCamp 1971; Bickerton 1971; Bailey 1973; Peet 1973). A strict two-valued implicational display demands that items be arranged in rows and columns as in Figure 5-4, where 1 indicates the presence of a category and 0 its absence. The presence of an item in any cell *implies* its presence in

0	0	0	0
0	0	0	1
0	0	1	1
0	1	1	1
1	1	1	1

Figure 5-4. Typical two-valued implicational pattern.

all cells to the right of it. Similarly, the absence of the item in any cell implies its absence everywhere to the left. Table 5-3 is convertible to a two-valued implicational pattern by arbitrarily deciding that, say, 50 percent output or greater represents the presence of final stop deletion and 49 percent or less represents its absence. The pattern is given as Table 5-4.

		Constraints Present		
CLASS	NONE	2ND	1ST	1ST, 2ND
Upper Middle	0	0	0	1
Lower Middle	0	0	1	1
Upper Working	0	1	1	1
Lower Working	0	1	1	1

Table 5-4. Data from Table 5-3 in two-valued implicational pattern format.

All the information in Table 5-4 is also captured by Table 5-3, but the latter clearly shows the differences between the upper and lower working classes, while they appear the same in Table 5-4. Also, that table does not show us, as does Table 5-3, that each 1 is larger than the one to the left

[10] The Guttman scale has been applied to a considerable extent in social sciences such as anthropology. For a review of its usefulness in anthropological research, see Pelto (1970:338–44).

of it or above it and each 0 is less than the one to the right of it or below it.

More information can be given by a three-valued implicational pattern. In a three-valued pattern, categorical (one hundred percent) presence, variable (between zero and one hundred percent) presence, and categorical absence are recognized. If we retain the symbol 1 for categorical presence and 0 for the categorical absence and introduce X to indicate variable presence, Table 5-3 can be represented as a three-valued pattern. To express the data as a three-valued pattern, let us assume that any output less than 10 percent is the equivalent of categorical absence and values in excess of 90 percent are the equivalent of categorical presence. Values in between are considered representative of variable presence. Table 5-5 is the result.

		Constraints Present		
CLASS	NONE	2ND	1ST	1ST, 2ND
Upper Middle	0	X	X	X
Lower Middle	X	X	X	X
Upper Working	X	X	X	1
Lower Working	X	X	X	1

Table 5-5. Data from Table 5-3 in three-valued implicational pattern format.

Table 5-5 is an improvement over Table 5-4. We know that stop deletion in the two lowest classes in the presence of both constraints occurs more often than under the other conditions, that is, approximately always. Similarly, we know that in the upper middle class stop deletion occurs less often in the absence of both constraints than under the other conditions, that is, approximately never. But the more and less relationships among the Xs are not revealed and the two lowest classes are not distinguished from each other.[11]

The fundamentally similar nature of all three versions of the Detroit stop deletion data should be clear. The three-valued implicational chart is simply more finely grained than the two-valued version and the frequency chart (which can be thought of as a multivalued implicational chart) in Table 5-3 is the most finely grained of all. Because data like those in Table 5-3 are not at all rare, but have come to be expected in the analysis of social dialects, we shall require of linguistic theory that it express the more and less relationships present in the table. It should be emphasized that the actual frequency values that appear in charts like Table 5-3 are rela-

[11] Of course, if we had chosen another threshhold for categorical presence, say, 95 percent, the two lowest classes would have been distinguished (although the two intermediate classes would then not have been distinguished without further gerrymandering).The point is that a frequency chart like Table 5-3 captures all the information of even a three-valued implicational chart, and more.

tively unimportant. To demand of a theory that the exact numbers in such displays be predicted would be to demand more than is justified by the facts. What is important are the relative relationships of more and less. Of course, more-less relationships would not be discovered without actual frequency values. But the tabulation of actual frequency values should be regarded as a discovery procedure for determining the more-less relationships rather than having direct theoretical status in itself.

Similar patterns exist for the outputs of different rules. Table 5-6 shows the outputs of three socially stigmatized rules in Detroit black speech: (1) the creation of syllable-final f from original θ (yielding the pronunciation *baf* for *bath,* for example), (2) the desulcalization or dropping of r after vowels, e.g., *ca'* for *car,* and (3) the final stop deletion rule. As we expect, based on the discussion in the previous chapter, the highest output frequencies for all three rules occur in the lowest class, with frequencies decreasing as we approach the highest class. Furthermore, all four classes

| | | *Rules* | |
CLASSES	f FROM θ	r-DESULCALIZATION	STOP DELETION
Upper Middle	.06	.21	.51
Lower Middle	.11	.39	.66
Upper Working	.38	.61	.79
Lower Working	.45	.71	.84

Table 5-6. Interaction of social class with three stigmatized rules in Detroit black speech (data from Wolfram 1969:60, 84, 110).

have the three rules ranked in the same order based on frequency; the final stop deletion rule has the largest output, r-desulcalization next and f from θ the least. It is easy to see that judicious selection of frequency thresholds would allow us to convert Table 5-6 to either a two- or three-valued implicational chart as we did for Table 5-3. Again, by so doing we would learn no more than we do from Table 5-6, and we would be obliged to give up the more-less information. For some language phenomena, apparently especially in the case of creole languages (DeCamp 1971; Bickerton 1971; Peet 1973), a two-valued or three-valued implicational display is adequate, but in the study of social dialects in the mainland United States, insights are lost if multivalued frequency displays are not employed.

A few moments' reflection will reveal how our earlier discussion of the various degrees of competence relates to the two-, three-, and multi-valued displays. A two-valued version of Table 5-6 would correlate with a linguistic theory that recognized only completely obligatory or completely absent rules. Such a theory is more conservative than any we presented earlier. A three-valued version of the same table would correspond to a theory that recognized only obligatory, optional, and, of course, absent rules. Any theory more powerful than this requires the recognition of multiple frequencies.

It is worth inquiring how it should come about that three rules like the ones in Table 5-6 should have differential outputs that repeat themselves so regularly for four social classes. Recalling our discussion of regional and time factors in Chapter Four, it is clear that time is one such factor. A rule that has come into a language earlier has had more time to generate a larger output. Reasoning this way, we would conclude that final stop deletion in Detroit black speech is the oldest rule, *r*-desulcalization is the next oldest, and the rule for the creation of *f* from θ is the most recent. For a number of reasons we need not investigate here, this is probably not the case. What is more relevant is *social evaluation* of rules. Although all three rules are stigmatized, black speakers in Detroit evaluate *f* from θ as the most stigmatized of the three, *r*-desulcalization as less stigmatized, and final stop deletion as least stigmatized.[12] In actual fact, time and social evaluation factors no doubt interact to produce frequency differentials, but in this Detroit case it appears that social evaluation is the paramount consideration.

Formalizing Variable Rules

We will illustrate the formal mechanism for expressing theoretically two of the three capabilities we find acceptable. As we have explained, we find it reasonable that a linguistic grammar account for variable rules indicating hierarchized variable constraints only, or that the hierarchized constraints with the margins of difference between them be indicated, or that the constraints be expressed and probability figures associated with each. We have also claimed that it is difficult to attempt to express the margins of difference between hierarchized constraints without also indicating probabilities. The formal rules we shall illustrate, then, express hierarchized constraints only and constraints with associated probabilities. Let us return for a moment to the information in Table 5-1. This is the final stop deletion rule with the effects of two of its constraints apparent. The first step is to write the rule, in a generative phonology format, including all constraints that *must* be present for the rule to operate. Given only the discussion associated with this table, we would know that the stop to be

---

[12] It is somewhat misleading to consider final stop deletion as a whole. Although deletion of final stops when a vowel does not immediately follow is barely stigmatized at all, deletion before a vowel is much more stigmatized; probably more so than *r*-desulcalization.

deleted must be word-final and must be preceded by a consonant.[13] These restrictions can be expressed in the following way:

$$C_{st} \rightarrow (\emptyset) \ / \ C\_\_\_\_\_\#\#$$

The symbol C_{st} should be taken to mean stop consonant. The symbols $\rightarrow (\emptyset)$ mean "becomes zero," i.e., is deleted. Placing $\emptyset$ in parentheses indicates that the deletion is variable and that the rule will not apply to every single instance of a stop in the position specified. The symbol $/$ means "in the environment of." The underlining which follows the slash indicates the position in which C_{st} must occur. The symbol $\#\#$ indicates an external word boundary meaning that the deletable stop consonant must appear at the end of an autonomous word, that is, not before a suffix. The next step is to include the two variable constraints. These are indicated by placing them in parentheses. The new version of the rule is:

$$C_{st} \rightarrow (\emptyset) \ / \ C_{(son)}\_\_\_\_\_\#\#\sim(V)$$

The subscript (son) in parentheses indicates that the rule is favored if the preceding consonant is in the class of sonorants (although the rule may delete consonants even if the preceding consonant is not a sonorant). The symbol $\sim(V)$ indicates that the *absence* of a vowel favors the rule. The symbol $\sim$ means "not" or "absence of." In order always to write rules so that the constraints *favoring* the rule are expressed, it is often necessary to express some constraints as not being one thing or another. This means that in such cases, like this one, we have to state that the constraint is the presence of the absence of a vowel. The constraint is there when the vowel is not; and the constraint is not there when the vowel is. This apparent perversity is necessary in the interests of consistency and must be kept in mind. Again, some consonants may be deleted even when a vowel is present, but fewer than when it is absent.[14]

We have yet to express the hierarchical arrangement. Before doing so, we will have to revise the symbolism we are using to prevent the entire rule from becoming too bulky, and to bring it into line with the way variable and other rules are actually written in the technical linguistic literature. The use of symbols like C and V do not allow sufficient precision, even with subscripts like st and son. It will be necessary to indicate the kinds of entities

---

[13] We learn later, in the discussion of the data in Table 5-2, that the presence of a preceding consonant is not absolutely necessary, but is another variable constraint. At this stage of the explication, however, we shall ignore this fact.

[14] It may appear that the difficulties could be avoided by having the rule specify the presence of a consonant rather than the absence of a vowel. This would be counterfactual. It is not the presence of a consonant that favors the rule but the presence of anything which is not a vowel—that is, a consonant or nothing at all.

we mean by means of *distinctive features*. If the concept of distinctive features is entirely new to the reader, he should consult other sources for details, but suffice it here to say that we will need to indicate all the relatively atomic attributes an entity must have in order to be the kind of entity the rule requires. In order to indicate precisely a stop consonant, we will have to specify it as [−nuc(lear)], [−son(orant)] and [−con(tinuant)]. "Nuclear" is the feature that distinguishes consonants and vowels and it means "capable of being a syllable nucleus." A segment with the feature [+nuc] would ordinarily be a vowel and [−nuc] usually indicates a consonant. Consonants which are [+son], as we have stated earlier, include nasal consonants and *l*. Consonants that are [−son], then, are the stops and fricatives. Of the [−son] consonants, fricatives are [+con] and stops are [−con]. Therefore we wish to specify the deletable consonant as [−son] and [−con]. If we use the same features to specify the environment segments and continue to put the variable constraints in parentheses, the new version of the rule is:

$$
\begin{bmatrix} -\text{nuc} \\ -\text{son} \\ -\text{con} \end{bmatrix} \rightarrow (\emptyset) \; / \begin{bmatrix} -\text{nuc} \\ (+\text{son}) \end{bmatrix} \underline{\hspace{1cm}} \#\# \sim ([+\text{nuc}])
$$

All that remains is to indicate which of the two variable constraints is the stronger. We saw that it can be inferred from Table 5-1 or Figure 5-1 that the absence of the following vowel is the stronger constraint. This is indicated by prefixing the portion of the rule written ([+nuc]) with an upper-case Greek letter alpha.

The feature [+son] in the preceding consonant is prefixed by an upper-case beta. Although many upper-case Greek letters are identical with the corresponding upper-case Latin letters, it is the Greek letters which are intended.[15] The final version of the rule, including the prefixes indicating the hierarchy, is: [16]

[15] In the original version of variable rules (Labov 1969), lower-case Greek letters, all of which are distinct from Latin lower-case letters, were used. We are not using lower-case Greek letters because (1) they already have another function in generative phonology and (2) our Greek letter prefixes have a somewhat different interpretation from the interpretation of Labov's lower-case letters. We choose upper-case Greek letters, rather than some other notation, to show continuity with Labov's work. An Arabic number prefix notation has also been used in place of lower-case Greek letters (Fasold 1970; Bailey 1973). Cedergren and Sankoff (1972) and Sankoff (1972) use lower-case Greek letters in a sense distinct from both Labov's and ours.

[16] The above rule formally includes only linguistic constraints on variability, but it may be possible to incorporate the types of social constraints we considered in Chapter Four into such rules as well. In order to do this, we naturally have to look at the relative effect of these social constraints as they intersect with the hierarchical effect of the independent linguistic constraints. If, for example, we found that the third-order constraint was style (nonformal style favoring deletion over formal style),

$$\begin{bmatrix} -\text{nuc} \\ -\text{son} \\ -\text{con} \end{bmatrix} \rightarrow (\emptyset) / \begin{bmatrix} -\text{nuc} \\ \text{B}(+\text{son}) \end{bmatrix} \underline{\quad\quad} \#\# \, \text{A} \sim ([+\text{nuc}])$$

Probabilities in Variable Rules

In order to compare the kind of variable rule we have just discussed with one that includes probability figures, we must introduce the rule for English contraction by Labov (1969:748). Contraction is the removal of the vowel in *am, is, are,* giving *'m, 's* and *'re* (e.g., *I'm here, He's writing, You're ugly*). The vowel is only removed if it has a weak accent and is reduced to a quality something like the sound *uh*. Contraction applies only to auxiliary verbs or forms of *be* functioning as copulas. At the point at which contraction applies, these are precisely the words in English which bear a tense marking—that is, designation of past and nonpast tense, and consist only of a vowel followed by a consonant. Writing contraction as an optional rule would result in:

$$\begin{bmatrix} +\text{nuc} \\ +\text{cen} \\ -\text{acc} \end{bmatrix} \rightarrow (\emptyset) / \quad \#\# \begin{bmatrix} \underline{\quad\quad} \\ +\text{TENSE} \end{bmatrix} [-\text{nuc}] \quad \#\#$$

This rule means that a segment having the features [+nuc] (a vowel), [+cen(tral)] (specifying the *uh* quality), and [−acc] (indicating weak accent) can sometimes be deleted (become zero) if it is the first sound in the word (specified by placing the dash immediately after the external word boundary symbol ##) and is followed by only one consonant (a segment with the feature [−nuc]), which is then immediately followed by another external word boundary. Furthermore, the word must have the grammatical feature +TENSE (we write grammatical features in all capital

---

we would designate formal style as Γ∼([+formal]). Similarly, if we found class to be the fourth-order constraint (working class favoring deletion over middle class) and sex to be the fifth-order constraint (male favoring deletion over female), then class and sex would be designated as Δ([+working class]) and E([−female]), respectively. The rule might incorporate these along with the linguistic constraints. Although there are a number of sociolinguists who maintain that social constraints should be incorporated into formal rules, only a few linguists have actually written such rules. There are still theoretical and practical issues which need to be resolved if such a position is to be maintained. For one, such rules extend the notion of a formal grammar beyond the individual and homogeneous speech community. Distinctions based on class, for example, involve such a step. Another issue involves imposing discrete category features (e.g. [+working class]) on what, in the real world, is a continuum of social relationships.

letters to distinguish them from phonological features). The rule in this form specifies what must be present in order for it to be even possible for the rule to operate. If a word fails to meet any of these specifications, contraction will never apply to it.[17]

Because contraction is a variable rule, it does not operate in all cases even when the specifications just described are met. But there are certain other factors that may or may not be present that favor the operation of the rule. Three constraints were found that affect the output of the contraction rule. The rule is favored if a verb follows [18] (e.g., an example like *John is going* is more likely to undergo contraction than an example like *John is good* or *John is a man*); if the preceding word ends in a vowel (e.g., *Joe is going* is favored over *John is going*); and if the following constituent, if not a verb, is a noun phrase (e.g., *John is a man* is favored over *John is good* or *John is in Chicago*). Table 5-7 is the array from which the hierarchical order of these features can be determined. The format is parallel to that of Table 5-2.

ENVIRONMENT			EXAMPLE	PERCENT DELETED
Preceding vowel	Following verb	Following noun phrase	(Not possible)	—
Preceding vowel	Following verb	No following noun phrase	Joe is going	86
Preceding vowel	No following verb	Following noun phrase	The play is a musical	80
Preceding vowel	No following verb	No following noun phrase	The tree is in the yard	70
Preceding consonant	Following verb	Following noun phrase	(Not possible)	—
Preceding consonant	Following verb	No following noun phrase	The men are going	65
Preceding consonant	No following verb	Following noun phrase	The women are leaders	37
Preceding consonant	No following verb	No following noun phrase	The children are fine	25

Table 5-7. Ranking of three linguistic factors favoring contraction.

[17] Our description of the contraction rule differs from Labov's, mainly because we have left out aspects of the rule the discussion of which would complicate the explication unduly. We have also noticed an inconsistency in Labov's formulation. His rule (Labov 1969:748) indicates that the absence of a following noun phrase favors the rule while the data in his Table 6 show that the rule is favored by the presence of a noun phrase. We are following the table rather than the rule.

[18] By "following verb" we mean any verb except *gonna* as in *He is gonna try*.

In Table 5-7, unlike Table 5-2, not all the logically possible combinations of three factors actually exist. In two places such combinations involve a contradiction. It is obviously not possible to have a following verb and a following noun phrase at the same time. In this case, however, the gaps are not too serious because it is still possible to infer that a preceding vowel is the first-order constraint, a following verb is the second-order constraint, and the presence of a following noun is the third-order constraint.[19]

If we add these three constraints to the optional rule we have already written, we obtain:

$$
\begin{bmatrix} +\text{nuc} \\ +\text{cen} \\ -\text{acc} \end{bmatrix} \rightarrow (\emptyset) \ / \quad A([+\text{nuc}]) \ \#\# \begin{bmatrix} \underline{\qquad}[-\text{nuc}] \\ +\text{TENSE} \end{bmatrix} \begin{array}{c} B([+\text{VERB}]) \\ \#\# \ \Gamma(\text{NP}) \end{array}
$$

Labov discovered another constraint on the output of the contraction rule. If a pronoun precedes (e.g., *He is running*), then contraction is heavily favored. Regardless of the preceding vowel or consonant or following constituent, contraction took place in over 97 percent of the cases in Labov's data. Labov took this figure to be the equivalent of categorical application. That is, if a pronoun precedes, the rest of the constraints can be ignored and contraction applies to every copula and auxiliary. The symbol for categorical application, given a certain environment in a variable rule, is the use of an asterisk prefix to that environment feature. Adding this "knockout" constraint to the rule yields:

$$
\begin{bmatrix} +\text{nuc} \\ +\text{cen} \\ -\text{acc} \end{bmatrix} \rightarrow (\emptyset) \ / \ *([+\text{PRONOUN}]) \quad A([+\text{nuc}]) \qquad \#\# \begin{bmatrix} \underline{\qquad}[-\text{nuc}] \\ +\text{TENSE} \end{bmatrix} \begin{array}{c} B([+\text{VERB}]) \\ \#\# \ \Gamma(\text{NP}) \end{array}
$$

Gillian Sankoff (1972) gives us the version of the variable contraction rule for the same data based on the stronger competence claim that imputes to the language user not only the knowledge of the hierarchical ordering of the constraints on variability but also the amount contributed by each to the probability of rule operation. To construct such a rule, it is necessary to begin with the data on which Table 5-7 is based. These data are given in Table 5-8.

---

[19] There are a number of instances in which missing cross products lead to difficulties in determining constraint hierarchies in various data sets for which attempts have been made to write this type of variable rule. Sometimes "commonsense" reasoning allows a solution, sometimes not. See Wolfram (1973b) for further discussion.

PRECEDING ENVIRONMENTS		FOLLOWING ENVIRONMENTS			
		—gonna	—Verb	—Noun Phrase	—Adj/Locative
C—	Observed	8/9	9/14	13/35	8/32
	Predicted	8.2/9	8.7/14	13.1/35	8/32
V—	Observed	6/6	12/14	51/64	16/23
	Predicted	5.8/6	12.1/14	50/64	17/23
Pro—	Observed	23/23	33/34	30/32	64/65
	Predicted	22.9/23	33.4/34	31/32	62.7/65

Table 5-8. Observed frequencies of contraction by preceding and following environment with frequencies predicted by a variable rule with probabilities (from G. Sankoff 1972).

Taking the top figure in each cell, which is the frequency of operation of the contraction rule observed by Labov, a statistical method called maximum likelihood can extract the probability to be associated with each preceding and following constraint. In addition, an "input probability" is calculated which is that invariant part of the rule operation probability not attributable to any one of the constraints, but which may well be decomposable, in whole or in part, into effects due to constraints which may favor the rule but have yet to be discovered. The contraction rule, in this format,[20] is:

$$\begin{bmatrix} +\text{nuc} \\ +\text{cen} \\ -\text{acc} \end{bmatrix} \rightarrow (\emptyset) \; / \; \begin{array}{l} ([+\text{PRONOUN}]) \\ ([+\text{nuc}]) \end{array} \quad \underline{\qquad} \begin{array}{l} [-\text{nuc}] \\ \#\# [+\text{TENSE}] \end{array} \quad \begin{array}{l} ([+\text{VERB}]) \\ (gonna) \\ (\text{NP}) \\ \#\# (\text{Adj/Loc}) \end{array}$$

Several differences between this version and the previous one should be noted. First, there are no prefixes analogous to the Greek letters indicating hierarchy of constraints. Second, the following environment contains an extra constraint compared with the earlier format. In the following environment, if *gonna,* another verb, or a noun phrase are not present, then an adjective or a locative is the only other possibility and so need not be stated in the first kind of rule. In this format, Sankoff retains the Adj/Loc specification for the sake of clarity. Third, the effect of the item *gonna* (as in *He is gonna come*) is considered here, while we ignored it in the other rule. Fourth, in spite of the extremely frequent operation of contraction when a pronoun is present, [+PRONOUN] is here considered a variable constraint, not a "knockout" constraint.

[20] Our notation differs from Sankoff's in that we use parentheses where she uses angled brackets ($< >$).

As it stands, the rule gives less information than the earlier one. The variable constraints are present, but there is no indication of the hierarchy, let alone the probabilities.[21] For this information, a list of the probabilities derived by the statistical method of maximum likelihood must be consulted. This list, called a "key" by Cedergren and D. Sankoff (1972), is as follows:

Input probability = .25
Pro__ = .86; ~Pro = 0
[+nuc] = .65; [−nuc] = 0
__NP = .16; __Adj/Loc = 0; Vb = .49; *gonna* = .89

When these probabilities are inserted into the formula on page 109, the predicted results are those given in the bottom figure in each cell in Table 5-8. It is clear that predicted frequencies are very close to the observed ones.

From the list of probability contributions, the hierarchy of constraints can be determined simply by listing them from the highest probability figure to the lowest (ignoring the input probability):

.89 __*gonna*
.86 Pro__
.65 V__
.49 __Verb
.16 __NP
   0 [+nuc]__, ~Pro__, __Adj/Loc

The order is entirely consistent with the one determined by the earlier method. The effect of *gonna,* here the first-order constraint, was not taken into consideration in the other version. [+PRONOUN] was the knockout constraint in the first rule, and so exceeded all the constraints labeled by Greek letters. Here it is the highest ranking constraint of all those considered in the first version. [+PRONOUN] was at the knockout level in the first rule but only .86 in this version because of a slightly different way of looking at the interrelation of [+PRONOUN] and [+nuc]. In the above list, the preceding vowel is the next strongest constraint, followed by a

---

[21] Sankoff points out (personal communication) that the hierarchy of constraints within each position in the environment could easily be indicated simply by listing constraints within each position in order from top to bottom. Following this convention, the preceding specific environment would appear as we have given it, but the following environment would be:

(*gonna*)
([+VERB])
(NP)
(Adj/Loc)

following verb then by a following noun phrase, in the exact order specified by the first rule. A preceding consonant and absence of a pronoun and a following adjective or locative phrase were left out of the first rule as not contributing to the operation of the rule; here they are last on the list with a zero probability contribution.

The study of social dialects has revealed that the linguistic control of variability is more patterned than has been commonly believed in the past. This linguistic control extends to the more and less relationships expressed in a frequency, or multivalued implicational chart. To express the regularities found in such an array, it is necessary for linguistic theory to include variable rules containing at least hierarchized constraints on variability and perhaps even the capability of associating probability values to such constraints.

6

SOCIALLY DIAGNOSTIC
PHONOLOGICAL FEATURES

In this chapter and the next we present some of the socially diagnostic features to be found in various social dialects of American English. In Chapter Six some of the socially diagnostic phonological features of English will be discussed, and in Chapter Seven we will deal with grammatical aspects. This kind of information is important for understanding social stigmatization of speech features and historical change in language. Social stigma is attached to language forms not because of inherent structural weakness in the forms themselves, but because of the position in society of the speakers who use the forms. By way of supporting at least the first part of this claim, we will show the often intricate and complex rules that govern nonstandard speech forms. With respect to historical change, because most of the features to be discussed are variable, they are candidates for new developments in the grammar and phonology of American English. It may seem unlikely to some that *stigmatized* aspects of language should be candidates for future developments because these variants are the ones condemned by leaders in society. But the most formal styles of the best-educated speakers are the most conservative with respect to linguistic innovation, so that new developments do not always or even usually begin with the upper class. Of course, in order to be established, innovations must ultimately be *accepted* by the leaders of the speech community, which is probably one reason that so few of the innovations introduced by the lower classes ever become established in the standard language, with the result that language changes rather slowly. Within the set of features to be discussed in these two chapters are no doubt some that will be part of the standard grammar and pronunciation of American English several generations hence.

Distinguishing Grammatical and Phonological Features

By placing pronunciation features in one chapter and grammar features in another, we assume that grammar and pronunciation features can be reliably distinguished. It may seem that there could be no problem in distinguishing the two kinds of features. It is true that a feature like *r*-lessness (pronouncing *car* like *ca'*) could hardly be a feature of grammar, nor is it plausible that a feature like the double negative could be due to pronunciation rules. But there are cases in which grammatical markers, such as suffixes, are variably absent and the question arises as to whether this is because of their status as grammatical markers or the phonological qualities of the sound segments by which the grammatical function is represented.[1] For example, in many kinds of Nonstandard English, the *-ed* suffix used to indicate past tense (*He walked home*), past participle (*They have been defeated*), and adjectives derived from nouns (*She's a blue-eyed girl*) can be absent. In many of these same dialects, the *-s* (or *-es*) suffix representing plural (*All those boys must go*), possession (*That's the man's hat*), and verbal concord for nonpast tense verbs with third-person singular subjects (*He fixes clocks*) can also be absent. Do these dialects have pronunciation rules for deleting final apical stops and sibilants? Or do they have grammar rules for deleting certain grammatical suffixes? This question is possible to answer given painstaking analysis of a sufficient amount of actual speech. The answer in these cases is that -ed is sometimes absent because of pronunciation rules and that variable -s absence is a grammatical phenomenon.

There are a number of reasons that allow us to state this with such confidence. First, there are words which are homophonous with words having the *-ed* or *-s* suffix but which do not have these suffixes. For example, *mist* is pronounced exactly the same way as *missed,* and *lapse* is homophonous with *laps.* The comparison of *-ed*-suffixed words with their homophones gives results different from the comparison of the *-s*-suffixed words

---

[1] In one or two cases (for example, copula and auxiliary deletion), pronunciation rules are treated in Chapter Seven because the rule involved affects only grammatical markers.

with their homophones. Both *missed* and *mist* end in the *st* sounds in actual pronunciation. The *t* sound of *missed,* where a grammatical suffix is involved, and that of *mist,* where there is no suffix, are both deleted under the same constraints and even at comparable frequency levels (the *t* representing -*ed* is somewhat less frequently deleted because its status as a suffix is a variable constraint on the phonological deletion rule). Similarly, the word *lapse* is identical in pronunciation to the *laps* of *The dog laps water* (or of *Babies often sit on laps* or *The first lap's best time is forty-eight seconds*). But the final *s* of words like lapse, in which *s* is part of the base word and not a suffix, is very seldom deleted in those dialects in which the suffixial -*s* can be deleted. Furthermore, the linguistic factors which influence the deletion of the *s* of *lapse* differ from those which constrain the deletion of grammatical suffixes.

Secondly, the absence of -*ed* is strongly affected both by its own phonetic shape and by the phonetic qualities of the following sounds. When -*ed* is suffixed to words ending in *t* or *d,* it is pronounced something like *id* (*lifted, scolded*). When it is suffixed to other words, it is pronounced as a single consonant, *t* or *d* (*slipped, tired*). It can be shown that the *id* pronunciation is much less frequently deleted than the *t* or *d* pronunciations. Analogously, the -*s* suffixes are pronounced somewhat like *iz* when the base word ends in a sibilant, but as single consonants (*s* or *z*) elsewhere. But in this case, the phonetic shape of the suffix makes no difference in frequency of deletion. Furthermore, the surrounding sounds (such as whether the next word begins with a consonant or a vowel) have a marked and patterned effect on the frequency of -*ed* deletion, but the frequencies of deletion of the -*s* suffixes are virtually impervious to the effects of the following sounds.

On the other hand, grammatical factors have a great deal to do with the frequency of deletion of the -*s* suffixes, but very little to do with -*ed* deletion. It does not matter very much whether -*ed* represents past tense, past participle, or derived adjectives (there is slightly less deletion of past tense -*ed*); all are deleted at comparable frequency levels. But in dialects which allow the deletion of all three -*s* suffixes (Vernacular Black English may be the only such dialect), which suffix is involved makes considerable difference. Plural -*s* is absent in Vernacular Black English less than 10 percent of the time, possessive -*s* is absent about 20 to 50 percent of the time, and verb concord -*s* is absent at frequency levels of 65 to 100 percent.

A third deciding piece of evidence is the case of irregular verbs. In the case of verb concord -*s,* there are three irregular verbs in English— *have, do,* and *say.*[2] *Do* and *say* undergo a vowel change when -*s* is suffixed,

---

[2] A fourth verb, *be,* is also irregular but follows an entirely different pattern.

and *have* loses the *v*. When verbal *-s* is absent from these verbs, these changes do not take place; where Standard English demands *has*, Nonstandard English has *have* (not *ha'*), *does* is *do* (not *doe'*), and *say* is pronounced so that it rhymes with *day* (rather than *se'*). Contrast this with verbs which undergo vowel change as well as suffixation in the past tense and past participle, e.g., *tell-told, leave-left, sleep-slept*. When the suffix is absent from these verbs, the vowel change has already taken place, resulting in *tol'* (not *tell*), *lef'* (not *leave*) and *slep'* (not *sleep*). These facts make it apparent for verbal *-s* and *-ed* that the *-s* is deleted on the basis of its grammatical function before it has a chance to affect the phonetic shape of the base verb, but that the past-tense suffix [3] is removed after it has caused a vowel change in the verbal base.

All three of these sets of facts converge on the conclusion that deletion of *-s* suffixes is grammatical, but deletion of *-ed* is phonological. Similar reasoning, we have found, can be brought to bear on any case of potentially ambiguous interpretation of a feature as due to either phonological or grammatical causes. It will be found, then, that *-ed* absence will be treated in this chapter as a special case of some pronunciation rules while the *-s* suffixes will be treated in the discussion of Chapter Seven as wholly grammatical features.

The evidence we use to distinguish grammatical and phonological features is all linguistic. But there are two sociolinguistic patterns which tend to correlate with grammatical as opposed to pronunciation features. Ordinarily, speakers are at either one or the other end of the spectrum for grammatical features. That is, they have either a very low frequency for the nonstandard form or a very high frequency, with very few speakers with frequencies of near 50 percent (see the discussion of sharp and gradient features in Chapter Four). Phonological features, on the other hand, have a tendency to show a normal curve of frequency distribution. That is, there are moderate numbers of speakers at the very high or very low ends of the frequency range with the highest numbers of speakers in the middle of the range. The other pattern has to do with variation and the lack of it. For most phonological features—final consonant cluster simplification, for example—the nonstandard variants are found in the speech of all social groups, but the frequencies are lower for the middle and upper classes. For most grammatical features, the higher social classes of speakers will use the standard variant only, while the rest of the community fluctuates between the standard and nonstandard variants.

---

[3] The *d* of *told* and the *t* of *left* and *slept* is really the same suffix as that of regular verbs, even though they are not spelled *-ed*. It should be pointed out that we are assuming a view of grammar, justifiable on independent grounds, in which grammatical operations are in some sense prior to phonological ones.

Categories of Stigmatized Features

There are several categories of stigmatized features that we are excluding in this chapter and the next. First, we exclude special usages of
individual words that can be found in various dialects. Some speakers
differ in their use of *leave* and *let* from the dominant standard pattern, so
that the following conversation is possible:

> The dog is outside scratching at the door. Leave him in.
> No, let him out!

Such usages will not be treated, nor will word usages like White Southern
and Vernacular Black English *upside the head* (as in *He hit him upside
the head*) or the Appalachian English use of *several* where Standard English
dialects would have *many*. We are more interested in pervasive patterns
that affect all words or constructions of a given type. For the same reason,
we will not typically deal with nonstandard grammar that affects only one
word or a few, like the use of *klum* as the past tense of *climb* or *brang* as
the past-tense form for *brought*. Similarly, nonstandard pronunciations of
individual or small sets of words are omitted, like *sink* pronounced *zinc*
(where there is no general breakdown of the *s-z* distinction); or *took* and
put pronounced *tuck* and *putt* (but *book,* for example, is never pronounced
buck); or Appalachian English *hit* for *it* (while *in* is never *hin*); or *creek*
pronounced *crick* (the only word affected; *peek* is never pronounced *pick*).

Other usages are not dealt with because we judge them not to be
really stigmatized socially, although they don't conform to the rules of
formal standard grammar. The construction *didn't useta* (the prescriptive
grammar books call for *used not to*) is common enough in normal educated
conversation to qualify as part of informal Standard English by our definition as is the use of *let's don't* for formal *let's not* as in *Let's don't go to
the beach today.*

There will also be no treatment of language features immediately
traceable to a foreign language, such as Spanish features in the English of
Americans of Chicano or Puerto Rican background, Swedish features in
the English spoken in parts of rural Minnesota, or Cherokee influence on
the English of North Carolina Cherokee Indians, as examples. It is likely
that some such features are more important socially than some we include
and some may even turn out to influence the future historical development
of American English, but an adequate description of such interference
features may well require a separate volume for each language involved.

Finally, there are no doubt a number of omissions that do not fit
any of the categories mentioned. These features do not appear in these

chapters because they were overlooked or simply because we do not know enough about enough nonstandard dialects to be aware of them. In the case of the pronunciation features in this chapter, the problem is especially acute, and we have no doubt left out numerous pronunciations with social significance in areas from which we do not have adequate information. This is particularly true of vowel pronunciations; we are somewhat more confident that our treatment of nonstandard consonant pronunciations is more complete because consonant variations seem less susceptible to geographical variation. In the case of the grammatical variables in Chapter Seven, we have made a serious attempt to be comprehensive, although we would not be surprised to learn that we have omitted a few important features.

Our major sources of information have been our own work on Vernacular Black English (very few features are found in other nonstandard dialects that do not also turn up in Vernacular Black English), White Southern nonstandard speech, and Puerto Rican English (Wolfram 1969, 1971, 1973; Wolfram et al. 1971; Fasold 1972). Other sources are Labov and his associates' work in New York City (Labov 1966; Labov et al. 1968), Robert Hackenberg's dissertation (1972) on Appalachian English, and the work of McDavid (1952, 1967) and Shuy, Wolfram, and Riley (1967) for general features of Nonstandard English.

Consonants

FINAL CONSONANT CLUSTER SIMPLIFICATION

Standard English words ending in a consonant cluster often have the final member of the cluster absent in nonstandard dialects. As we have pointed out, the reduction of some clusters which are formed by the addition of the -*s* suffix can be attributed to a grammatical difference between standard and nonstandard dialects. Cluster simplifications in which the deletable final member is a stop consonant, however, do not result from grammatical differences, but are the product of a pronunciation rule. Words such as *test, desk, hand,* and *build* are pronounced as *tes', des', han',* and *buil',* respectively. Because of this, we find that pairs of words such as *build* and *bill, cold* and *coal,* and *guest* and *guess* are sometimes pronounced identically.

It is important to distinguish two basic types of clusters that are affected by this sort of reduction. First, clusters in which both members of the cluster are an inherent part of the same word can be reduced, as in *tes', des', han',* and *buil'.* But reduction also affects the final *t* or *d* which results when the suffix *-ed* is added to a word. We have already mentioned the fact that when *-ed* is suffixed to a word ending in *d* or *t,* the *-ed* suffix is pronounced something like *id* (e.g., *wantid, countid*), and no cluster results. When the word ends in a voiced sound, it is pronounced as *d,* so that words with *-ed* like *rubbed* or *rained* are actually pronounced as *rubd* and *raind,* respectively. Consonants like *b, n,* and *g* are pronounced with vocal chords vibrating, that is, they are *voiced.* If the base word ends in a voiceless consonant, the cluster ends in *t,* so that *messed* and *looked* are actually pronounced as *mest* and *lookt,* respectively. Consonants such as *s, k,* and *f* are pronounced without the vibration of the vocal chords, that is, they are *voiceless.* In Nonstandard English, when the addition of the *-ed* suffix results in either a voiced or voiceless cluster, the cluster may be reduced by removing the final member of the cluster. The list of clusters affected by this process and the examples of the two types of consonant cluster reduction are given in Table 6-1: Type I represents clusters that

PHONETIC CLUSTER	TYPE I	*Examples* * TYPE II
[st]	test, post, list	missed, messed, dressed
[sp]	wasp, clasp, grasp	
[sk]	desk, risk, mask	
[št]		finished, latched, cashed
[zd]		raised, composed, amazed
[žd]		judged, charged, forged
[ft]	left, craft, cleft	laughed, stuffed, roughed
[vd]		loved, lived, moved
[nd]	mind, find, mound	rained, fanned, canned
[md]		named, foamed, rammed
[ld]	cold, wild, old	called, smelled, killed
[pt]	apt, adept, inept	mapped, stopped, clapped
[kt]	act, contact, expect	looked, cooked, cracked

Table 6-1. Consonant clusters in which the final member of the cluster may be absent. (*Where there are no examples under Type I and Type II, the cluster does not occur under that category.)

do not involve *-ed* and Type II represents clusters that result from the addition of the *-ed* suffix.

Note that in the table, such clusters as *mp* (*jump, ramp*), *lt* (*colt, belt*), *nk* (*crank, rank*), *lp* (*gulp, help*), *ps* (*lapse*), and *ks* (*six, box*) are not included. The reason is that the reduction rule operates only when the second member is a stop consonant (eliminating *ps* and *ks*), and only when both members of the cluster are either voiced or voiceless (eliminating *mp, nk, lp,* and *lt*). Words like *lapse, six,* and *box* end in a fricative, not a stop.

Words like *mind, cold,* or *rained* (pronounced *raind*) end in two voiced sounds, *n* and *d*. Words like *jump, belt,* and *help* end in one voiced and one voiceless sound; *m, n, l,* and the *ng* sound of *n* in *nk* (the phonetic symbol is [ŋ]) are voiced while *t, k,* and *p* are voiceless. Because final consonant clusters can be reduced only when both consonants are voiced or when both consonants are voiceless, these words ending in one of each kind of consonant never have reduced clusters.[4]

The rule deleting the final member of the consonant cluster operates in standard dialects as well as in nonstandard dialects, but there are differences in the conditions affecting the rule. In Standard English, the final member of the cluster may be absent if the following word begins with a consonant, so that *bes' kind, col' cuts,* and *wes' side* are common and acceptable in spoken Standard English. In Standard English, however, this reduction can *only* take place when the following word begins with a consonant. Although *col' cuts* does not violate the pronunciation rules of Standard English, *col' egg* does. This restriction does not apply to Nonstandard English, where simplification not only takes place when the following word begins with a consonant but may also take place when the cluster is followed by a vowel. Thus *wes' en', bes' apple,* and *col' egg* are all acceptable in Vernacular Black English, for example, and probably in other nonstandard dialects as well. Items such as *Yesterday he mess' up* occur because of this pronunciation rule and not because past tense is absent in any of these dialects. In Standard English it is not at all unusual to hear a sentence such as *Yesterday I burn' my hand,* because the potential cluster in *burned* is followed by a word beginning with a consonant. But a sentence such as *It was burn' up,* acceptable in Vernacular Black English, would not be acceptable in Standard English because the potential cluster is followed by a word beginning with a vowel. Even in nonstandard dialects, the presence of a following vowel has a partial inhibiting effect. Clusters are less frequently simplified if the next word begins with a vowel than if it does not. Another major constraint on deletion frequency is whether or not the final member of the cluster represents *-ed*. If it does, there will be a lower frequency of simplification than if the final member is an inherent part of the word. Table 6-2 illustrates the effect of these two constraints on cluster simplification in Detroit black speech. Recalling the discussion in Chapter Five, it can be seen that, of these two constraints, a following vowel is the first-order constraint and the grammatical suffix status of the final member of the cluster is the second-order constraint.

Related to the reduction of the final consonant clusters is a particular

---

[4] Whether it is actually voicing agreement or other factors which make some clusters eligible for simplification and not others is disputed by linguists who have studied the phenomenon (see Fasold 1972:81–82 for a summary). But there is less disagreement as to the facts about which clusters can be simplified and which cannot.

| | *Social Classes* | | | |
ENVIRONMENTS	UPPER MIDDLE	LOWER MIDDLE	UPPER WORKING	LOWER WORKING
Following vowel Final member is -ed	.07	.13	.24	.34
Following vowel Final member is not -ed	.28	.43	.65	.72
Following consonant Final member is -ed	.49	.62	.73	.76
Following vowel Final member is not -ed	.79	.87	.94	.97

Table 6-2. Linguistic effects on frequency of final consonant cluster simplification in Detroit black speech (adapted from Wolfram 1969:59–69).

pattern of pluralization involving the -s and -es plural forms. This pluralization pattern is usually associated with Vernacular Black English, but there is also some evidence that white nonstandard dialects in Appalachia and the deep South have a similar pluralization pattern. In order to describe this pattern, it is first necessary to understand that in all varieties of English, there are several different phonetic forms for the plural suffix. If the word ends in a sibilant such as s, sh, z, zh, the plural suffix is formed by adding -es, pronounced something like iz. Thus bus, bush, and buzz are pluralized as buses, bushes, and buzzes, respectively. If the word does not end in an s-like sound then -s is added; phonetically this is z after voiced sounds and s after voiceless sounds. Thus, the plurals of pot, coat, bud, and pan are pots, coats, buds (pronounced budz), and pans (pronounced panz), respectively. In Vernacular Black English, words ending in s plus p, t, or k add the -es plural instead of the -s plural. Thus, words like desk, ghost, wasp, and test are pluralized as desses, ghosses, wasses, and tesses. Because the p, t, and k are so often removed by the rule discussed in this section, these plurals are formed as if desk, test, and wasp ended in s instead of sk, st, or sp. It is essential to understand that the pluralization pattern is perfectly regular, once the final consonant has been deleted.

Attempting to learn Standard English pluralization patterns, speakers will sometimes pluralize words like desk and test as deskes and testes, respectively. These forms result from a tendency to pluralize the same words in the same way, even when the cluster is maintained intact. This is an example of structural hypercorrection—a phenomenon we will describe in greater detail in connection with some of the features in Chapter Seven.

Because consonant clusters occur so infrequently at the end of words in nonstandard dialects, one might ask whether these word-final clusters can be considered an integral part of the dialect system. This question can be answered most clearly by observing what happens when suffixes beginning with a vowel are added to a base word ending in a cluster in Standard English. This includes *-ing* as in *testing* or *scolding, -er* as in *tester* or *scolder,* and *-est* as in *coldest* or *oldest.* If a consonant cluster is present in such constructions (e.g., *testing, tester*), we may assume that the speaker is fully acquainted with the cluster, but that it can be reduced in places where it is not possible in Standard English. For the vast majority of nonstandard dialect speakers, this is exactly how the rule concerning consonant clusters operates. These speakers may reduce the cluster in the context of *tes' program* or *tes' idea,* but retain the cluster in *tester.* There is, however, a group of Vernacular Black English speakers, most typically Southern children, who not only show the absence of the final member of the cluster in *tes' program* or *tes' idea,* but in *tesser* as well. For these speakers, final consonant clusters of the type we are discussing may not be part of the dialect system at all. Even for those varieties of Vernacular Black English in which final *t* is always present in words with suffixes like *-ing* and *-er,* so that *tesser* or *tessing* never occur, there are some speakers for whom *st, sp,* and *sk* clusters must always be deleted everywhere else (Labov et al. 1968:126). For such speakers there is no *test idea* or *test program;* only *tes' idea* and *tes' program.* There is some indication that some Vernacular Black English speakers of whom this is true have only *st* clusters, even when there is a suffix beginning with a vowel. For them, Standard English *risking* is *risting* and *clasping* is either *clapsing* or *clasting.* This situation can be maintained because of the frequency with which final *k* and *p* (as well as *t*) can be eliminated from consonant clusters and the relative paucity of words ending in *sk* or *sp* in English. The one very common word which does end in *sk* in standard English, *ask,* is often pronounced *aks* in these and other varieties of Vernacular Black English, as well as in Appalachian nonstandard dialects. The form *aksing* which would occur instead of Standard English *asking* would not provide any information about the presence of *sk* clusters.

Our observations about word-final clusters are summarized in Table 6-3, which represents how Standard English and various nonstandard dialects function with respect to final consonant clusters. On the basis of the information summarized in the table we can make some reasonable statements about the social significance of consonant cluster simplification. We see, for example, that all the dialects, even Standard English, allow simplification when the following word begins with a consonant. Therefore, simplification of a cluster has little social significance in this context. When the word ending in a cluster is followed by a vowel, however, simplification is socially stigmatized. Absence of the final member of the cluster is most heavily stigmatized when a suffix beginning with a vowel is added.

Variety of English	Cluster Simplifications			
SE	sometimes *tes' program*	always *test idea*	always *testing*	always *risking*
Most VBE and some WNS speakers	usually or always *tes' program*	sometimes *tes' idea*	always *testing*	always *risking*
Some WNS Some VBE speakers	always *tes' program*	always *tes' idea*	always *testing*	always *risking*
Some WNS Some VBE speakers	always *tes' program*	always *tes' idea*	usually or always *testing*	usually or always *risting*
Some VBE speakers (especially Deep South children)	always *tes' program*	always *tes' idea*	always *tessing*	always *rissing*

Table 6-3. Consonant Cluster Simplification. SE—Standard English; WNS—White Nonstandard English dialects; VBE—Vernacular Black English.

THE *th* SOUNDS

There are actually two sound segments spelled *th* in English. The voiced apico-dental sound occurs in such words as *this, mother,* and *lathe,* while the other sound, a voiceless consonant, occurs in *think* and *path.* The words *thy* and *thigh* are identical except that *thy* has the voiced *th* sound and *thigh* has the voiceless one. Both sounds have variant pronunciations which have social significance, as well as variations which are acceptable in Standard English. Under certain circumstances, the *th* sounds can assimilate to (become similar or identical to) surrounding sounds or even disappear altogether without losing acceptability in Standard English (Wolfram et al. 1971:70–74). Labov (1966; Labov et al. 1968) maintains that the affricate pronunciations of these sounds (when words beginning with these sounds are pronounced as if they had a *t* or a *d* as part of them—e.g., *tthing, dthere,* where *tth* and *dth* are single consonants) are somewhat stigmatized, but there is some indication (Wolfram et al. 1971) that the affricate and fricative (pronunciations without the *t* or *d*) are all but indistinguishable and probably are not noticed as different in normal conversation. It may even be true that the stop pronunciations (where the voiceless *th* is pronounced as *t* and the voiced *th* is pronounced as *d*—e.g., *ting, dem*) are part of Standard English provided that the *t* or *d* is pronounced with the tongue against the upper teeth rather than against the roof of the mouth just behind the teeth and provided that the *t* in these *th* words is not aspirated (i.e., does not have the small puff of air normally accompanying initial *t*'s in English).[5] The precise facts about which pronunciations of affricates and stops in *th* words are acceptable in Standard English are not known, but we will assume that affricates are completely acceptable and that stops are completely nonstandard. These assumptions are no doubt oversimplifications.

To adequately understand the socially stigmatized pronunciations of *th* it is necessary to consider the beginnings of words separately from the middle and ends of words. At the beginnings of words, voiced *th* is sometimes pronounced as *d* and voiceless *th* can become *t* (*dose apples, the ting I told you about*). Of the two cases, the use of *d* for voiced *th* is less stigmatized (and fairly frequently used by speakers of Standard English), used at higher rates of frequency (i.e., of, say, 100 voiced *th* words and 100 voiceless *th* words, many more of the voiced *th* words would be pronounced with *d* than voiceless *th* words pronounced with *t*, no matter who the speaker is), and more widespread geographically. In New York City, at least, the voiced and voiceless stop pronunciations for *th* have parallel social significance for white speakers. But for the black speakers in New York City studied by Labov and his associates (Labov et al. 1968:92–99), the use of *t* for voiceless *th* was not only less frequent than the use of *d* for voiced *th*, but did not show the same clear evidence of social stigmatization (in particular, the pattern of style stratification typical of stigmatized linguistic features was not clear). In the case of black adults who had been raised in the South, there was very little use of *t* for voiceless *th* at all, although the use of *d* for voiced *th* was common. These facts led Labov and his associates to the conclusion that "the parallel treatment of (th) [i.e., voiceless *th*] and (dh) [i.e., voiced *th*] is essentially a white phenomenon which is being acquired slowly in the Northern ghettoes" (Labov et al. 1968:98).

Where *t* is used for voiceless *th*, it is somewhat more frequent if the *th* precedes *r* than if it does not (Wolfram et al. 1971:64). That is, *thrill* is slightly more likely to be pronounced something like *trill* than *thin* to be pronounced *tin*. The pronunciation *f* for voiceless *th* is possible only before *r*, giving *free* for *three* and *frough* for *through*. This is more often a feature of language acquisition by children than an actual social dialect feature.

Within a word, it is fairly common in many nonstandard dialects for voiced *th* to be pronounced as *d* (*My faduh and moduh never boduh me much*). The stop pronunciation is much less common at the end of words, but sometimes occurs; *lade* is occasionally used for *lathe*, for example. With the exception of words in which *th* occurs next to a nasal consonant and the preposition *with*, the use of *t* for voiceless *th* in the middle or at the end of a word is very rare for Vernacular Black English, although it is more

---

[5] It will be very difficult to appreciate exactly what is meant by this comment unless the reader has had training in phonetics.

common in Northern white nonstandard dialects. More common in Vernacular Black English is the conversion of medial and final voiceless *th* to *f*, so that such pronunciations as *bof* in place of Standard English *both* and *nuffin* for *nothing* can be observed. This phenomenon is to be found mostly within Vernacular Black English and in dialects influenced by it, like Puerto Rican English in New York City, but occasionally a speaker without a background in these dialects will be found to use these pronunciations. In black communities in some Southern areas, the use of *f* lacks social stigmatization to the extent that many middle-class speakers who do not use other features of Vernacular Black English still retain the use of *f* in voiceless *th* words on a variable basis. For some speakers of Vernacular Black English, the use of *f* in medial and final position for *th* is so frequent that some observers have believed that voiceless *th* had merged with *f* completely (e.g., Stewart 1970). But it can be shown convincingly by linguistic analysis that speakers of Vernacular Black English have not merged voiceless *th* and *f* at deeper levels even when *f* is nearly the exclusive pronunciation on the surface (Wolfram et al. 1971:86–90).

There is a parallel use of *v* for voiced *th* in the middle and at the ends of words in some varieties of Vernacular Black English, giving *brovuh* for *brother* and *breave* for *breathe*. But this is much less frequent than the use of *f* where Standard English has voiceless *th*. Furthermore, there seems to be a difference in geographical distribution. Although most varieties of Vernacular Black English have *f* as a variant of voiceless *th*, *v* as a variant of voiced *th* is far more common in Atlantic Coast speech than further inland. Both *f* and *v* occur less frequently in the middle of words than at the ends.

If voiceless *th* occurs next to a nasal consonant in actual pronunciation, it can be pronounced *t* in many nonstandard dialects, even when it is not so pronounced medially in other words. Because of the contiguous nasal consonants, the pronunciations *aritmetic, mont,* and *nuttn* (Standard English *arithmetic, month,* and *nothing,* respectively) are possible. In its standard pronunciation, of course, *nothing* does not have *th* contiguous to a nasal, but in nonstandard dialects there is a pronunciation in which *th* is actually immediately before *n*. The preposition *with* can be pronounced *wit* (or *wid*) [6] even in dialects which do not otherwise have *t* for final voiceless *th*. Apparently, this is a peculiarity of the word *with*.[7]

---

[6] The standard dialects vary in the use of voiced and voiceless *th* in *with*. While we are involved with individual words, we might mention that *something* has the pronunciation *sumpm* in which *th* is absent altogether, but this pronunciation is to be found in Standard English and *something* is the only word of this type.

[7] One could also say that this pronunciation possibility is a feature of all English prepositions ending in *th*, but *with* is the only one that does.

VOICED FRICATIVES BEFORE NASALS

When the voiced fricatives *th* (as in *heathen*), *z* (as in *wasn't,* where the *s* is pronounced as *z*), and *v* (as in *seven*) occur before a nasal sound, they may become voiced stops in some varieties of English. In order to understand how this rule operates, it is necessary to note that in unaccented syllables, the vowel sound preceding *n* and *m* may be absent. If this takes place, the *m* or *n* may be the center of the syllabic pulse. This is sometimes referred to as a *syllabic nasal.* When the syllabic nasal follows, *th* and *z* may become *d.* The *z* to *d* rule affects items like *isn't, doesn't, wasn't,* and *hasn't.* These items may now be pronounced as *idn't, doedn't, wadn't,* and *hadn't,* respectively. In the case of *hasn't,* it should be noted that there is now no distinction between the negativized past tense form of *had* and the present form *has.* Both of them may now be pronounced as *hadn't.* The rule affects *th* in a word like *heathen,* so that it is now pronounced as *headn.* The rule is quite prevalent in some parts of the South, but can also be found in selected areas of the North. In the case of *v,* words like *seven* and *even* may now be pronounced with a *b*-like sound. When *v* is pronounced as *b,* the following nasal spelled *en* is pronounced as an *m.* The appropriate pronunciation of *seven* and *even* would then be *sebm* and *ebm,* respectively. This particular pronunciation pattern seems to be restricted to Southern varieties of English and is not particularly stigmatized in certain parts of the South.

FINAL STOP DEVOICING

Another socially significant consonantal pronunciation is the devoicing of stop (and, to some extent, fricative) consonants at the ends of words, when they are not in consonant clusters. In all varieties of English, the vowels of stressed syllables are lengthened before voiced consonants. In other words, it takes a few fractions of a second longer to say the *i* in *kid* than the *i* in *kit.* In actuality, it is this vowel length to which English speakers respond more than the voicing of the final consonant in distinguishing the voiced and voiceless counterparts of stop consonants. In other words, *kid* can be pronounced with a *t* (which is the voiceless counterpart of *d*) and it would still be heard as *kid* provided the *i* sound is held for the proper length of time. As a matter of fact, it is likely that stop consonants in this position are only barely voiced, if at all, in any variety of American English. The absence of voicing is not noticed because the length of the preceding vowel in a sense compensates for it.

But we have claimed that final stop devoicing is socially significant, which would not be possible if it were never noticed. Some speakers devoice final consonants in a way that *is* noticeable—namely by an abrupt cutoff of the voicing simultaneously with or even a little before the stop occlusion in the mouth. This results in a voiceless stop of a type known to phoneticians as a "glottalized consonant".[8] The kind of devoicing that is not noticeable consists of a more gradual "trailoff" of voicing during the duration of the stop occlusion. When the devoiced stop is *d,* but not when it is *b* or *g,* the oral occlusion may not be made at all and the *d* will be represented only by the abrupt stoppage of the voicing in the larynx, creating a "glottal stop." The full social significance of this feature depends crucially on the stress in the syllable containing the final stop. If the syllable is unstressed (as in *acid, hundred,* or *decided*) the final stop can be devoiced by an abrupt cutoff of voicing not only in Nonstandard English but in the speech of many Standard English speakers as well.[9] Abrupt devoicing in monosyllables (*kid, rag, cub*) seems to be distinctive of Black English. It is quite common in Vernacular Black English, but its social stigmatization among black speakers is so low that abrupt devoicing of final stops in monosyllabic words is often retained in the speech of middle-class black speakers who have no other distinctive syntactic or segmental pronunciation features associated with Vernacular Black English.

Devoicing of final stops can affect the grammatical suffix *-ed.* When *-ed* is suffixed to a verb ending in a vowel, like *play,* it is actually pronounced more like *playd.* This final *d* is subject to abrupt devoicing, so that it can end in "glottalized" *t.*

A glottalized *t* may also occur when *d* is followed by a syllabic nasal, so that *couldn't* may be pronounced something like *coultn(t).* This particular pronunciation pattern is not restricted to Vernacular Black English, but can be found in some Southern and Northern white varieties as well. When *l* in an unaccented syllable follows *t* as in words like *bottle* or *little,* the *t* may also take on this glottalized type of sound as well. These pronunciations, although restricted to only a few items, may be quite noticeable. In many instances, they may become the focus of overt comments about certain stigmatized phonological patterns.

ABSENCE OF FINAL *d* AND *t*

In Nonstandard English, it is possible to find cases of the absence of the stop consonants *d* and *t* at the ends of words even when they are not in consonant clusters (we have already discussed the conditions under which final stops, *d* and *t* included, can be deleted in final consonant clus-

---

[8] When speakers with this feature read word lists, it is often easy to hear the difference between devoiced *d* and *t* because the original *d,* unlike the *t,* is released with a "pop" of pharyngeal air rather than lung air.

[9] Although we have no data to support it, we strongly suspect that devoicing of final stops in unstressed syllables among middle-class speakers is far more common in women's speech than in men's.

ters). This means that the pronunciation *goo'* can occur where Standard English has *good* and *ba'* for standard *bat.* This kind of final consonant absence seems to be largely restricted to just these two stops; the absence of final *k, g, p,* or *b* is far less frequent. Just how widespread among non-standard dialects the deletion of *t* and *d* actually is is not known, but these deletions occur at least in Vernacular Black English and in Puerto Rican English in New York City, and at higher frequencies in Puerto Rican English than in Vernacular Black English.

Like most variable rules, the rule for *t* and *d* deletion will apply more or less frequently depending on various linguistic constraints. Of the two consonants, *d,* the voiced member of the pair, is more frequently deleted than is the voiceless *t.* If a word beginning with a vowel follows a word ending in single *t* or *d,* deletion will be less frequent than if a consonant is the next sound. If the final stop is in a stressed syllable, deletion is less frequent than if the stop ends in an unstressed syllable; *rabi',* then, for either standard English *rabid* or *rabbit* is more likely than *bi'* for either *bid* or *bit.*[10]

The deletion of final *d* is promoted if the word has an *-s* suffix. As a result, *roads* will sound like *rows,* and this pronunciation will be more frequent than *row* for *road.* The same effect is not found for final *t.* Although the word *kids* or *bleeds* will sometimes be pronounced *kizz* or *bleez* (recall that *-s* suffixes sound like *z* after voiced sounds like *d*), *kits* and *bleats* will not be pronounced *kiss* or *bleas.*

The deletion of final *d* intersects with grammatical markings in the case of the *-ed* suffix applied to verbs ending in a vowel, as we have seen. The actual pronunciation of a verb like *played,* to repeat our earlier example, is *playd.* When the rule for final single *d* deletion is applied to a verb like this, it is pronounced *play.* Such pronunciations do not indicate that nonstandard dialects allowing this pronunciation lack past tense or that speakers who use these pronunciations have a language deficit, as is sometimes assumed. The *-ed* suffix is understood, but its phonetic manifestation can be removed by a variable pronunciation rule. When the *-ed* is involved, however, deletion occurs systematically less often. That is, there will be fewer instances of *towed* being pronounced *tow',* proportionally, than of *toad* being pronounced *toa',* even though the two words are homophonous. Furthermore, there is some evidence that the *function* of the *-ed* suffix has an effect on deletion frequency. The *-ed* suffix can function as a marker of the past tense (*He eyed the man carefully*), as a marker of past parti-

---

[10] Recall, however, from our discussion of final stop devoicing, that vowels preceding voiced consonants are longer in duration than vowels preceding voiceless consonants. Thus, *bi'* from *bid* is not homophonous with *bi'* from *bit* because the vowel in *bi'* from *bid* is noticeably longer. In the case of the unstressed pair *rabbit* and *rabid,* *rabi'* will be much harder to identify with one or the other word because vowels tend to lose duration in all unstressed syllables.

ciple (*That man is eyed by everyone who comes in here*), or as a marker of an adjective derived from a noun (*He's a blue-eyed Scandinavian type*). Some of the data we have collected indicate that there is systematically less deletion when the construction marks past tense than when it marks past participle or derived adjectives.

r AND *l*

The pronunciation rules for *r* and *l* can differ in various American English dialects. At the beginning of a word, *r* and *l* are always pronounced, as in *run, lip, rub,* or *lamp.* In other positions, however, *r* is sometimes "vocalized" and pronounced something like *uh.* The most important context to recognize in discussing the so-called "loss" of *r* is when it follows a vowel (technically called *postvocalic*). In such items as *sister* or *bear,* only a "phonetic vestige" of *r* is pronounced, so that we hear *sistuh* and *beauh,* respectively. Preceding a consonant in a word (e.g., *wart, heart*), some speakers do not have any phonetic vestige of *r;* this means that in some dialects in which the vowels are pronounced identically, *heart* and *hot* may be pronounced the same. In some areas of the South, non-standard dialects may also reveal no vestige of *r* following the vowels *o* or *u.* For these speakers, *door* and *doe, four* and *foe,* and *sure* and *show* may be pronounced alike.

In some *r*-less American English dialects the word that follows *r* is important in determining whether or not *r* vocalization and loss may take place. For example, in the *r*-less dialect of New England, *r* is consistently absent when the following word begins with a consonant, as in *brothuh Mike* or *fouh people;* when followed by a word that begins with a vowel, the *r* is consistently present, as in *brother Ed* or *four apples.* In dialects of Southern origin, however, it may be absent in both types of contexts, although it is more frequently absent when followed by a word beginning with a consonant (e.g., *fouh people*) than when followed by one beginning with a vowel (e.g., *fouh apples*). In *r*-less dialects in New England, *r* can be inserted in words that are not spelled with *r* when a word beginning with a vowel follows (*This bananar is not ripe*).

In Vernacular Black English and in some white Southern varieties, it is possible for *r* to be absent after a vowel and before another vowel within the same word. The result is pronunciations like *sto'y, ma'y,* and *te'ific* for *story, marry,* and *terrific,* respectively. If the vowel directly before the *r* belongs to a prefix and *r* belongs to the base, then *r* cannot be deleted, so that *be'eave* and *re'un* are *not* possible pronunciations for *bereave* and *rerun.* However, intervocalic *r* deletion within a word is much less frequent than postvocalic *r* deletion at the end of a word or before a consonant.

The vocalization of *l* (vocalized *l* sounds like *oo* with *l*-coloring) and its deletion after vowels is possible but is much more heavily restricted. In addition, although *r* vocalization and deletion is one of the most widely studied variable phenomena in American English, *l* vocalization and loss has been studied much less often and linguists disagree both on the facts and how to account for them. We will largely follow the description in Labov et al. (1968). They report that for Vernacular Black English, at least, before the consonants *w, r,* or *y, l* is virtually never heard. This is true whether *l* is at the end of a word and one of these glide consonants at the beginning of the next (as in *all week, all wrong,* or *will you*) or whether *l* and the glide occur in the same word (as in *always, already,* and *million;* the second *i* in *million* is phonetically a *y*). A following consonant seems to be virtually essential in order for both vocalization and deletion to take place. Pronunciations for *hall* like *haoo* or *ha'* in a context such as *The hall on the second floor* are almost nonexistent, although either pronunciation could occur in a consonant context like *The hall downstairs.* Between vowels, *l* is not deleted so that *foo'ish* is not a possible pronunciation for *foolish.*

A preceding back rounded vowel (the sounds of *u, o,* and *aw*) favors vocalization and deletion far more than a front or central vowel. This means that *l* is far more often vocalized or deleted in *pooled, cold,* or *salt,* for example, than in words like *mild, felt, bulk,* or *scalp.* Only before a labial consonant in the same syllable may there be no phonetic vestige of the *l.* Thus, *woof* and *wolf, help* and *hep,* and *shelf* and *chef* are homophonous. This is characteristic of some white Southern dialects and Vernacular Black English.

The consistent absence of *r* at the end of a word has led to several mergers of vocabulary items. That is, because of the similarity of two words after a particular pronunciation rule has operated, one word has assumed the function of what was originally two words. For example, when the phonetic vestige that replaces the *r* is removed, there is only a small difference that separates *they* from *their* or *you* from *your.* The deletion of *r* is one source of the forms *they* and *you* being used as possessives, as in *It is they book* or *It is you book.* Another source for nonstandard treatment of case in pronouns will be presented in Chapter Seven.

Like *r* loss, the loss of *l* may have important implications for grammatical functions. The most crucial of these deals with the loss of *l* on a contracted form of the future modal *will.* We may get a sentence such as *Tomorrow I bring the things* or *Tomorrow I'uh bring the things* for *Tomorrow I'll bring the things,* where *will* becomes *'ll* and then is vocalized and reduced or lost completely. This pronunciation process accounts for the use of *be* as an indicator of future time, as in *He be here in a few minutes.*

Before leaving our description of the rules for *r* and *l,* we must note that in certain words *r* may be absent when it follows a consonant. Two main types of contexts can be cited to account for this phenomenon. First, *r* may be absent when preceded by voiceless *th* and followed by either *o* or *u,* so that we get *th'ow* for *throw* and *th'ough* for *through.* Second, *r* may be absent in unstressed syllables, so that *protéct* and *proféssor* are pronounced as *p'otéct* and *p'oféssuh,* respectively.

Unlike a number of the features presented so far, in which standard and nonstandard pronunciations could be sorted out with little intersection with regional variation, the vocalization and deletion of *r* and *l* can hardly be universally designated as nonstandard. In the case of *r* deletion, the absence of *r* is actually socially favored over its presence in many parts of the country. And as we have seen in Chapter Four, it may differ according to age. Even in those geographical areas in which postvocalic *r* vocalization and deletion bears social stigma, the stigma is likely to be rather slight. In most linguistic contexts, *l* vocalization and deletion would never be thought of as nonstandard in many regions. The absence of *l* is most likely to be marked socially as nonstandard in the single word *help* and in sentences in which contraction of *will* and subsequent removal of *'ll* by *l* deletion has totally removed the indicator of future time reference.

NONSTANDARD TREATMENT OF NASAL CONSONANTS

In this section we will deal with nonstandard pronunciations of nasal consonants themselves as well as their effect on variant vowel pronunciations. One of the best known of these nonstandard pronunciations is the dropping of the *g* in some words ending in *ing.* Phonetically, *ng* is a single nasal consonant. When the *g* is dropped, the *ng* consonant [ŋ] is replaced by *n.* The *in* pronunciation of *ing* occurs in all nonstandard dialects at a high frequency level and is used in standard dialects as well with considerable frequency. Labov et al. (1968) found that the *in* pronunciation was extremely frequent in both black and white nonstandard speech in New York City and was very sensitive to style context. The use of *in,* they found, would drop from frequencies in excess of 90 percent in conversational style to well below 50 percent in reading styles.

The *in* pronunciation is very heavily influenced by the stress of the syllable in which *ing* appears. In monosyllables that automatically receive primary word stress in English, *in* is not used, so that *sing* is never *sin.* In the words *anything* and *everything, ing* ends a syllable with an intermediate stress level. Under such stress conditions, *in* is an uncommon pronunciation. In separate tabulations of *in* for *ing* by two students of one of the authors, *anything* was never pronounced *anythin'* and *everythin'* was recorded for *everything* only once out of twenty examples of the word. When the syllable containing *ing* is unstressed, as in the *-ing* verb suffix or the words *nothing* and *something*, the *in* pronunciation is very common in nonstandard dialects. In the tabulations referred to above, all instances of *nothing* ended in *in* in both counts; *something* was never pronounced with *ng* in one count and was pronounced with *ng* only twice out of 84 instances in the other. As we have pointed out already in connection with *th*, *something* was most often pronounced *sumpm* in both counts with the syllabic *m* representing *ing*. In the case of the -*ing* verb suffix, the *in* pronunciation was tabulated 84 percent of the time in one count and 91 percent of the time in the other. In unstressed syllables, *in* is far more common than *ing* in nonstandard dialects, while *in* for *ing* in syllables with even secondary stress is very seldom observed.

It is often reported that the suffix -*ing* can be absent in Nonstandard English. There is a context in which -*ing* can be removed, but in most cases it is a rather restricted one. When -*ing* is added to a verb that ends in unstressed *en* (like *listen* or *open*), the *in* pronunciation of -*ing* causes the verb to end in two identical syllables (*lissinin* or *opinin*). There is a tendency in language, called haplology, for sequences of identical syllables to be reduced to one. This tendency can apply to forms like *listening* and *opening* and leave *He was listen to it* or *He is open a can*. There are other pronunciation processes by which -*ing* can be reduced so that it is hardly discernible by Standard English speakers. When -*ing* is added to a verb that ends in a consonant, the suffix can be pronounced *n* (which carries syllable beat). In these cases, *getting,* for example, can be pronounced *gettn.* If the next word begins with voiced *th,* the *th* can assimilate to the *n,* even in Standard English, so that *getting the book* can be pronounced something like *gettnuh book.* In rapid speech, the *n,* which in effect stands for both -*ing* and the *th* of *the,* can easily be missed entirely, so that *gettnuh book* sounds to the untrained listener like *get the book.* As we shall show in the next paragraph, a final nasal consonant, like the *ng* of -*ing* (or the *n* of -*in*) can be removed entirely, so that *He was showing me* is pronounced *He was showuh me* with a nasal quality to the vowel *uh.* It is also easy to fail to hear this reduced, nasalized vowel and to hear *He was show me.*

Another variable pronunciation feature involving nasal consonants is the deletion of nasal consonants at the end of syllables. A "trace" of the deleted nasal is always left in the form of nasal quality with the preceding vowel. The reason for this is that in English, vowels that precede nasal consonants assume nasal quality in anticipation of the articulation of the nasal consonant. Anticipatory vowel nasalization takes place, in a sense, before nasal consonant deletion so that the nasal quality is present with the vowel even when the expected consonant is not present. This is phonetically something like the nasalized vowels of French. Deletion of nasal consonants is very common in Standard English when a consonant follows. Pronunciations like *ju^{n}p* for *jump* and *co^{n}sideration* for *consideration* (the raised ^{n} indicates the nasal quality with the preceding vowel) are very frequent in the standard dialects and are not socially stigmatized. In some nonstandard dialects, a nasal consonant may also be removed at the end of a word (although apparently not between vowels within a word). In these dialects (Vernacular Black English is one), *run, rum,* and *rung* can all sometimes be prounced ru^n.

Finally, we should mention the influence that nasal consonants have on the vowels *i* and *e*. Before a nasal consonant, *i* and *e* do not contrast, making words such as *pin* and *pen, tin* and *ten,* or *Minnie* and *many* sound identical. This pronunciation rule is a feature of some standard varieties of Southern speech, and only has social significance in a Northern context. Even there, its social significance is minimal.

OTHER CONSONANT FEATURES

A consonant feature that is quite limited is the absence of *s* in a word that ends in *x* (phonetically *ks*). This pattern results in the pronunciation of *box* as *bok* and *six* as *sik* (homophonous with *sick*). For the most part, this feature is limited to a few items ending in *x* in Vernacular Black English and is more frequently found in Southern speakers than it is in Northern speakers. We may also mention a nonstandard pronunciation of the *str* clusters in such words as *stream* and *street,* which may be pronounced as *skream* or *skweam* and *skreet* or *skweet,* respectively. Most often these pronunciations are found in the speech of younger children and *skr* and *skw* are given up automatically as the children grow older.

Another consonantal pronunciation with social significance is a *y* sound between a consonant and the vowel *u*. This pronunciation is word-specific and has prestige when used with the appropriate words, although its absence is not nonstandard. Some words are always pronounced with the *y* sound— for example, *few* is always pronounced *fyoo,* never *foo.* In other words, there is variation; a word like *due* is pronounced *dyoo* by some speakers while others pronounce it *doo.* Some speakers of this prestige dialect create a *ch* out of *t* and this *y* and a *j* out of *d* and *y*. For these speakers, *Tuesday* is identical with *choose-day* and *dune* and *June* are also homophonous. In still other words, including all those in which the *u* sound is spelled *oo,* the *y* sound is only inserted by people attempting to acquire the prestige pronunciation in adulthood without knowing just which words actually take it. The pronunciation *nyoon* for *noon* is an example of such hyper-correction.

The treatment of words beginning with *wh* and words that begin with *hu* is another case of social and regional significance overlapping. In large areas in the Northeast, there is no distinction between *wh* and *w* so that *witch* and *which* and *whale* and *wail* are homophonous. In most other regions, there is a distinction between the two sets of words. In regions where there is no distinction, the pronunciation of *wh* words without the *h* is part of the standard dialect, although it may be stigmatized elsewhere. In parts of the mid-Atlantic states, *h* is not pronounced in words beginning with *hu,* so that *human* sounds like *yooman* and *humor* is pronounced *yoomor.* Again, these pronunciations are thoroughly standard in regions where they are native, but not well-accepted elsewhere.

Vowel Features

Vowel features, as we have mentioned, are more likely than consonant features to be subject to a combination of regional and social significance. To research and report the social and regional variation of vowel sounds around the country would be a prohibitive undertaking. As a result, we will deal with only a few vowel features in a way that should be taken as more illustrative than comprehensive.

In the pronunciation of "long" *i* (we are not dealing with duration as we were when we spoke of vowel length in connection with consonant devoicing, but rather of the difference between *bit* and *bite*), used in standard Northern dialects, there are actually two sounds, a full vowel *ah* followed by what phoneticians call an off-glide which sounds like *ee.* The variant pronunciations we are interested in are those in which the off-glide is preserved (as in *pie* as pronounced in the North) compared with those in which the off-glide is absent (as in *pah*). The linguistic context has a considerable influence on the frequency with which pronunciations without the off-glide will be heard. The off-glide is most likely to be deleted in words that end in the vowel, such as *lie, sky,* and *hi.* If a consonant follows the vowel, the off-glide is most often deleted if that consonant is voiced (all consonants except *p, t, ch, k, f,* voiceless *th, s,* and *sh* are voiced in English). There are some dialects of English in which the off-glide can be removed only if no consonant or a voiced consonant follows the vowel. That is, the off-glide may be absent in *sigh* or *side,* but not in *sight.* The deletion of the off-glide, of course, is fully standard in Southern dialects, at least at the end of a word or before voiced consonants. In other areas, there is a slight social stigma associated with the off-glide absence.

It is not necessarily the case that the deletion of the off-glide creates widespread homophony, as speakers of Northern dialects of English often assume. Even when *side* is pronounced roughly *sahd,* it is consistently kept distinct from both *sod* and *sad* by the quality of the *ah* vowel.

A similar situation exists with the *y* sound in *boy* and *boil* being variably deletable in dialects of Southern origin. As in the *side* example just cited, the removal of the off-glide does not necessarily create homophony between words like *boil* and *ball*. Even in the absence of the off-glide, the vowel quality in *boil* keeps it distinct from the vowel in *ball*, for some speakers.

There is socially significant variation in the vowels of such words as *bad* and *bat* on the one hand and *ball* and *talk* on the other. In the New York City area, pronunciations of *bad* which sound like *bay-ud* or *bee-ud* are socially stigmatized. Similarly, pronunciations of *ball* and *talk* which sound like *boo-ul* and *too-uk* are considered nonstandard at least by middle-class speakers. Whether these pronunciations have the same social significance in other mid-Atlantic areas is not known. In the Great Lakes area from upstate New York west, the *bay-ud* and *bay-ut* pronunciations for *bad* and *bat* are common and do not carry social stigma (these pronunciations may be what is meant by the expression "Midwestern twang"). The *boo-ul* and *too-uk* pronunciations for *ball* and *talk* apparently do not occur in this area. There are a number of other vowel variations we might mention, but most of these are regionally restricted.

Pronunciation of Articles

The pronunciation of the articles *a/an* and *the* varies with regional and social significance. In standard Northern dialects, these articles are pronounced differently depending on whether or not the next word begins with a vowel or a consonant. If the next word begins with a consonant sound, *a* is used (*a dog, a ukelele*). If the next word starts with a vowel, *an* is selected (*an animal, an order*). Similarly, *the* is pronounced like *thuh* if a consonant follows (*thuh dog, thuh ukelele*) and like *thee* if a vowel follows (*thee animal, thee order*). In some Southern standard dialects, *a* and the *thuh* pronunciation for *the* are used everywhere (*a dog, a animal, thuh dog, thuh animal*). In those varieties in which *a* appears before vowels, the word *a* is often absorbed into the initial vowel of the following word if that vowel has the same quality as the article *a*. In a sentence *He has a ugly face*, the quality of the vowel spelled *u* in *ugly* is the same as the quality of *a* so that the sentence is spoken as *He has ugly face*. In cases like this, what appears to be a difference in the grammar of articles turns out to be explainable on purely phonological grounds. In other regions, these pronunciations are somewhat stigmatized, especially in the case of *a* and *an*, where there is a spelling difference to match the pronunciation difference.

Verb Forms with to

There are several verb forms which take infinitive complements with *to* (called "quasi-modals" by Labov and his associates) and which have varying pronunciations in these constructions. Pronunciations such as *hafta* for *have to, useta* for *used to, wanna* for *want to, wanda* for *wanted to,* and *gonna* for *going to* are examples. All of these pronunciations are part of Standard English and should not be taken as examples of non-standard dialect pronunciations. However, there are further reductions of *gonna* which apparently carry a certain degree of social stigma. With *I* as a subject, *I'm gonna* can be further reduced to produce *I'ngna, I'mana, I'maw* and *I'ma* (each of these can be taken as further reduction of the preceding). With other subjects, *gonna* is sometimes reduced to *gaw^n* in some nonstandard dialects, as in *He gaw^n do it.*

Suprasegmentals

Most of the studies of socially diagnostic features of English have been concentrated on the segmental characteristics. That is, they describe only the consonant and vowel patterns. This does not necessarily mean, however, that there are no differences between dialects on a suprasegmental level. Included in the suprasegmentals we have stress or accent patterns and sentence intonation. For the most part, stress operates quite similarly in various regional and social dialects of American English. There are, however, stress differences that may affect small subsets of items. One such case is the placement of stress on the first or the second syllable of a word. For example, the pronunciation of *Detroit* with stress on the first syllable (*Détroit*) instead of the second syllable (*Detróit*) may indicate that a speaker is not a resident of the city. Words like *pólice* for *políce, hótel* for *hotél,* and *Júly* for *Julý* are characteristic of Vernacular Black English and some Southern white varieties. In a Northern context, this stress pattern may be somewhat stigmatized. Another difference related to stress is the absence of the first syllable of a word when the first syllable of a polysyllabic word is normally unstressd. Words like *'rithmetic, 'member, 'cept,* and *'bout* all result from this pattern.

At this point, we know little about the specifics of intonation as it relates to social dialectology. For the most part, intonation patterns do not become crucial indicators of social class in speech. Because they usually lack social diagnosticity, nonstandard speakers who learn a standard variety may retain indigenous intonational patterns. Although intonation is not typically recognized as an indicator of social class, it appears to be one of the main reasons why some standard-speaking blacks may be identified ethnically. Tarone (1972), in a recent study of white and black intonation patterns, concluded that there are several main intonational differences: (1) Vernacular Black English patterns were characterized by a wider pitch range, extending into higher pitch levels than the corresponding nonstandard white dialect (or the formal black speech style), (2) a falsetto register was used more often in Vernacular Black English, and (3) more rising and level final contours were used in Vernacular Black English. Tarone points out that intonation, like many of the other features we have already discussed, cannot really be studied apart from the social situation. An individual's use of certain socially stigmatized or prestigious features may fluctuate considerably depending on the formality of the speech situation.

Conclusion

We have seen in our discussion of nonstandard pronunciations that a number of generalizations can be made. First, for most nonstandard speakers the standard and nonstandard pronunciations both occur. For many features, the nonstandard variants also occur to some extent in the speech of speakers of the standard dialects, but less frequently. The nonstandard pronunciations are not due to carelessness but are controlled by rules sensitive to linguistic context. The social significance of many of the features, especially vowel features, intersects with regional variation, so that whether the feature is nonstandard or not depends on what regional standard dialect is spoken in the area under consideration. Although we have not been exhaustive in our treatment of socially significant pronunciation variation in American English, we expect that these generalizations will be true of features we have not mentioned as well.

7

SOCIALLY DIAGNOSTIC
GRAMMATICAL FEATURES

The grammatical features of Nonstandard English can be considered more interesting than pronunciation aspects for several reasons.[1] Pedagogically, teachers are likely to be more concerned with the former because it often appears that a student who does not use standard grammar is being imprecise in his speech. We will attempt to show that not only is this not the case, but in some areas various nonstandard dialects can make precise distinctions more easily than standard grammar can. Socially, it has been demonstrated (Wolfram 1970) that nonstandard grammar is more likely than nonstandard pronunciation to arrest the attention of speakers of the standard dialects and thus lead to negative reactions on their part. Middle-class speakers are generally sharply divided from working-class speakers linguistically by the fact that they use nonstandard grammar features far less frequently. Many forms of nonstandard pronunciation are present in varying degrees in the speech of educated middle-class speakers, but in the case of grammar, Standard English speakers virtually always use a given feature called for by the rules of informal standard grammar while speakers of nonstandard dialects use the standard and the equivalent nonstandard

[1] Some of the features we will discuss are technically pronunciation features. We deal with them in this chapter because they have a strong effect on grammatical features.

forms in varying proportions. With respect to language change, if the variation between standard and nonstandard forms is symptomatic of change in progress, then the change will be more profound if a grammatical change is being introduced than if a pronunciation is changing. Many of the grammar features we are dealing with, however, involve variation that is either relatively stagnant or is moving in the direction of Standard English.

Verb Forms

THE -ed SUFFIX

As we have seen already, the -ed suffix, which marks past tense and past participial forms as well as derived adjectives, is sometimes not pronounced in Nonstandard English because of pronunciation rules (pp. 130 and 139). When -ed is added to a verb base ending in a consonant, as in *missed,* it can be removed by application of the consonant cluster reduction rule. When -ed is added to a verbal base that ends in a vowel, as in *played,* it can be removed by the rule for deletion of syllable-final *d.* As we have already pointed out, the *d* deletion and consonant cluster reduction rules apply much less often when the following word begins with a vowel rather than a consonant.

When -ed is added to a base ending in *t* or *d,* it is pronounced something like *id.* In this form, it is not absent very frequently in any nonstandard dialect. However, this *id* form can be reduced to *d* alone in nonstandard dialects and also in Standard English by some fairly complex, but very regular rules. In casual speech, the words *want* and *start* are the most frequently occurring verbs eligible for these rules. If these rules apply, the *i* sound of *id* can be eliminated. The verb then ends in *dd* or *td,* which is simplified to *d.* These operations result in sentences like *He stard crying* (from *He started crying*) and *He wanda go* (from *He wanted to go*). Such sentences are common in all varieties of American English and are not considered nonstandard. In the case of *stard,* Vernacular Black English (but not Standard English) has a rule for the elimination of the remaining *d,* especially when the verb occurs before a gerund, as in *He sta crying* (the *r* of *start* is absent for reasons we have already discussed). The verb *started* is virtually the only verb to undergo this process.

These rules are pronunciation rules. This means that the missing -ed suffix does not reflect a grammatical difference between Nonstandard and Standard English. The suffix is a part of the grammar of both kinds of English. That is, all English speakers know the -ed suffix; they simply do not always pronounce it.

IRREGULAR PAST-TENSE FORMS

A number of verbs in Standard English form their past tenses not by adding *-ed,* but in various irregular ways. For example, the past tense of *give* is not *gived,* but *gave;* of *do,* the past tense is *did; teach* is *taught* in the past tense; and there is a fairly large number of similar examples. It is sometimes claimed that it is typical of Nonstandard English for such verbs to turn up in their nonpast forms in past contexts. That is, sentences like *My dad come here in about 1910* are assumed to be the general usage. It is not necessary to distinguish among several nonstandard dialects in order to make realistic statements about this feature. In Vernacular Black English, Fasold (1972:38) discovered that the use of a present form in a past context was quite rare and that there were no individual speakers who did not use the standard irregular past forms most of the time. Similar discoveries were made by Labov et al. (1968) for Vernacular Black English in New York City and by Wolfram (1971) for Harlem Puerto Rican English. In Vernacular Black English, however, the verb *say* seems to be something of an exception, with *say* being used for Standard English *said* fairly frequently. Labov et al. (1968:138–39) claim greater frequency for the use of present forms of irregular verbs in past contexts for White Nonstandard English than for Vernacular Black English. In his analysis of Appalachian English, Hackenberg (1972) found 77 instances of this feature in recorded interviews with 39 speakers, but it is important to note which verb is involved. Sixty-seven of the cases involved *come* and *run* and 9 of the remaining 10 were cases of *give* for Standard English *gave.* In general, we have been unable to find evidence that this feature is very widespread or that it implies any basic differences between the tense systems of standard and nonstandard grammars.

Another phenomenon involving irregular verbs is a tendency to regularize some of them. Verbs that are irregular in Standard English are given regular *-ed* past forms occasionally by some nonstandard speakers. This feature was noted as very rare for Vernacular Black English by Fasold (1972) and for Appalachian English by Hackenberg (1972). Among Hackenberg's 39 speakers there were only 17 examples and 12 of these were *knowed* for *knew.* In looking at the verb systems of nonstandard dialects, as wholes, nonstandard treatment of irregular verbs is linguistically not very significant, although apparently these treatments are very noticeable to Standard English speakers.

PRESENT AND PAST-PERFECT TENSES

It seems safe to say that both the present and past-perfect are intact in the varieties of Nonstandard English with which we are familiar. Because of the frequency of the deletion of auxiliary *have* and the break-down in the distinction between past tense and past participle in Nonstandard English, features we will discuss directly, it sometimes appears that there is no distinction between the past tense and the past-perfect tense. It can appear that a sentence *I seen it* demonstrates the collapse of the standard English distinction between *I saw it* and *I've seen it*. This is not the case, as we shall see, although the collapse of the distinction is very possible as a future development. The use of the past-perfect tense (*I had seen it*) is a striking feature of Vernacular Black English narrative style. The construction is used liberally in stories about events in the past.

THE COMPLETIVE ASPECT WITH *done*

Some nonstandard dialects have an additional perfective construction made with *done* and the past tense or past-participial form. Use of this construction results in sentences like *I done tried hard all I know how* (by a Vernacular Black English speaker) and *He's done went home* (by an Appalachian English speaker). This construction is attested in both Vernacular Black English and Appalachian English and no doubt is to be found in other nonstandard dialects, especially those of Southern origin. The construction is not a substitute for the present-perfect tense in Standard English, but is in addition to it. The general meaning of the completive aspect construction is to emphasize the completeness of the action. In spite of its usefulness in adding an aspectual distinction to English, the completive aspect seems to be dying out in both Vernacular Black English and Appalachian English.

THE REMOTE TIME ASPECT WITH *been*

A similar construction using *been* as an auxiliary is used only in Vernacular Black English to emphasize the remoteness of an action from the current interests of the speaker. An example we have observed is *You won't get your dues that you been paid*. A sentence like this is quite likely to be misunderstood by a speaker of Standard English as involving a passive construction, but the meaning is active (i.e., dues were not paid to you, you paid them to someone else). It is possible for Vernacular Black English speakers to combine the completive and remote time constructions in sentences like *I been done went there* or *I done been went there*. Such sentences are rare, not because their grammaticality within Vernacular Black English is questionable, but because situations requiring such fine aspect distinctions seldom arise. In any event, the *been* construction, like the *done* construction, is dying out in spite of its potential usefulness.

THE PAST PARTICIPLE

Although it is quite clear that the tenses formed grammatically with *have* and *had* are part of the nonstandard dialects we have investigated, it is less clear whether or not there are past participles in their grammars. In Standard English, most past participles are formed with the -*ed* suffix and so are identical with the past-tense form (e.g., *moved, has moved*). But there are a number of semiregular and irregular verbs for which the past participle and past tense are formally distinguished (e.g., *came* versus *has come; ate* versus *has eaten,* etc.). In some nonstandard dialects there is some evidence that there may not be any irregular verbs for which the past tense and past participle are invariably kept distinct. Sometimes the Standard English past-participle form is generalized to serve both functions (*He taken it; He has taken it*), but more commonly the simple past form is used in both kinds of constructions (e.g., *He came; He has came*). For a few verbs, some speakers generalize one and some the other (e.g., *He done it; He has done it; He did it; He has did it*). It is possible, then, that some nonstandard equivalents of the present and past-perfect tenses do not consist of forms of *have* plus the past participle, but rather involve a form of *have* plus a general past form.

Wherever there is a Standard English distinction that is weak in nonstandard dialects, hypercorrection, the overextension of a Standard English pattern, is likely to occur. Because the distinction between past-tense and past-participial forms is less definite in nonstandard grammar, it is sometimes observed that nonstandard speakers supply a distinct participial form where Standard English has identical past-tense and participial forms, giving rise to sentences like *They haven't cutten all them trees.* In general, hypercorrect forms are much less frequent in occurrence than are instances of the construction causing the hypercorrection, and they can be considered incorrect from the point of view of nonstandard grammar as well as standard grammar. In the participial case, hypercorrections like *have cutten* are much less frequent than instances like *I seen a movie* or *They just taken him away a minute ago.*

THE PRESENT-TENSE SUFFIX

In perhaps every American English nonstandard dialect the standard -*s* (or -*es*) suffix marking nonpast tense when the subject of the sentence is third-person singular is variably absent. It is usually also the case that sentences in the nonpast tense with subjects other than third-person singular *do* sometimes have the suffix. When the suffix is absent, sentences like *He don't come here anymore* result. When the suffix occurs with other kinds

of subjects, the result is sentences like *They doesn't come here anymore.*
But it is *not* the case that the grammars of all these dialects are the same
with respect to nonpast tense. In order to understand these somewhat
subtle, but linguistically and pedagogically important differences, it is necessary to review the present-tense concord grammar of the standard dialects.

In Standard American English, the suffix *-s* (or *-es*) is used to identify
the present tense of a verb only if the subject of that verb is in the third-
person singular. The paradigm is:

SINGULAR	PLURAL
I walk	we walk
you walk	you walk
he walks; the man walks	they walk; the men walk

In a sense, the use of the *-s* suffix to mark present tense with third-person
singular subjects is an irregularity, because no suffix is used to mark present
tense with other persons. Vernacular Black English on the one hand, and
Appalachian English on the other have developed variable grammatical
rules which tend to regularize the standard paradigm. But they have done
so in opposite ways. Vernacular Black English has variably and categorically, depending on the speaker, eliminated the rule that requires *-s* when
the subject is third-person singular. Appalachian English has variably extended the rule so that (with one special exception) *-s* can be suffixed to
verbs with third-person subjects, regardless of number. To highlight the
difference, we will give the paradigms that would exist in both systems if the
rules were all categorical rather than variable. In Vernacular Black English
the paradigm would be:

SINGULAR	PLURAL
I walk	we walk
you walk	you walk
he walk; the man walk	they walk; the men walk

In some varieties of Appalachian English, it would be:

SINGULAR	PLURAL
I walk	we walk
you walk	you walk
the man walks	the men walks

The above paradigms are completely accurate only for some speakers. For
other speakers, *He walk* and *The man walk* actually vary with *He walks* and
The man walks. For Appalachian English speakers, *The men walks* varies
with *The men walk.*

Hackenberg (1972) was unable to find a single example of the absence of -s from a nonpast-tense verb when the subject was third-person singular, except in a few instances in which the verb involved was *don't* (for more on this phenomenon, see below). Furthermore, there is an interesting special exception to the rule that -s can occur with third-person subjects, both singular and plural. If the subject of a nonpast-tense verb is third-person plural, the suffix can only appear if the subject is a noun. If the subject is the pronoun *they,* use of -s is forbidden. In other areas of the South, there are restricted cases in which -s third-person singular may be absent even when *don't* is not the verb form.

Special mention should be made of the three English verbs that take special nonpast forms. The verbs *have, do,* and *say* have forms that undergo other changes when -s is added. As a result, *have* takes the form *has* rather than *haves, do* becomes *does* rather than *dos,* and *says* from *say* is pronounced *sez* rather than the expected *saze.* When these verbs occur without -s, they do not undergo any of these secondary changes. In nonstandard dialects like Vernacular Black English *He have, He do,* and *He say* are heard rather than *He ha', He doe',* and *He se'.* In spite of the fact that *He have a bike* may appear to be a different phenomenon from *He ride a bike,* both sentences are the result of the same grammatical rule.

The form *don't,* as in *He don't walk,* seems to promote -s absence more than other verbs, and even more than *do* without the *not* contraction. There are nonstandard dialects, such as Appalachian English, as we have already pointed out, and also the Northern white nonstandard dialect Labov et al. (1968:147–48) investigated, that allow nonpast tense -s to be absent with third-person singular subjects *only* when the form involved is *don't.*[2] In these dialects, *He don't walk* is occasionally heard, but *He walk* is never heard. In other nonstandard dialects, like Vernacular Black English, in which the -s suffix may be absent from any verb, it is more frequently absent in the case of *don't* than in other cases (Fasold 1972:124).

In Vernacular Black English, the tenuous status of the verbal -s suffix in the grammar of that dialect leads to hypercorrection. That is, the suffix is added to sentences in the nonpast tense with other than third-person singular subjects, giving *I/You/We/They/The men walks.* These sentences make it appear that this dialect is somewhat like Appalachian English in allowing verbal -s with third-person plural subjects, but this is not the case. Such sentences from Vernacular Black English speakers are violations of the rules of grammar for their dialects and are inspired by an attempt to use the standard suffixation rule without control over

---

[2] Labov et al. do not report the use of -s with other than third-person singular subjects for this dialect, however.

restrictions on the standard rule. The grammar of Appalachian English, on the other hand, calls for such sentences. There are three reasons why we know this is true. First, the -s suffix is not weak in Appalachian English: evidently it is possible to omit verbal -s only with *don't* and then only at low-frequency levels. The -s suffix is absent in Vernacular Black English from all verbs at frequencies often higher than 75 percent. Thus there is a structural reason for hypercorrection in this dialect, but not in Appalachian English. Second, the -s suffix is occasionally extended even to non-finite verb constructions in Vernacular Black English, giving sentences like *He want to goes* and *They get caughts.* This is a good indication that the suffix is being applied largely by guesswork and not by rule. Sentences like these would never occur in Appalachian English. Finally, the use of -s when the subject is not third-person singular is relatively infrequent and limited to a relatively small number of speakers in Vernacular Black English. For example, Fasold (1972) found that only 6 of 47 working-class black speakers used hyper-s at all and in the speech of the 6, it was observed only about 13 percent of the time. The absence of verbal -s where Standard English demands it, on the other hand, was observed in the speech of 44 of the 47 speakers at a rate of over 65 percent of the time. Hackenberg (1972) found that -s was used with third-person plural subjects in his Appalachian English corpus 30 percent of the time and by a majority of his speakers.

Verbal -s is used with subjects other than third-person singular in connection with the so-called historical present in some varieties of White Nonstandard English. This is especially associated with sentences with first-person singular subjects in examples like *I goes downtown and I sees this man and he says to me....* Although mentioned as a characteristic of Northern White Nonstandard English, this feature has not been investigated in detail, so the rules governing it are not known.

CONCORD WITH FORMS OF *be*

A well-known feature of nonstandard speech is the use of *is* and *was* with all persons and numbers. The case of *is* is very similar, in Standard English, to the case of verbal -s: *is*, like -s, is used in the nonpast tense but only when the subject is third-person singular. The nonpast form of *to be* when the subject is first-person singular (*I*) is *am;* all other persons and numbers take *are. Was* is the past-tense concord form for first- and third-persons singular with *were* used elsewhere in Standard English. In some nonstandard dialects, sentences like *I/You/We/They/The boys is (was) here* appear. Although absence of concord is a common feature, it functions differently enough in various nonstandard dialects so that it will be necessary to discuss the nonstandard uses of *is* and *was* separately, and for each of the dialects we have investigated.

There is some evidence that Vernacular Black English is not as uniform for the *is* concord feature as it is for other aspects of grammar and pronunciation. For younger children and rural Southern communities, it may be the case that *is* is the only present-tense form of *to be* and the grammar of these dialects calls for its use regardless of person and number. *Are* and *am* are used rather infrequently and often hypercorrectly, as in *There she are* and *You am a teacher.*

For Northern urban Vernacular Black English, the rule that restricts *is* to third-person singular subjects seems to be variable. It is difficult to get reliable tabulations of the frequency of *is* where the subject is not third-person singular because of the frequency with which present-tense forms of *to be* can be deleted in these dialects (see Labov et al. 1968:220–21 and Wolfram et al. 1971:326–28 for discussion), but it is certain that the grammar allows the standard forms *am* and *are* to vary with *is*. The hypercorrect use of *am* and *are* when the subject is third-person singular (*He are, He am*) is almost nonexistent. With expletive *there* or *it, is* is always used regardless of subject, giving *There's (It's) four boys here.*

In the white nonstandard dialect investigated by Labov and his associates in New York (1968), the use of *is* with subjects other than third-person singular is virtually nonexistent.

For Appalachian English, Hackenberg was able to show convincingly that the *is* concord rule is the same rule as the verbal *-s* concord rule. Just as *-s* can be used with regular verbs variably with third-person plural subjects, so *is* can be used with these subjects, but is so used a little more frequently. The special constraint that prevents the use of *-s* when the subject is *they* (but allows it when the subject is a plural noun) also operates in the case of *is* concord; that is, *The men is here* is possible, but *They is here* is not. It turns out that the use of expletive *there* strongly favors the use of *is* where *are* would be required in Standard English, so that *There's flies everywhere* would be more common than *Flies is everywhere.*

In all the nonstandard speech varieties we have investigated, the use of *was* where Standard English demands *were* is much more frequent than *is* for *am* and *are*. We have no evidence differentiating varieties of Vernacular Black English on the basis of *was* concord, but in both Wolfram et al. (1971) and Labov et al. (1968) it was found that the use of *was* when the subject is second-person or plural (i.e., where Standard English takes *were*) is very frequent for Vernacular Black English; so much so that Labov et al. suggest that *were* is not part of Vernacular Black English at all. The past-tense paradigm for *to be,* then, would be:

SINGULAR	PLURAL
I was	we was
you was	you was
he was; the man was	they was; the men was

The use of *were* for Standard English *was* is not too common, although there is a pronunciation in Vernacular Black English for *was* in which the final *s* is articulated very lightly if at all (*wa'*), which often sounds like *were* to Standard English speakers.

The white nonstandard dialect mentioned in Labov et al. (1968) has the nonstandard *was* concord rule but it is applied rather infrequently.

In Appalachian English, the use of *was* for Standard English *were* is noticeably more common than *is* for Standard English *am* and *are*. *Was,* unlike *is,* can be used with first- and second-person subjects as well as third-person plural. That is, *I/You/We/They was here* is possible along with *The men was here.* The frequency of nonstandard *was* concord is higher in the expletive *there* construction so that *There was a lot of people there* is more frequent than *A lot of people was there.* Examples like *There was a lot of people there* are fairly common in informal Standard English.

AUXILIARY DELETIONS

In Standard English, the auxiliary forms *have, has, had, will,* and *would* and the copula and auxiliary forms *am, are,* and *is* can be contracted giving *'ve* for *have, 'll* for *will, 'm* for *am, 're* for *are, 'd* for both *had* and *would,* and *'s* for both *has* and *is.* In Vernacular Black English, but apparently in no other dialect with the same lack of restrictions, all of these contractions can be deleted except *'m* and *'d.* The following sentences are then possible:

> *I gone there lots of times.* (contraction and deletion of *have*)
> *He gone there lots of times.* (contraction and deletion of *has* or *have*)
> *He go there tomorrow.* (contraction and deletion of *will*)
> *They over there all the time.* (contraction and deletion of *are* or *is*)
> *He over there all the time.* (contraction and deletion of *is*)

A number of clarifying comments are necessary. The contraction *'d* can also be eliminated, but by a different pronunciation rule. This rule operates by causing *'d* to be absorbed by the following consonant if the following consonant is a labial (e.g., *b, p*) or velar (e.g., *g, k*). This rule is part of Standard English as well, giving such commonly heard sentences as *If he were nominated, he get a lot of support* (with *would* contracted to *'d* and *'d* absorbed by the *g* of *get*). The same "absorption" rule sometimes applies to *'ve* and, to a lesser extent, to *'ll* in Standard English, giving *I been waiting here an hour* and *He be here when he can*. However, such sentences are much less frequent than they are in Vernacular Black English. Notice that the absorption rule does not apply to *'s* so that *is* is never deleted in Standard English. *Is* is deletable only in Vernacular Black English except that *is* deletion may occur in Southern white nonstandard dialects if the next word is *gonna* (giving *He gonna go*).

For some speakers of Vernacular Black English, especially children and rural Southern speakers, present-tense forms of *to be* are removed as wholes without the intermediate contraction step. Their use of sentences such as *He good* is not related to contractions like *He's good,* which may not even occur in their speech, but are the result of a rule that deletes the whole form *is*. Speakers with this *is*-deletion rule are in the minority among Vernacular Black English speakers compared to those with the rule for the deletion of *'s*.

The form *are* is present less often than the form *is* in the speech of Vernacular Black English speakers. *Are* is also absent in white Southern dialects of English that do not allow the absence of *is*. The English contraction rule, as we have pointed out, provides for the removal of all but the final consonant of certain auxiliaries (*are* to *'re, will* to *'ll, have* to *'ve,* etc.). In dialects that lack *r* after most stressed vowels, *are* has no final consonant (i.e., it is pronounced *ah*). Applying the contraction rule to this pronunciation eliminates the word *are* entirely, without utilizing the Vernacular Black English rule for removing the consonant. Because of this there are speakers who have *are* absence but do not have *is* absence.

By now it may have occurred to some of our readers to question the claim that the present-perfect tense is intact in Vernacular Black English and other nonstandard dialects. Note that the present-perfect tense is formed with a present-tense form of auxiliary *have* and the past participle of a verb, e.g., *He has worked*. Except for a closed list of irregular verbs in Standard English, the past tense and past participle are identically formed, e.g., *He worked, He has worked*. In addition, we have already pointed out that in Nonstandard English the distinction between past and past participle is somewhat tenuous even for irregular verbs, so that *I seen it* and *I've seen it* are both possible. We have just seen that in Vernacular Black English at least, *have* forms can be deleted by contraction and deletion. In effect, we are claiming that a sentence like *I tried (done) that many times* and *I tried (done) that yesterday* are distinct in Nonstandard English. The first example is in the present-perfect tense and the second is in the simple past. The *have* auxiliary has been removed (by contraction and either deletion or absorption) in the first example and *done* is possible as a simple past form in the second example because of the lack of consistent distinction between past participle and past tense. It may appear equally reasonable to claim that the distinction between past tense and past participle has been lost and that both sentences are examples of a general past tense. Such an analysis has, in fact, been proposed for Vernacular Black English by Marvin Loflin (1970). Although we admit that such may be a future development for Nonstandard English and even Standard English,[3] we maintain that the distinction is still effective for the overwhelming majority of the various nonstandard dialects for three reasons. First, even though the past-tense/past-participle distinction is weak in Nonstandard English, the distinction seems to be maintained as often as not for irregular verbs. Second, forms of *have* as an auxiliary are never completely absent in the samples of Vernacular Black English and Appalachian English we have investigated. Finally and most importantly, in constructions in which *have* forms cannot be contracted, they are *never* deleted in Nonstandard English. We have tested over 50 black working-class Washington residents for the sentence sequences *He been living there for a long time; I know he has* and *He been a bus driver for ten years; I know he has.* The form *have* or *has* was invariably supplied in the second sentence of both sequences.

Auxiliaries can be deleted without contraction in inverted direct questions. In both content and yes–no questions, the auxiliary (in content questions, along with the content question word) is moved to the front of the sentence. The question equivalent of *He has been here* is thus *Has he been here?* and of *He is going somewhere* the content question equivalent is *Where is he going?* In this position, some of these elements are especially vulnerable to deletion. This gives questions like *He coming with us?* (deletion of *is*), *Where you been?* (deletion of *have*), and *You understand?* (deletion of *do*). Although this is frequently cited as a feature of the various nonstandard dialects, deletion of these auxiliaries in direct questions is part of spoken Standard English as well.

INVARIANT *be*

When the verb *to be* is used as a main verb in Standard English, it appears as one of the five variant inflected forms *is, are, am, was,* or *were,* depending on the verb tense and the person and number of the subject. In Vernacular Black English, the form *be* can be used as a main verb, regardless of the subject of the sentence, as in *I be here this afternoon* and *Sometime he be busy.* This use of invariant *be* has two explanations; deleted *will* or *would* and distributive *be.*

The *'ll* contraction of *will* is often absent before *be.* This is fairly

---

[3] A sign that the distinction is weakening in Standard English is the frequency with which the simple past tense is used with *yet* and *already* (*I didn't do it yet; I did it already*). Standard English in the recent past demanded the present-perfect tense with these adverbs (*I haven't done it yet; I've done it already*).

common in Vernacular Black English, but also happens in other non-standard dialects and occasionally even in Standard English, giving sentences like *He be here pretty soon.* The contracted form of *would* is *'d*, which can be absorbed by the *b* of *be.* This process is another source of invariant *be* in nonstandard dialects and is quite common in the standard dialects as well. A sentence like *If you gave him a present he be happy* is possible both in standard and in nonstandard dialects.

The other source for invariant *be* is very different. This type of invariant *be* occurs because *be* is possible in Vernacular Black English with a meaning something like "object or event distributed intermittently in time." This use of *be*, as in *Sometime he be here and sometime he don't*, occurs only in Vernacular Black English and is usually misunderstood by Standard English speakers. It is common for Standard English speakers to take this use of *be* as a deviant form of *am, is,* or *are*, when in fact it contrasts with these forms. To say *I be good* means that the speaker is good only intermittently. Unlike the cases of invariant *be* which are derived from *will be* or *would be*, this *be* usage is highly stigmatized socially. Because there are three ways in which *be* can appear as the main verb of a Vernacular Black English sentence, *If somebody hit him, Darryl be mad* is potentially ambiguous in three ways. If its source is by *'ll* deletion from *If somebody hit him, Darryl will be mad*, it is a prediction about Darryl's future reaction to being hit. If it is derived from *'d* absorption from *If somebody hit him, Darryl would be mad*, it is a hypothesis about Darryl's probable reaction to being hit. If it is an example of distributive *be*, it is a statement about Darryl's usual reaction to being hit. The last interpretation, of course, is possible only in Vernacular Black English, although the first two could arise in other dialects, even standard ones. In negative sentences in which *not* is contracted, contraction of *will* and *would* is impossible and there is no ambiguity in the corresponding negative sentences. The three sentences in the negative, in order, are:

If somebody hit him, Darryl won't be mad.
If somebody hit him, Darryl wouldn't be mad.
If somebody hit him, Darryl don't be mad.

A-VERB-ING

Another verb construction that is unique to a single dialect is the use of constructions consisting of a past or nonpast form of *to be* plus the present participle of a verb with the prefix *a-* (Hackenberg 1972). Example sentences are *She's a-working on her Master's degree* and *I was a-farming in those days.* This construction occurs only in Appalachian English of the dialects we have investigated and it is observed beside the standard present-participial constructions with a slightly different meaning. *She's working* to a speaker of Appalachian English who has both *She's working* and *She's a-working,* can mean that she is currently engaged in a relatively short-run task. *She's a-working* has a uniquely durative meaning and would have a meaning something like "She's engaged in doing a relatively long-term job." This Appalachian durative participial construction, then, is not used to express momentary actions, so that a sentence like *He's a-jumping over the fence this very second* would not occur. The use of this verb form appears to be on the wane within Appalachian English.[4]

Negation

THE USE OF *ain't*

One of the best-known and most widespread nonstandard grammatical features is the use of *ain't*. It is probably part of every Nonstandard American English dialect. There are three basic correspondences between *ain't* and Standard English forms. *Ain't* is used where Standard English rules specify *am not, isn't,* or *aren't* (*I/He/They ain't here*), where Standard English has *haven't* or *hasn't* (*I/He ain't done nothing*), and where Standard English would have *didn't* (*He ain't see it*). The correspondence between *ain't* and negativized forms of *be* and *have* occur in all nonstandard dialects; *ain't* for *didn't* seems unique to Vernacular Black English and seems more common along the Atlantic coast than elsewhere.[5] It is important to note also that *ain't* is not categorical in any nonstandard dialect. For all the dialects for which we have detailed information, *ain't* varies in speech samples with *am not, isn't, aren't, haven't, hasn't,* and, for Vernacular Black English *didn't.* Wolfram et al. (1971) discovered that for Puerto Rican English (and the same facts would appear to be true of other nonstandard dialects), *ain't* was proportionately more likely to correspond to *isn't* or *aren't* than to *am not.* In addition, *ain't* is favored if the clause also contains an instance of negative concord. *I ain't done nothing,* in other words, is more likely than *I ain't done it.*

NEGATIVE CONCORD

Another universally nonstandard feature of English grammar is <u>negative concord or the double or multiple negative</u>. Sentences like *He ain't got*

---

[4] Hackenberg (1972) also collected two examples of the *a-* prefix with the past participle; e.g., *It was a-worked out.* In both examples the semantic force seemed to be something like "thoroughly depleted."

[5] Labov et al. (1968) report one example of *ain't* for Standard English *didn't* in the white nonstandard dialect they investigated.

nothing come to mind immediately in connection with nonstandard speech. Actually the grammar of negative concord is completely regular and fairly complex, as we shall show.

In order to understand negative concord thoroughly, we will make use of a derivational approach to grammar. We start with an abstract "underlying string" which is never actually said. The underlying strings we will use in our illustrations are

NOT + ANY-BODY + DO-Z + KNOW + ANY-THING

and

NOT + HE + DO-Z + KNOW + ANY-THING

There are three rules that serve to generate the kinds of sentences in which we are interested in various English dialects. The first rule is the one that places NOT, the negative marker, into the main verb phrase of the sentence. Informally stated, it is:

1. In a negative sentence, place NOT in the main verb phrase.

Rule 1 places the NOT in the main verb phrase DO-Z + KNOW + ANY-THING of both our illustrative underlying strings. The first string requires the application of Rule 2 and the second string eventually comes out as *He doesn't know anything.*

Rule 2, like Rule 1, is the same for all English dialects.

2. In a negative sentence, if there is an indefinite element preceding the main verb, remove NOT from the main verb phrase and incorporate it into the indefinite element.

The effect of this rule is to remove NOT from the verb phrase DO-Z + KNOW + ANY-THING of the first illustrative string and to incorporate it into the ANY of ANY-BODY. Other rules of English whose forms do not concern us here will then create the sentence *Nobody knows anything,* if the nonstandard version of Rule 3 does not apply. Rule 2 applies without exception in every dialect of English, standard or not. No variety of English allows *Anybody doesn't know anything* or *Anybody knows nothing* or *Anybody doesn't know nothing.*

The third rule has a standard and two nonstandard versions:

3a. (Standard English version.) For elegant emphasis, remove NOT from the main verb phrase and incorporate it in the first indefinite *after* the main verb phrase.

    3b. (First Nonstandard English version.) For emphasis, incorporate a *copy* of the NOT which is in the main verb phrase or pre-verbal indefinite in *all* indefinites after the main verb phrase, but leave the original NOT intact.

    3c. (Second Nonstandard English version.) For emphasis, incorporate a *copy* of the NOT which is in the main verb phrase or the pre-verbal indefinite into the main verb phrase (if it is not there already) and in *all* indefinites after the main verb phrase, but leave the original NOT intact.

Working with the underlying string NOT + HE + DO-Z + KNOW + ANY-THING, we find that Rule 1 places NOT in the main verb phrase, and Rule 2 does not apply (there is no indefinite ANY preceding the main verb phrase). Rule 3a is optional; if it is not used, *He doesn't know anything* results, as we have seen. If a Standard English speaker wishes to express a kind of elegant emphasis, he can elect to apply Rule 3a, which takes NOT out of the verb phrase and incorporates it into the ANY of ANY-THING. The result is *He knows nothing.*

In many varieties of Nonstandard English, Rule 3a is replaced by Rule 3b. Rule 3b differs from 3a in that it is a copying rule and in applying to *all* postverbal indefinites instead of just the first. Taking the same underlying string, we find that Rule 1 places NOT in the main verb phrase and Rule 2 is not applicable, as before. Now Rule 3b applies, but it does not remove NOT from the verb phrase as 3a does, but creates a new NOT and incorporates it into the ANY of ANY-THING. The result is *He doesn't know nothing.*[6] The fact that the same underlying string, with only one NOT, is the source for both the standard sentences and the nonstandard one makes it clear that the proposition expressed by the sentence is negated only once. It is not true that the "two negatives make a positive" in the nonstandard sentence because the second negative is simply a copy of the first and does not exist at the underlying level which expresses the real meaning of the sentence.

We have written Rule 3b so that copies of NOT can be incorporated into *all* postverbal indefinites. As a result, Rule 3b generates not only double negatives but multiple negatives. For example, Wolfram (1969) reports the sentence

We ain't had no trouble about none of us pulling out no knife.

in which three copies of the original NOT are made in postverbal indefinites.

For most nonstandard dialects, Rule 3b is variable. In these dialects, both *He doesn't know anything* and *He doesn't know nothing* are possible.

---

[6] We are ignoring the obvious fact that verbal *-s* may well be absent, so that the sentence is quite likely actually to be *He don't know nothing.*

In separate studies of New York City adolescent speakers of Vernacular Black English (Labov et al. 1968; Wolfram et al. 1971), the conclusion was that Rule 3b is obligatory for these speakers. This means that only *He doesn't know nothing* is possible; *He doesn't know anything* is a violation of the grammar rules of the dialect. Wolfram found the same to be true of those Puerto Rican English speakers who identified most closely with black peers. For at least some varieties of Vernacular Black English and dialects strongly influenced by these varieties, then, every postverbal indefinite must be redundantly marked with a negative element.

Rule 3c, which allows a copy of the negative element that is in the preverbal indefinite to be copied into the main verb phrase, does not exist in many nonstandard dialects. In some nonstandard dialects, including Vernacular Black English and some white nonstandard dialects, it is possible to have negative elements in both places without the two negatives cancelling each other out. In these dialects, the sentence *Nobody doesn't like it* can occur with the meaning "Nobody likes it."

Negation can be expressed with the negative adverbs *hardly* and *never* as well as in verb phrases and by incorporation into ANY. Multiple negation can be expressed by a negative adverb and also by another negative element elsewhere in the same sentence. The result is the utterance of sentences like *He doesn't hardly come to see us any more,* or more commonly, *He doesn't come to see us any more, hardly.* Standard English speakers who never use other kinds of multiple negation sometimes use sentences like this. In Vernacular Black English, the marking of negation in the verb phrase or with indefinite ANY in sentences that contain *hardly* is the rule rather than the exception.

In our work with Nonstandard English, we made an interesting discovery about the variability of multiple negation when the sentence contains a copula or a negative adverb (Wolfram 1971:227–31). We discovered that even for those speakers for whom Rule 3b is not variable, so that *He don't know anything* is ungrammatical, there is variation between the following types of sentences:

> *They're no good.*
> *We hardly play with that.*

and

> *You ain't nothing.*
> *I don't hardly go with them.*

In both cases, it is possible to have sentences with a single negative following a verb phrase. When a negative adverb or copula is not present, however, a single postverbal negative is not possible, so that *He know nothing* is ungrammatical. It is noted that in both *You ain't nothing* and *I don't hardly go with them,* the two negative elements are next to each other, but they are separated in sentences like *He don't know nothing.* The solution is to add Rule 4, a variable rule which says:

> 4. If two negative elements occur next to each other, remove the first one variably.

Thus, to derive *They're no good* from its underlying string NOT + THEY + BE-Z + ANY + GOOD, NOT is placed in the verb phrase by Rule 1. A copy of NOT is incorporated into ANY by Rule 3b. A rule of English whose details do not concern us reverses the order of NOT + BE-Z to BE-Z + NOT. This gives the string THEY + BE-Z + NOT + NOT-ANY + GOOD. Rule 4 removes the first NOT and the sentence ultimately comes out *They're no good.* To derive *They ain't no good,* exactly the same process is followed, except that Rule 4 is not applied and BE-Z + NOT is ultimately converted to *ain't.*

In some sentences, an indefinite expression or the adverb *either* can be used appositionally to modify a whole clause, rather than being an integral part of that clause. In Nonstandard English, such sentences can variably bear negative concord, as in:

> *Your mother ain't good looking either (neither).*
> *He don't get a second try or anything (nothing).*

In such cases, there are no nonstandard dialects in which negative concord is obligatory and in all dialects negative concord is less frequent in these appositional clauses than within the same clause.

Occasionally, but very rarely, it is possible for negative concord to occur across clause boundaries. This results in sentences like *There wasn't much I couldn't do,* with the meaning "There wasn't much I *could* do." Labov et al. (1968) maintain that this phenomenon is restricted to Vernacular Black English, but it has been reported to us that it can occur in Southern white nonstandard speech as well. In any event, such examples of negative concord are extremely rare.

NEGATIVE AUXILIARY PREPOSING

If a sentence has an indefinite noun phrase with or without a negative marker (*nobody, nothing, no dog, anyone*) before the verb, the negativized form of the verbal auxiliary (*can't, wasn't, didn't, won't*) may be placed at the beginning of the sentence in nonstandard dialects of Southern origin, including Vernacular Black English. The result is sentences like *Can't nobody do it, Wasn't nothing wrong, Didn't no dog bite him,* and *Won't anyone believe that.* Although these sentences appear to be questions in their written form, the intonation of the spoken form in these dialects makes it clear that they are statements. If the noun phrase before the verb does not contain an indefinite, pre-position of the auxiliary is not possible, so that a sentence like *Don't the man do it* will not occur as a statement. If the auxiliary is *ain't,* there are two possible grammatical sources for sentences with preposed auxiliaries. A sentence like *Ain't (wasn't) nobody here* can be derived from *Nobody ain't (wasn't) here* by negativized auxiliary preposing, or from the expletive *there* construction *There ain't (wasn't) nobody here* by deletion of *there.*[7] There are dialects with the *there* deletion rule that do not have the preposing rule. As a result, some nonstandard speakers say *Ain't (wasn't) nobody there,* but never *Can't (Won't, Didn't, etc.) nobody do it* because there is no *There can't (won't, didn't) nobody do it.*

Clause Syntax

RELATIVE CLAUSES

We will present two nonstandard aspects of relative clause formation. At least certain aspects of both, unlike the other features we have presented, seem to be moving into the standard dialects. The first feature has to do with the deletion of relative pronouns. It is an undisputed fact about Standard English that a relative pronoun can be absent in relative clauses if the pronoun replaces the object of the subordinate clause. In a sentence like *That's the dog I bought,* the clause *I bought* is a relative clause without a relative pronoun. It is also possible, of course, to say *That's the dog which (that) I bought.* In this sentence, the relative pronoun *which* or *that* replaces the noun phrase *the dog* from the embedded sentence *I bought the dog.* For most Standard English speakers, a relative pronoun is obligatory if the relative pronoun represents the subject of the subordinate clause. In *That's the dog which (that) bit me,* the relative pronoun replaces *the dog* of the embedded sentence *The dog bit me.* For this reason, Standard English does not allow *That's the dog bit me.* But sentences of this form are allowed by the grammar of many nonstandard dialects in English. A detailed analysis of this feature is given by Hackenberg (1972) for Appalachian English, and subject relative pronoun absence has been observed informally by the authors in other dialects, black and white. Hackenberg

---

[7] Some dialects sometimes have *it*—Standard English has expletive *there,* as we shall see. Expletive *it* can also be removed by this rule.

discovered that the expletive *there* construction favored the relative pronoun absence feature markedly. That is, *There's a man comes down the road every day* is more likely than *I met the man comes down the road every day.* In fact, subject relative pronoun absence in expletive *there* sentences seems to be ordinary spoken usage in many standard dialects and appears to be gaining wider acceptance among educated speakers.

Another heretofore nonstandard relative clause usage that appears to be moving into the standard dialects is the associative or conjunctive use of *which.* The generally accepted standard usage allows *which* to replace inanimate noun phrases or whole sentences or phrases. In the sentence *He goes to the school which is only two blocks from here, which is fine with me,* the first *which* replaces the noun phrase *the school* and the second *which* replaces the whole sentence up to the comma. In both cases it is possible to find an antecedent in nominal form for each *which.* To the question "What is only two blocks from here?" the answer is "The school" —the antecedent of the first *which.* The answer to "What is fine with me?" gives the antecedent of the other *which*—"His going to the school which is only two blocks from here." But there is another use of *which* that does not allow this kind of analysis. The following two sentences are examples:

> *He gave me this cigar which he knows I don't smoke cigars.*
> *His daughter is marrying Robert Jenks which he doesn't approve of her marrying a divorced man.*

The analogous *what* questions are not answerable and are not even well-formed questions. The questions would be:

> *What does he know I don't smoke cigars?*
> *What doesn't he approve of her marrying a divorced man?*

Part of the reason for the appearance of this type of sentence is situations in which relative clause formation by the standard rule would give sentences that are at least somewhat awkward. For example:

> *I'm going to get a new car which I don't know what make will be.*
> *There are some people who I like who it is obvious don't like me.*
> *This is one of those words which I don't know where to break at the end of a line.*

In ordinary conversation, these awkward constructions, if they are not circumvented altogether through paraphrase, are likely to be solved, respectively, in the following ways:

I'm going to get a new car which I don't know what make it will be.
There are some people who I like who it is obvious that they don't like me.
This is one of those words which I don't know where to break them at the end of a line.

In these cases, *which* or another relative pronoun appears in the sentence without replacing its noun-phrase referent. The existence of such sentences in the spoken language may be the thin edge of the wedge for the introduction of sentences in which the relative pronoun *which* not only does not replace its referent, but does not even have a proper referent.

NONSTANDARD RELATIVE PRONOUNS

There are speakers of Nonstandard English who use forms other than *who, whom, which,* and *that* as relative pronouns. These speakers seem largely to be speakers of white rural varieties of English. Examples appear in *A car what runs is good to have* and *There's those as can do it.* As far as we know, these usages have not been studied in detail by linguists, so we do not know what the syntactic rules are that govern them.

QUESTION INVERSION

In Standard English, there are two patterns for dealing with both yes–no and content questions. In direct questions, the content question word, if any, followed by the auxiliary, is moved to the beginning of the sentence. For the statement *He finished the job somehow,* the content question is *How did he finish the job?* and the yes–no question is *Did he finish the job somehow?* (with *did* serving as the tense-bearing auxiliary). In indirect questions, the forward movement of content words and auxiliaries does not occur and the conjunctions *if* or *whether* are introduced if the indirect question is a yes–no question, giving:

I wonder how he finished the job.
I wonder if (whether) he finished the job somehow.

It is fairly common in Nonstandard English, especially Vernacular Black English and Southern White English, for indirect questions to follow the direct question rules. This gives sentences like:

I wonder how did he finish the job.
I wonder did he finish the job somehow.

This represents a regularization of the question formation rules, so that the same rules apply regardless of the direct-indirect distinction. It is reported for some nonstandard dialects (Gordon and Lakoff 1971:76) that there is a distinction between *I wonder how did he finish the job* and *I wonder how he finished the job*. The first question counts as a request for information and requires an answer such as *I don't know* or *He did it by convincing his friends that whitewashing a fence was a privilege*. To answer *I wonder how did he finish the job* from a speaker of such a dialect by saying *Yeah* or *It would be nice to know* would be rude. But because *I wonder how he finished the job* can count as a statement about something the speaker is curious about and need not be interpreted as a request for information, these latter two answers would not be out of place. In this dialect, it would not be possible to say *I wondered how did he finish the job but I found out later* because one would not request information he already has. Whether this restriction is operative in all dialects that have direct question syntax in indirect questions is not known.

In Vernacular Black English, some speakers occasionally use direct questions according to the rules of indirect question syntax. Sentences like *He took it?* and *Why he took it?* result. The first question in print looks like the kind of echo question that might occur in a Standard English dialogue like the following:

You know, he took it.
He took it?
Yeah.
I never would have believed it!

In Vernacular Black English, intonation and context would make it plain that many questions of the form *He took it?* are not intended as echo questions. In the case of content questions, it is not always clear whether a speaker has followed Standard English direct question syntax and then deleted the auxiliary (as in *What you doing?* from *What are you doing?*) or has followed indirect question syntax and deleted the auxiliary by contraction deletion (as in *What you doing?* from *What you're doing?*) However, there are enough unambiguous cases like *Why he took it?* which could not be a result of preposed auxiliary deletion, to make it clear that indirect question syntax is actually being followed. It seems fairly clear that there are fewer speakers who use this pattern than speakers who use direct question syntax in forming indirect questions, but we have no information as to how widespread this pattern is among nonstandard dialects. The relationship between these two question patterns awaits further study.

LEFT DISLOCATION

A frequently cited example of nonstandard clause syntax is the "double subject," pronominal apposition, or pleonastic pronoun (technically, *left dislocation*). Operation of the left dislocation rule results in sentences like *My mother, she works at home.* What seems to a speaker of Standard English to be an unnecessary redundancy is actually an effective stylistic focusing device in nonstandard oral narrative. To understand how left dislocation works, it is necessary to have in mind a basic fact about pronominalization in English. If a noun with the same referent occurs twice in the same sentence, one of them, ordinarily the second, is pronominalized. Rather than say *My brother is coming to town today and I'm going to meet my brother at the airport,* we pronominalize the second instance of *my brother* and say *My brother is coming to town today and I'm going to meet him at the airport.* In the many nonstandard dialects which allow left dislocation, a copy of one of the noun phrases is made at the extreme left side of the sentence. From *My mother works at home,* left dislocation produces *My mother, my mother works at home.* Then the ordinary rule of pronominalization converts the second of the two identical noun phrases to the appropriate pronoun, giving *My mother, she works at home.* The pedagogical term *double subject* is not quite accurate as a label for left dislocation because it is not only nouns in subject position which can undergo dislocation. Possessive noun phrases can be dislocated, giving examples like *Mr. Smith, I got one F in his class one time,* as can objective noun phrases, resulting in such sentences as *That girl name Wanda, I never did like her.* A similar rule exists in some standard dialects, but it is not a copying rule like left dislocation and it applies only to noun phrases in object position, giving sentences like *Him, I like, but her, I don't.* Left dislocation itself is acceptable to many, if not most, speakers of Standard English but only if there is considerable modifying material between the dislocated noun phrase and the pronoun. Fasold has tested the acceptability of the sentence *That man that I met on the train to Chicago last week, he turned out to be a Congressman* numerous times with groups of graduate students and public school teachers and invariably the great majority find it acceptable. There seems to be a great deal of difference in the frequency levels with which left dislocation is used.

NONSTANDARD *there* CONSTRUCTIONS

Where Standard English uses *there* in an expletive or existential function, dialects of Southern origin sometimes use *it.* This results in sentences like *It's a boy in my room name Robert* and *Is it a Main Street in this town?* where Standard English would have *There's a boy. . . .* and *Is there a Main Street. . . ?* This difference in the choice of one word in a single construction affects the understanding of a considerable number of sentences in normal conversation. For example, if a speaker of a dialect with expletive *it* were waiting for water in ice cube trays to freeze, he could ask *Is it ice yet?* To him, this would mean "Is there (any) ice yet?" To speakers of most standard dialects, it means "Has it become ice yet?"

Speakers of Vernacular Black English of elementary school age often use the expression *There go* or *Here go* where speakers of Standard English and older speakers of Vernacular Black English use *There (here) is.* Youngsters of this age are often heard to say things like *There go a candy store* or *Here go my house.* This is one nonstandard syntax feature that is strongly age-graded. As children who use these phrases move into adolescence, they ordinarily give up these expressions of their own accord as being part of "little kids' talk."

PLEONASTIC CONJUNCTIONS

Nonstandard speech of Southern origin sometimes contains conjoined sentences with two conjunctions where Standard English has only one. Conjunctive sentences like *He's not very good at basketball and plus he's a showoff,* and disjunctive sentences like *He's high or either he's messed up* result. The use of *and plus* is not unlike the elegant Standard English use of *and in addition,* as in *We can't afford it and in addition it would be poor business practice.*

USE OF *at* IN *where* QUESTIONS

A very frequent and widespread socially stigmatized construction is the use of *at* at the end of *where* questions, such as *Where is my shirt at?* In Standard English, *where* questions are derived from structures like *My shirt is at someplace* by the content-questioning of *at someplace.* In the standard dialects, the word *where* replaces the whole locative phrase *at someplace* and yields *Where is my shirt?* through a derivation which assumes that the underlying form of the sentence includes the content-question symbol *Wh.* Starting with *Wh my shirt is at someplace, Wh* is first incorporated, giving *My shirt is Wh-at-someplace.* Next, the *Wh* phrase and the copula *is* are brought to the beginning of the sentence, giving *Wh-at-someplace is my shirt.* Finally, *Where* replaces *Wh-at-someplace.* In many nonstandard dialects and, it seems, with increasing acceptability to speakers of Standard English, *Wh* is incorporated at a different position in the sentence, yielding *My shirt is at Wh-someplace,* so that *where* replaces *Wh-someplace* only, and *at* is left intact.

Nominal Constructions

PLURAL

In Vernacular Black English, the plural suffix *-s* (or *-es*) is occasionally absent in sentences like *He took five book* or *The other teacher, they'll yell at you.* Plural suffix absence is rather infrequent in occurrence and it is rare to find a speaker who deletes more than one plural suffix in ten. It is sometimes claimed that plural suffixes are always or more often absent when the plural noun is modified by a quantifier like *two, some,* or *all kinds of,* but several careful studies of speech records have shown that the plural suffix is not *always* absent in the presence of a quantifier and results are conflicting as to whether it is more often absent when a quantifier is present. Some nonstandard rural dialects besides Vernacular Black English allow the plural suffix to be absent only with nouns of measure, giving *four mile up the road* or *about seventeen ton.* It seems that plural suffix absence is more frequent with measure nouns than with other kinds of nouns.

Nonstandard dialects sometimes form regular plurals from nouns that have irregular plurals in Standard English. For example, *sheep* in Standard English is identical in form whether singular or plural. A noun like *foot* forms its plural by vowel change rather than by suffixation, and the plural is *feet.* Nouns of both types are likely occasionally to appear with regularized plurals in Nonstandard English, e.g., *sheeps* and *foots.* Another phenomenon that can sometimes be observed is the addition of the plural suffix to nouns that are also pluralized in another way, giving *feets, peoples,* and *childrens.* These double plurals, of course, can be formed only with a small subset of English nouns.

In Vernacular Black English and perhaps in other dialects as well, there is an associative plural construction *and them* (more accurately *an' 'em*), as in *Freddy an' 'em ain't going today.* The meaning is "Freddy and those associated with him." In this example, a real one, it means "Freddy and his younger siblings."

POSSESSIVE

Where the *'s* possessive appears in Standard English, in nonstandard dialects (at least in Vernacular Black English) possession is indicated by the order of the words. The phrase *The boy hat* corresponds to *The boy's hat* in the standard dialects. In Northern urban Vernacular Black English, apparently no one uses the zero form of the possessive exclusively; it alternates with the *'s* form. In Southern varieties of the dialect, it seems possible that speakers exist who do not use *'s* for the possessive at all. There is some reason to believe that the presence of the *'s* possessive suffix is more common at the end of a clause (i.e., in absolute position, as in *The hat is the boy*['s]) than in the attributive possessive (*The boy*['s] *hat*). It has been claimed that the *'s* in this situation is regularly present. However, the absence of the *'s* suffix in the absolute possessive suffix has been observed with some frequency in the speech of Northern urban Vernacular Black English speakers and has been found to be extremely common in Southern Vernacular Black English data.

Because the position of the *'s* possessive is somewhat unstable in the grammar of Vernacular Black English, some speakers use the *'s* suffix inappropriately with personal names when attempting to speak Standard English. In Standard English, of course, the rule is that the *'s* is attached to the surname when the possessor is identified by his full name (*Jack Johnson's car*). Occasionally, a Vernacular Black English speaker will attach the *'s* suffix to both names (*Jack's Johnson's car*), or to the first name (*Jack's Johnson car*). This feature is not part of the grammar of the dialect but is another example of hypercorrection based on relative unfamiliarity with the Standard English construction.

Some Vernacular Black English speakers, especially elementary school-aged children, may occasionally use the nominative or objective case of personal pronouns in possessive constructions. Sentences like *James got him book* or *She want she mother* result. This rather uncommon construction is actually part of a wider pattern in which case is not differentiated in the pronoun system. For such speakers a single Standard English case, always either the accusative or the nominative, is used in all sentence positions. These speakers use sentences like *Him gave him him bike* or *Read we a story out of we book*. Even more rare are cases in which gender distinctions are not maintained either, so that sentences like *He a nice lady* (of a woman) result.

In Standard English the absolute possessive form of the personal pronouns pattern according to the following paradigm:

Singular	Plural
mine	ours
yours	yours
his, hers, its	theirs

Except for *mine,* all of these forms end in *-s* (*his* ends in *-s* but is irregular in other ways). Some nonstandard dialects regularize the paradigm by adding *-s* to *mine* as well, so it is grammatical to say *That's mines.* Other nonstandard dialects tend to move in the opposite direction toward regularization and add *-n* to some of the other pronouns, producing *yourn, hisn, hern, ourn,* and *theirn.*

INALIENABLE POSSESSIVE
ARTICLE REPLACEMENT

Standard English has a rule whereby certain possessive pronouns can be replaced by the article *the* in a construction following a verb of physical contact.[8] In a construction consisting of a verb of physical contact, followed by an animate noun or personal pronoun, followed by a prepositional phrase of location of which the object is an inalienably possessed body part modified by a possessive pronoun coreferential with the object of the verb, the possessive pronoun is replaced by *the.* Resulting sentences are *I punched the man in the nose* or *He touched her on the arm.* In all such cases, the noun phrases like *the nose* and *the arm* refer to body parts belonging to the person receiving the physical contact. In some nonstandard speech (it has been particularly noticed among younger speakers of Vernacular Black English), this rule does not obligatorily operate. The result of the suspension of this Standard English rule is the utterance of sentences like *I punched the man in his nose* and *He touched her on her arm.*

DEMONSTRATIVES

There are two very common nonstandard usages with respect to demonstrative pronouns. Most Nonstandard English speakers use *them* where the standard dialects demand *those* so that such sentences as *I want some of them candies* are heard. Other nonstandard dialect speakers add *here* and *there* to the demonstratives *these* and *them* and produce sentences like *I like these here (dese 'ere) pants better than them there (dem 'ere) ones.*

REFLEXIVES

In many varieties of Nonstandard English, reflexive pronouns are formed with the possessive form of the personal pronoun plus forms of *self* for all personal pronouns. In Standard English, first- and second-person reflexives are formed with the possessive pronoun (*myself, yourself, ourselves*), but the third-person reflexives are formed with the accusative form (*himself, herself, itself, themselves*). In nonstandard speech, the

---

[8] The term *physical* is not to be taken too literally because the rule operates after *looked* in *I looked him in the eye.*

possessive form is often extended to third-person reflexives as well (*hisself, herself, itself* [the latter two are actually ambiguous], *theirselves* [*self*]). Because of phonological rules discussed above, *theyselves* (*self*) may also occur.

PLURAL FORMS OF *you*

In Standard English, the pronoun *you* is used regardless of number (*You are two of the nicest people I know, You are one of the nicest people I know*). Various English dialects have plural forms of *you*. The use of *you-all* (*y'all*), although amusing to speakers of Northern dialects, is hardly nonstandard in the South. In Northern Nonstandard English, the pronoun *youse* (more often than not pronounced something like *yiz*) is the plural form supplied, as in *Youse mad at each other*? Some rural dialects have *you'uns* as a second-person plural pronoun, although these dialects often also have *we'uns* as a first-person plural form.

Conclusion

In our discussion of the pronunciation and grammar features of Non-standard English we have attempted to be fairly comprehensive, though no doubt there are features we have overlooked. The features we have presented are socially diagnostic in one way or another and many represent potential changes in the structure of English. Most of these will not become established in the language because they will not be accepted by leading groups in American society. A few are actually gaining acceptance in Standard English and we have given our opinion as to which these are in some cases.

All of the features we have discussed are controlled by rules of the various nonstandard dialects. Throughout, we have tried to give some indication of the form of these rules. In spite of the social stigma attached to these nonstandard aspects of speech, it is not accurate to consider them as merely careless deviations from Standard English.

8

SOCIAL DIALECTS AND EDUCATION

The study of social dialects has particular relevance for many kinds of pedagogical problems involving language variation. Public education in our society serves the function of inculcating in children the values that are shared by the society in which they will be participating members. Included in these values are attitudes and beliefs about language and language varieties. Where the value system being promoted by the school matches that of the sector of society from which the children come, the value-socialization process of public education is served fairly well. In the area of language, the notion of what is correct in speech and what is not simply reinforces the values the children have already begun acquiring at home.[1] What the teacher says is correct English will in most details be not only what the child has already been told is correct, but will also be what he has heard adults using all his life.

When the value system of the educational institution differs from that of the community from which the children come, an obvious conflict arises. In the area of language, a child from a sector of society in which a nonstandard dialect is the real medium of community life will be told by his teacher that certain things in the language patterns he is used to are wrong. Even so, Labov (1966) was able to show that speakers of non-

[1] Rosenthal (1973) has shown that many preschool children have remarkably consistent notions on what is "correct" and "not correct" in language. Many also are able to make accurate judgments about the ethnicity of a speaker from speech alone.

standard dialects share with the rest of the larger community the overt opinions that nonstandard speech is bad and pass these overtly conscious opinions on to their children. But the child will have heard Nonstandard English being used effectively by adults and older children all his life. The day-to-day proof that nonstandard language is, in fact, adequate for the needs of those closest to him simply overwhelms the occasional remarks he hears to the contrary. We see, then, that although the overt opinions about speech may match those of the dominant social class, on a covert level the nonstandard dialect is obviously preferred for actual usage.

The overwhelming majority of teachers of children from such communities, even those who have come from the same communities, feel that part of their duty is to upgrade (as they see it) the nonstandard dialect of their students. Few teachers are even exposed to the linguist's position on the inherent adequacy of nonstandard varieties and so they simply accept the prevalent idea among educated people that differences from "correct" English represent deficiencies to be overcome. As he is taught to read and write, as his classroom recitations are corrected, as he is assigned to speech therapists for special language work, as his standardized test scores are misinterpreted, the child gradually is taught that the dialect he has always known only as an efficient tool of communication is considered a distortion of proper English.

In the course of their study of social variation in language, many sociolinguists have realized that what they were learning had potential for educational application. The lists of the publications of almost all of the linguists who have studied social variation include some written for educators. In addition, a few have worked directly with teachers in schools (see Shuy 1971). This involvement has led to the realization that language differences per se are only a small part of the problems faced by educators of economically impoverished children. Nevertheless, most sociolinguists are convinced that language differences are far from being a negligible part of the picture and that the application of the insights of their research is likely to have a beneficial effect. It is our intention to summarize these insights in this chapter.

Teacher Attitudes

Our experience in working with teachers has indicated that the most crucial contribution that the study of social dialects can make to education is in the area of teacher attitudes. A teacher who has been freed from the opinion that nonstandard dialect is simply distorted English will be a better teacher even without new materials and techniques specifically designed to deal with language variation. A teacher with this insight into language will be slower to correct grammatical and phonological manifestations that differ from standard dialects—he or she will spend less time on nonstandard pronunciations and grammar in oral reading and get on with the teaching of the reading skill itself. This teacher will not be so ready to conclude that a child has a speech pathology that requires the services of a speech clinician simply because his speech is not standard. Furthermore, he will be less likely to conclude low intelligence on the basis of Nonstandard English and will be skeptical of the results of standardized tests that contain segments presuming mastery of a standard dialect of English.

In a well-known experiment, Rosenthal and Jacobson (1968) were able to show that teacher attitudes toward students can have a profound effect on the students' performance. In their experiment, certain students were selected at random and their teachers were told that they had been found very gifted. At the end of the experiment, these particular children were actually performing better than their classmates. Presumably, the opposite belief about students on the part of a teacher could have a deleterious effect on the performance of a student of adequate intelligence. Therefore it is of considerable importance that teachers learn not to infer lack of intelligence from the use of nonstandard speech. Although we consider attitudinal change to be of central importance, it is an arduous task to realistically bring about such changes.

Spoken Standard English

In the remainder of this chapter, we shall examine the insights provided by social dialect study in the areas of teaching spoken Standard English, teaching reading, teaching comprehension, and evaluating the language aspects of standardized testing. Before we discuss the methodology of teaching spoken Standard English to speakers of nonstandard dialects, we need to outline the possible goals and the prospects for success, given a classroom environment.

POSSIBLE GOALS

Exhausting the logical possibilities, there are four conceivable goals of teaching spoken English. Of these, one has been the historic goal of educators and has only been questioned recently, two are recently proposed and quite controversial, and the remaining goal is nonsense. Figure 8-1 displays the four goals in terms of the control of language an individual

		STANDARD ENGLISH	
		Yes	No
NONSTANDARD	No	1	2
ENGLISH	Yes	3	4

Figure 8-1. Combinations of control over Standard and Nonstandard English which are conceivable as goals for an individual as a result of a spoken language curriculum.

should have as a result of the spoken language curriculum. The cell labeled 1 means the individual should control Standard English and should have given up Nonstandard English. Cell 2 means that Nonstandard English would be eradicated, but Standard English not explicitly taught. Cell 3 corresponds to the goal of teaching Standard English while allowing the retention of the nonstandard dialect, and cell 4 indicates the retention of nonstandard dialect as a goal without the teaching of Standard English. Of the four, cell 2 can be dismissed as nonsense. To attempt to eradicate Nonstandard English without teaching Standard English in its place would entail the student's becoming mute as a result of the spoken language curriculum! As ridiculous as this sounds, it appears that some teachers, in trying to achieve the goal designated by cell 1, inadvertently come closer to the goal of cell 2, achieving the "mute child" result. Certainly no teacher would intentionally aim at such a result, but by constantly correcting nonstandard speech without providing effective Standard English instruction, some teachers convince children that it is better to not respond in school at all rather than risk having every sentence corrected.

The cell 1 goal, called *eradicationism,* is the one historically accepted by educators. Indeed, it probably has not occurred to some educators that any other alternative is possible. The goal of eradicationism is to eliminate the negative concord, zero copula, and other nonstandard grammar and pronunciation features from the speech of students completely, replacing them with the Standard English equivalents. Much of the motivation for setting this goal is based on the conviction that Nonstandard English is a corruption of Standard English that leads to cognitive deficits and learning disabilities. The indefensibility of this view weakens the position of eradicationism as a goal. Another incentive for the eradicationist approach is based on the premise that Nonstandard English, although perhaps linguistically the equal of the standard dialects, still confers a social stigma on its speakers, and should therefore be eliminated in order to eliminate the stigma and allow the student full opportunity to enter the mainstream of society. Even this line of reasoning is questionable, as we shall see in our discussion of the goal indicated in cell 4. If it is valid, the line of reasoning based on social stigma leads more directly to the goal of cell 3. A further problem with the eradicationist approach is that the goal is usually pursued with methods of questionable effectiveness. The traditional methods of random correction of a child's oral recitations, the rote learning of grammar rules, and the use of written exercises cannot be expected to have much effect on a student's habitual use of the language. From the point of view of a linguist who has studied socially diagnostic language variation, the eradicationist approach has little to recommend it.[2]

Bidialectalism, the goal indicated by cell 3, means that Standard English is to be taught, but with no effort to eradicate the student's native nonstandard dialect. At the end of the spoken language curriculum, the student ideally would be able to use either Standard or Nonstandard English as the situation required. In classroom, job interview, or similar settings, Standard English would be selected from the individual's dialect repertoire, and Nonstandard English would be used in more normal situations. Unlike the eradicationist position, the bidialectalism position overtly rejects the notion that Nonstandard English is inherently inferior. Like the eradicationist position, it assumes that social stigmatization of Nonstandard English is both significant and inevitable. With bidialectalism as a goal usually goes the adoption and adaptation of some of the techniques of foreign language teaching as part of the methodology, but there is no reason why these techniques could not also be used in pursuit of the eradicationist goal. The majority of sociolinguists who have studied social dialects advocate the bidialectalist position.

The goal designated by cell 4 calls for the retention of Nonstandard English with no attempt to teach Standard English either as a replacement dialect or a second dialect. Advocates of this goal reject the notion that Nonstandard English is inherently inferior (as do advocates of bidialectalism), but they also reject the idea that language prejudice is significant and inevitable. This rejection of Standard English acquisition as a goal has been called to the attention of mainstream educators in two widely read articles by the linguist James Sledd (1969, 1972). In a scathing attack on bidialectalism and its proponents, Sledd questions the moral adequacy of assuming the inevitability of language prejudice and formulating educational goals so as to accommodate it. Rather than teach standard English to speakers of Nonstandard English, Sledd would devote attention only to an attack on the negative language attitudes of wielders of power in the

---

[2] There is a possible position, which we call "enlightened eradicationism," that is more defensible. Under this position, the bidialectal goal (cell 3) is pursued, but with the idea that eradication is the likely result if the curriculum is successful at all. The reason given for this is that the maintenance of two dialects is not possible because there are not enough linguistic distinctions between them. The attitudes, motivation, and methods of enlightened eradicationism, however, are those of bidialectism, not eradicationism as we have described it.

mainstream of society. Some black scholars also have raised the question of the significance of nonstandard speech as a force in limiting opportunities for Blacks (R. Williams 1971; Wiggins 1972). They see racial prejudice on the part of the white society as the real problem and the language question as something of an attempt to dodge the central issue.

In connection with this position, it is sometimes advocated that a stigmatized dialect such as Vernacular Black English be taught in schools serving white Standard English-speaking students as a means of fostering understanding. Although this proposal has a certain appeal to some liberal whites, it seems to us to be completely unworkable. The parents of the white students involved would almost surely reject the idea as a subversive attempt to undermine the language of their children. Blacks who do not accept the validity of the concept "Vernacular Black English" may see it as a racist attempt to teach whites that Nonstandard English is associated with blacks. On the other hand, blacks who do recognize Vernacular Black English might not accept the effort to teach it in white schools as valid if carried on by whites, and they would probably not consider it to be a project of sufficient priority to engage in it themselves.

One of the important considerations in teaching Standard English must be the desires of the community. It would be a mistake to conclude that Nonstandard English-speaking communities do not want Standard English taught. According to recent research (Taylor 1973), most black parents profess to want their children to learn the standard dialect. Although the fourth goal, that of teaching the stigmatized dialect, is the most radical, it nonetheless deserves careful consideration along with the others. We have no information on whether or not this position is taken in connection with other Nonstandard English-speaking communities, but it would not be surprising to learn that it is. Wherever it is advocated, it is bound to be controversial.

There is no "safe" position among these proposals. Advocates of eradicationism face the ire of all who accept the legitimacy of nonstandard dialects. To accept bidialectalism invites the criticism of traditional educators and language purists on the one hand and of the more outspoken members of minority communities and their allies on the other. Taking the position that Standard English should not be taught or that a nonstandard dialect should be taught means being resisted by all those who for one reason or another believe in the importance of Standard English in American society.

PROSPECTS FOR SUCCESS

Aside from the question of what goals should be set as the aim of spoken Standard English programs on a priori grounds, it is useful to ask what degree of success can be expected if the teaching of Standard English as a spoken dialect is to be the goal. There seems to be reason for a fair amount of pessimism. It is possible to come to the conclusion that what the English teacher does in the classroom with regard to spoken Standard English is irrelevant. Speakers who start out speaking Nonstandard English but find that they need to learn Standard English will learn it, and those who do not will not, almost independently of what their English teachers do. The reason is that learning spoken language is unlike any other kind of learning. It cannot be taught only with the methods, materials, and motivational strategies used to teach other subjects. It is even open to serious question that one very necessary factor in learning new spoken skills, whether a new dialect or a whole new language, *can* be supplied in the classroom. It is crucial that there be a viable expectation and desire on the part of the learner to become a member of the group represented by the speakers of the new language, dialect, or style. If this factor is present, other methods and motivations may also contribute to successful learning of new spoken language skills. But if it is missing, nothing that goes on in the classroom can make up for its absence.

Psychologists and others interested in second language acquisition—which is different in degree but not in kind from second dialect acquisition—have realized the crucial importance of group reference to successful language learning. Discussing the learning of Hebrew by immigrants to Israel, Professor Simon Herman (1961:162–63) states:

> If, as our analysis would indicate, group references play an important part in the choice of a language, it would follow that the readiness of a person to learn and use a second language may depend in part on the measure of his willingness to identify with the group with which the language is associated—or, at any rate, on his desire to reduce the social distance between himself and that group.

Whyte and Homberg (1965:13) found that this factor sometimes outweighed even inborn language-learning ability in predicting the success of U.S. businessmen in learning a second language in Latin America:

> A strong psychological identification with the other people and culture may more than make up for below average learning ability whereas a man of superior language ability may fail to make the necessary psychological identification and make poor progress.

John Gumperz (1966) gives an example which illustrates that absence of this group reference factor can nullify the tendency for people to learn the speech habits of those who have superior social status. There are three tribes in South India who have lived together for hundreds of years. Two of these tribes occupy a socially subordinate position to the third. Yet members of these tribes do not learn the prestige language of the third tribe because the castelike social system precludes the possibility that they will ever be accepted as members of the higher group.

If similar studies of second dialect learning were available, the same observations would no doubt be made. Without an expectation of acceptance on the part of the learner, there is small hope of success in language or dialect teaching. If this expectation is present, the new language or dialect is likely to be learned, even in the absence of formal teaching. Some Nonstandard English speakers have such an expectation with respect to the Standard English-speaking community; others do not. There seems to be no really effective way that it can be provided in the classroom for those who do not.

Practically any English speaker can provide himself with a feel for the sort of rejection of prestige speech that is involved here. There are certain points of grammar that are taught as correct, and most Standard English speakers will admit that they "should" use them, yet they don't. Some examples of these appear in the list below.

RULE	ONE "SHOULD" SAY	ONE OFTEN SAYS
Use nominative forms of pronouns when they are the subjects of understood verbs.	He is human, just as you or I.	He is human, just like you or me.
Never end a clause with a preposition.	The slot in which it goes.	The slot it goes in.
Use "may" to request permission.	May I have another piece of pie?	Can I have another piece of pie?
Use "whom" as direct object.	Whom did you meet?	Who did you meet?
Make the *t* sound distinct from the *d* sound between vowels.	bet-ter	bedder

Most English speakers who have been through elementary school will recognize these rules as some of those which govern "correct" English. Yet honest reflection will no doubt reveal that some or all of these rules are usually ignored in ordinary conversation. This poses an interesting dilemma. Why do so many educated speakers fail to use what they would admit is correct English? Many people would say that they are just not as careful with their speech as they should be. But the reason most people are not more "careful" is that to follow these rules would actually render their speech socially unacceptable. Not unacceptable because it is "sloppy" but unacceptable because it would be considered "snobbish." Although impeccably "correct" speech may be impressive in some situations, we all know the feeling we have when someone will not "relax" his speech. In spite of eminently good reasons for *not* using overprecise speech, most Americans still have the vague feeling that ordinary speech is basically careless and that they really should follow the rules. A very similar situation exists for some Nonstandard English-speaking youngsters. They may well have the feeling that their speech is not as good as it should be; they may even be able to cite the rules they are violating. But the cost in terms of damaged reputation among their peers is so high that the assumption of Standard English forms is not likely to take place unless they begin associating with youngsters who use Standard English. The average school teacher probably will not find himself in the position to join the "upper crust" of society, but if this opportunity were to arise, the teacher would fairly quickly and largely unconsciously adopt the speech appropriate to that social class. Similarly, a Nonstandard English-speaking individual, if he feels that he has a viable chance to become a member of a social group which uses Standard English, and if he desires to do so, will also fairly quickly and largely unconsciously adopt Standard English—and probably not before.

In summary then, language or dialect learning is a unique kind of learning which depends very heavily on a psychological factor of group reference. If this is not present, the best efforts of the English teacher are in grave danger of being completely nullified. If it is present, nonstandard dialect speakers can be expected to learn Standard English, with or without formal teaching.

METHODOLOGY

If the group reference factor is present and the student is oriented toward learning Standard English, a well-designed methodological program developed particularly for spoken skills may be of significant help in guiding the student toward his goal. Techniques developed by linguists for teaching foreign languages to speakers of English or English to speakers of other languages, such as contrastive analysis, mimicry, and pattern practice, can be used with good effect, *if* the differences between second language and second dialect learning are taken into account. There are a number of programs available which purport to apply the methodology of second language teaching to teaching spoken Standard English as a second dialect that are so unimaginatively adapted that they are likely to produce no results other than profound boredom.

One of the best adaptations of these second language techniques has been made by Irwin Feigenbaum. His approach is described and illustrated in two articles (Feigenbaum 1969, 1970a) and applied in materials he has developed for use in public schools (1970b). The drill techniques are designed to overcome boredom in several ways (1970a). First, it is suggested that they be used for brief periods of time. Second, the pace should be quick with a minimum of explanation. Third, the sentences being drilled are given content with a certain amount of inherent interest. Finally, the sequential progression of the drills is programmed so that each activity is more difficult than the last—thus the student is constantly being challenged. The final drills in each sequence allow for a degree of free expression that begins to approach normal conversation.

A typical lesson designed by Feigenbaum has five types of drills.[3] The first is a *presentation* of less than half a minute. If the feature to be taught is the Standard English verbal -*s*, two sentences such as *He work hard* and *He works hard* are presented and it is quickly pointed out to the students how they differ and which one is standard and which is nonstandard (Feigenbaum prefers the terms *formal* and *informal* in classroom situations). The next activity is a *discrimination* drill. In this drill, the class hears pairs of sentences like the following:

> *He work hard.*
> *He works hard.*
> *He work hard.*
> *He work hard.*
> *He works hard.*
> *He works hard.*

They respond "different" to examples like the first pair and "same" to examples like the second and third pairs.

Next follows an *identification* drill. In this drill, the students hear only one sentence, which they must identify as standard or nonstandard (or formal or informal). Examples might include:

> *He work hard.*
> *He works hard.*
> *Paula likes leather coats.*
> *She prefer movies.*

Only one socially diagnostic feature—the one being taught—distinguishes standard and nonstandard sentences. The appropriate response to the first and fourth of the above sentences is "informal" and to the second and third "formal."

Various types of *translation* rules are next. In these activities, the

---

[3] This description is a summary of Feigenbaum 1970a:92–99. Readers interested in developing lessons of this type should consult this source.

teacher gives either a standard or nonstandard sentence and the student is to respond with the corresponding sentence of the opposite type. This requires the students to demonstrate two skills. First, it must register with them whether the original sentence was standard or nonstandard. Then they must know what the corresponding sentence is in the other dialect and produce it. One of the unique aspects of Feigenbaum's program is translation from Standard to Nonstandard English as well as the reverse. Some examples of teacher stimuli and student responses follow:

TEACHER STIMULUS	STUDENT RESPONSE
He work hard.	*He works hard.*
He works hard.	*He work hard.*
Paula likes leather coats.	*Paula like leather coats.*
She prefer movies.	*She prefers movies.*

A variety of *response* drill activities conclude the lesson. In these exercises, the student is required to supply a certain amount of original content as well as the correct sentence in the appropriate dialect. A little imagination can lead to considerable variety, so the example given here is more an illustration than a pattern. In this drill, the instructor asks a question with either standard or nonstandard grammar. The student supplies his own answer, but it must be in the same dialect grammar in which the question was asked. For example, if the question is *Do your brother get good grades?* the answer might be *Yes, he do,* or *No, he don't; he get lousy grades,* or *In some subjects he do and in some he don't.* Regardless of the answer, if the question comes in nonstandard grammar, the answer must be in nonstandard grammar also. If the question is something like, *Does your English teacher give hard homework?* the answer may be *She certainly does!* or *No, she gives easy homework,* or any other sort of content the student feels is appropriate. But the answer must include the *-s* suffix because the question was asked in Standard English.

The approach taken by Feigenbaum, where both students and teacher are required to use nonstandard grammar in the course of the drilling, is clearly designed to implement the bidialectal approach. Teachers frequently object to those parts of the exercise calling for the use of nonstandard grammar. But the use of nonstandard grammar is necessary to focus on the point of contrast between standard and nonstandard grammar. Some teachers complain that they have difficulty producing nonstandard structures. Others express the fear that they will teach or reinforce Nonstandard English by using it in the classroom exercises. But the lessons are designed to be used with speakers who already control a nonstandard dialect. The few times that they are required to use nonstandard sentences in the drills will have no effect on the grammar they have internalized already. Furthermore, wherever Nonstandard English is required, it is always in direct contrast with the equivalent standard construction, so that the difference between the two is foremost in the student's mind. In classes in which there are students who already speak Standard English, there is negligible danger that they will learn the nonstandard from the drills. First of all, it will always be clear that the goal is learning the standard sentences, not the nonstandard ones. Second, while it is assumed that at least some of the Nonstandard English speakers are motivated to learn Standard English, there will be no Standard English speakers who will be motivated to learn the nonstandard dialect, at least not from their schoolteacher. The possibility of Standard English speakers learning nonstandard patterns from the drills, then, seems to be rather minimal.

Teaching Reading

The child who speaks a nonstandard dialect faces two problems when he is being taught to read, while the Standard English-speaking child has only one. The Standard English-speaking child primarily needs to learn the process and mechanics of reading: of deriving meaning from the printed page. The child who speaks a nonstandard variety must learn the reading process, but must also learn the language of the reading materials at the same time—and this is a language variety which matches his spoken language very poorly.[4] The match between spoken and written language is very important, because spoken language is primary and writing derived from it. Speaking is not an attempt to approximate written forms, but written forms are basically attempts to reflect speech. Therefore any mismatch between speech and writing, whether at the level of spelling, vocabulary, or grammar, reflects a failure of the writing system, not of spoken language.[5] In learning to read, a student is really learning to see his speech on the printed page. To the degree that his speech is not represented on the pages of the material being used to teach him to read, an obstacle is being raised for him.

This view of the relationship of spoken and written language is basically the only one the linguist has to contribute as a linguist. But there are a number of applicational strategies consistent with this principle. It

[4] It has been pointed out (e.g., Weber 1969:38) that the language of the typical reading text does not match the speech of the Standard English-speaking child very well either. But the degree of difference is greater if the student does not control spoken Standard English.

[5] Some qualification of this statement is necessary, because written language probably represents a level of formality never used in spoken language in most cases. However, the basic relationship between speech and writing is the one we have described.

is important to note that there is no unitary "linguistic approach"—that mythical but marketable item that has become a token of prestige in language arts curricula. Rather, there are several alternatives which attempt to eliminate the possible effect that dialect differences may have in the acquisition of reading skills. As will be seen, there are no easy solutions. The advantages and disadvantages of each alternative we shall present must honestly be faced if we are going to arrive at a feasible solution. The fact that we have no infallible alternative should not, however, be taken to mean that all alternatives that attempt to deal with the discrepancy between the language of the primer and the indigenous language of the child are equal. As the different approaches are evaluated, it should be apparent that some can be more highly recommended than others.

Although there are idiosyncratic aspects of practically every proposed reading program, the various alternatives can be roughly divided into two main groups. Some call for different methods in teaching reading with extant materials and others call for the development of new types of reading materials.

If the linguistic diversity between the dialect of children who speak Nonstandard English and the dialect of the reading materials is going to be neutralized without altering basic materials, then two options are open; either the child's language patterns must be changed to conform to Standard English patterns prior to the teaching of reading, or some accommodation to the dialect in the traditional type of reader must be made. The feasibility of these two alternatives is discussed below.

TEACHING STANDARD ENGLISH
PRIOR TO READING

To neutralize the difference between the "language of reading" and the language which the lower-class child brings to school with him, it has sometimes been suggested that the teaching of Standard English should precede the teaching of reading (McDavid 1969; Venezky 1970). Although this may appear to be similar to the simultaneous teaching of reading and Standard English that is often engaged in, it is essential not to confuse these procedures. When teachers correct children for dialect interference in reading as well as for the usual types of errors that occur in learning to read, the teaching of Standard English is usually accomplished in a haphazard and unsystematic way. Furthermore, legitimate dialect interference and reading problems arising from the incomplete mastery of the reading process are often not distinguished from each other.

The approach suggested here, however, first concentrates on the systematic teaching of Standard English before any reading is taught; when a child has adequately acquired Standard English, the teacher may proceed to the teaching of reading—the teaching of reading begins with the assumption that the source for dialect interference has been eliminated. This is not necessarily to say that the child's indigenous dialect will be eradicated, only that he will have capacity in Standard English as well as the vernacular.

Most school curricula call for the teaching of Standard English eventually, but the program described here inevitably means that Standard English will be taught at the initial stages of the child's experience, because the acquisition of reading is obviously one of the earliest priorities of formal education. One might further suggest that because Standard English will probably be taught anyway, it is most reasonable to teach it before the failure to learn it can inhibit reading development.

If we were simply dealing with linguistic considerations, teaching Standard English prior to reading would certainly be an attractive alternative, as well as a seemingly obvious procedure. We know that children are quite adept at language learning, so why not take advantage of this fact and teach them Standard English at an early age? Before we accept the potential advantages of this alternative, we must realistically consider the total sociolinguistic situation, for potential linguistic advantages cannot be treated in isolation from sociocultural facts.

Probably the most essential sociolinguistic point that militates against this alternative is the fact that teaching Standard English may not even be possible without the group reference orientation we have discussed earlier. Children want to speak like their peers, and the conflicts between school and indigenous value systems have repeatedly shown that school values will most often come out on the short end of a compromise.

Given the pessimistic but realistic predictions about the teaching of Standard English, it is therefore surprising that Venezky observes that the teaching of Standard English may only involve a delay of several months in the introduction of reading. He observes:

> There is no reason to believe that a delay of a few months in the introduction of reading will seriously impede any child's natural development.
> (1970:342)

Kochman, who seriously questions the wisdom of teaching Standard English at all, bases part of his argument for not teaching it on what he calls the "efficiency quotient" (1969:87). By this he means the excessive time that must be spent in order to produce even a mediocre and restrictive performance in Standard English. He notes that with maximum cooperation, for example, it takes several months of drills simply to get a student to say *ask* where he formerly said *aks*. Kochman therefore concludes that "the input in time and effort is prodigious and the results negligible" (1969:87).

Even if we take a more optimistic view on the teaching of Standard English, we cannot assume that the first grade is the most conducive age for teaching it. Some sociologists and educators suggest that it is most reasonable to start teaching Standard English at an age when there is an increasing awareness of the social consequences of using certain nonstandard features of speech. According to Labov, the social perceptions of speech stratification start to match the adult norms around the ages of 14 to 15 (Labov 1964b:91; but see also Rosenthal 1973). If the 5 to 6-year-old child perceives little social differentiation in speech, it may be argued that it is senseless to teach Standard English at the first-grade level, the level at which reading skills are expected to be developed. Rather, Standard English should be initiated at a secondary level, when students have acquired the notion of social appropriateness for different types of behavior more fully.

Before we could endorse teaching Standard English as a prerequisite for reading, we would have to have evidence that it can be extensively taught given the current sociocultural facts, and that it is most effectively taught at the initial stages of education. At this point, the sociocultural facts that inhibit the widespread acquisition of Standard English even as a second dialect do not suggest this alternative as a reasonable solution.

DIALECT READINGS OF
EXTANT MATERIALS

The other alternative that retains the traditional materials does not involve the teaching of Standard English in any form. Rather, it involves the acceptance of dialect renderings of Standard English reading materials. Goodman is probably the most explicit spokesman for this position when he states:

> No special materials need to be constructed but children must be permitted, actually encouraged, to read the way they speak.   (1969:27)

This child is given the standard types of reading materials and simply asked to read them aloud in a dialect-appropriate manner. In silent reading, this approach is irrelevant, but it must be remembered that oral reading is the primary basis for evaluating a child's reading skills in the incipient stages. If a child can read the passage in such a way that it systematically differs from Standard English where his indigenous dialect differs, he has successfully read the passage. For example, if a lower-class black child reads a standard sentence such as *Jane goes to Mary's house* as *Jane go to Mary house,* he is considered to have read it properly, because third-person singular -*s* and possessive -*s* suffixial absence are part of the lower-class black child's vernacular. It is held that by permitting the child to read the traditional materials in his own dialect, the teacher can focus on the essentials of the reading process and the child will not be confused about reading problems that may result from dialect interference and legitimate types of reading errors arising during the course of the acquisition of reading skills.

There are several assumptions implicit in accepting what Goodman suggests as the only practical alternative for the reading problem among children with nonstandard speech, and our evaluation of its relative merits is based on these assumptions. In the first place, it assumes that the Standard English contained in the beginning materials is comprehensible to the child. Claims about the comprehension of Standard English by Nonstandard-speaking children vary greatly, but we still lack definitive empirical evidence on this question. At this point, the most reasonable position seems to be that for the most part, the dialect speaker has a receptive competence in Standard English. (The converse, Standard English speakers comprehending lower-class dialects, may not necessarily be true to the same extent because of the sociopsychological factors which enter into the comprehension of the speech of a socially subordinate class by a superordinate one [see Wolff 1959].) This position seems to be most realistic for several reasons. For one, the majority of differences between the child's vernacular and Standard English appear to be on the surface rather than the underlying levels of language (Labov and Cohen 1967). One might expect that differences on the surface level would usually affect comprehension less than differences on the underlying levels of language. A more important reason for this position is found, for example, in the indirect evidence that we have from the lower-class child's ability to perform certain types of tasks based on the receptive competence of Standard English. In performing a sentence repetition test devised by Baratz, lower-class black children could comprehend Standard English sentences that focused on the areas of difference between the child's vernacular and Standard English sufficiently well to repeat them in the nonstandard dialect (Baratz 1969). That these children were able to give back a nonstandard equivalent was indicative of the basic comprehension of the content of the sentence.

This position on comprehension does not, however, preclude the possibility of some information loss when reading Standard English. The loss of information would not be as great, of course, as it would be if the readers were written in a foreign language. We would certainly not argue that a speaker of a nonstandard dialect is going to understand as little Standard English as a monolingual German speaker reading English. When some information loss does occur because of dialect differences, what should be done about features that might be unfamiliar to the Nonstandard English speaker? Are these unfamiliar features sufficiently infrequent to warrant their retention in the materials, inasmuch as any child can expect some unfamiliar constructions in reading material; or will the unfamiliar constructions be sufficiently great to impede the reading process? These are empirical questions, but ones that must be faced squarely if no change in traditional reading materials is advocated.

Another factor that must be considered in using extant materials concerns the orthography, particularly if the phonics approach to reading is employed. It appears that the traditional orthography is not totally inappropriate for the dialects of children who do not speak Standard English (Fasold 1969). Hence, we do not consider this factor to be a major disadvantage as long as the teacher knows the type of sound-symbol relations appropriate for the dialect.

Our reference to the teacher's knowledge of the appropriate sound-symbol relations brings out another assumption of this alternative; namely, that the reading teacher is thoroughly familiar with the dialect of the children. When Goodman says that the student should be encouraged to read the way he speaks, this assumes that the teacher knows what particular dialect rendering of a given passage can be expected. Otherwise, there is no way of distinguishing legitimate reading problems arising from an incomplete mastery of the sound-symbol relations and reading differences that are the result of dialect interference. For example, if a lower-class black child reads the word *thought* as *fought,* the teacher must know whether this is simply a problem of sound-symbol relations due to the incomplete mastery of these relations or a legitimate dialect rendering of *th.* In this case, the pronunciation cannot be attributed to dialect interference because there is no known dialect rule which renders *th* as *f* in word-initial position. But what if the student reads *Ruth* so that it is identical with *roof?* In this case, it is a legitimate dialect pronunciation and should not be corrected. The type of discernment which might correct the homophony of *thought* and *fought* but not the homophony of *Ruth* and *roof* assumes that the teacher knows the dialect rule that realizes *th* as *f* at the middle or end of a word, but not at the beginning. Some teachers may inductively arrive at such types of discernment because of consistence in the oral reading of nonstandard dialect speakers, but if the alternative proposed by Goodman and others is to be adopted on an extensive level, it will require the training of teaehers in the structural patterns of the dialect. (An acquaintance with the structural patterns does not, of course, mean that the teacher will be able to speak the dialect.)

Although this alternative has several potential disadvantages, it does have one very practical advantage: it can be established much more immediately than some of the other alternatives. For example, it can be adopted while further experimentation with other alternatives which require more drastic curriculum reorganization is carried out. Indeed, the teacher who thoroughly acquaints himself with the description of the dialect features and is convinced of the legitimacy of the dialect as a highly developed language system is in a position to start initiating this alternative. Chapters Six and Seven were designed to provide this kind of information.

A seemingly more drastic alternative to the reading problem for speakers of nonstandard dialects involves the incorporation of new types of materials into the reading curriculum for lower-class children. Basically, there are two approaches that have been proposed—one involving the elimination of all features that might be unfamiliar to the Nonstandard-speaking child and one that involves the writing of new sets of materials designed specifically to represent the language and culture the child brings with him when he enters school.

THE NEUTRALIZATION OF DIALECT DIFFERENCES

One method of revising current materials for nonstandard dialect speakers is to simply eliminate features that might predictably be problematic for the nonstandard speaker because they are not an integral part of his linguistic system. This alternative essentially follows the suggestion of Shuy that grammatical choices in beginning material should not provide extraneous data. Shuy observes:

> In the case of beginning reading materials for nonstandard speakers, the text should help the child by avoiding grammatical forms which are not realized by him in his spoken language (third singular verb inflections, for example). (Shuy 1969:125)

It should be noted that this alternative would *not* incorporate any nonstandard features present in the dialect but absent in Standard English.[6] For example, the use of *be* to indicate distributive action in a sentence such as *He be here every day* would not be used, because this feature is unique to nonstandard speech. Accommodation would be made only by excluding features in Standard English that do not have isomorphic correspondences in the dialect. It capitalizes on the similarities of large portions of the grammar of these dialects so that the possibility of grammatical interference is eliminated. This alternative would only concentrate on grammatical differences, because differences in pronunciation would involve most of the words in the English language. It thus appears that this choice involves the neutralization of grammatical differences along with the acceptance of dialect pronunciations of reading materials, as was suggested in one of the previously discussed alternatives.

---

[6] In the article by Shuy in which this procedure is suggested, this is only one of several types of changes that Shuy recommends for materials to be used by nonstandard dialect speakers.

There are several assumptions which form the basis of this alternative, and it cannot be evaluated apart from these. For one, it assumes that there is a sufficient common core between the standard and nonstandard language system which allows for the practical implementation of these suggestions into our reading materials. The validity of this assumption is an empirical question, and on the basis of our research, we can answer that there are many similarities, at least between Standard English and the varieties of nonstandard dialects we have been discussing. The inventory of similarities is certainly greater than the inventory of differences. But the fact remains that there are differences and so we must ask if they might be of the sort which would make it difficult to effectively incorporate this type of change into materials.

To examine this problem more closely, we can take one of the sample inventories of the prominent features of lower-class black dialect, and see what changes would have to be made in order to neutralize the grammatical differences between it and Standard English. For example, consider the sample inventory that Shuy delimits, which seems to be a fairly typical list:

WRITTEN EXPRESSION	LINGUISTIC FEATURE	ORAL EXPRESSION
1. John's house	possession	John house
2. John runs	3rd sing. pres.	John run
3. ten cents	plurality	ten cent
4. He jumped	past	He jump
5. She is a cook	copula	She a cook
6. He doesn't have any toys	negation	He aint't got no toys
		He don't have no toys
		He don't got no toys
7. He asked if I came	past conditional question	He asked did I come
8. Every day when I come he isn't here	negative + be	Every day when I come he don't be here
		(Shuy 1969:128)

What would be involved if we were to eliminate the above types of constructions from extant reading materials at the beginning level of reading? For No. 1, possession, it would mean that we could only express possession via the preposition *of* or the verb *has,* or avoid possessive constructions altogether. For some items such as *John's hat* or *Bill's bike,* the use of *of* might be stylistically unacceptable even though it might be grammatical (e.g., *the hat of John, the bike of Bill*). Using the construction

John has a hat or *the hat which John has* every time we wanted to indicate possession might lead us into even more serious stylistic difficulties. Thus a sequence of sentences in discourse such as

> *John's new bike is blue. Mary's new bike is red. John's bike is bigger than Mary's.*

might be restructured something like

> *John has a new blue bike. Mary has a new bike too and it is red. The bike John has is bigger than the one Mary has.*

It seems that the only way one could eliminate such stylistic unacceptability would be to avoid the possessive construction. When we look at No. 2 on Shuy's list, we find that a problem with the use of third-person singular present tense -*s* occurs. The use of *has* in our above sentence is therefore unjustified if we are to hold to our stated principle. In fact, this difference eliminates virtually all stories in the present tense that call for the use of third-person singular forms, a rather restricting limitation to be placed on reading materials. As for No. 3, which has plurals that might not appear in the nonstandard vocabulary of the child, this would probably take even more ingenuity if, in fact, there is any way anyone could deal with this. The elimination of structures calling for copulas, as in No. 5, would certainly add a further restriction to a growing inventory of structures to be avoided, although one might maintain that copulas can be used as long as the full form (e.g., *He is big*) and not the contracted form (e.g., *He's big*) is used, based on the conclusion that the full form of the copula is an integral part of the dialect whereas the contracted form may not be. Item No. 6 involves the elimination of potential negative concord sentences so that sentences such as *He doesn't have any toys* would not be permitted. One might suggest that this may be remedied by using only a negative indefinite (instead of a negative auxiliary and indefinite) such as *You have no toys,* but this is not feasible because the rule that transfers the negativized auxiliary to the indefinite form (e.g., *You don't have any toys* to *You have no toys*) is not an integral part of the dialect. The embedded question in No. 7 could be handled fairly simply by making a direct question out of it, such as *He asked, "Can I come?"* instead of *He asked if he could come.* If one wanted to avoid constructions where the dialect might potentially use *be,* discourses involving certain types of habituality would have to be avoided, a stringent limitation if the principle is to be followed faithfully.

The above exercise demonstrates several important points with respect to the accommodation of materials for at least lower-class blacks. First, it shows that the feasibility of neutralization varies from feature to feature.

There are some that can be handled by minor adjustments in current materials; others, however, require the elimination of significant portions of narratives or the cumbersome use of certain circumlocutions. It should be noted that when there are a number of different features that must be avoided in a particular type of passage, the problem of restructuring a narrative with these in mind can become quite difficult. Even if the overall differences between the standard and nonstandard dialect are significantly less than the similarities, the clustering of differences may make this strategy virtually unusable for particular types of passages.

Materials developers would not necessarily have to be as rigorous in their avoidance strategy as we have described above. One might just avoid certain types of grammatical differences while disregarding others. For example, a decision might be made to avoid grammatical differences which involve lexical changes, while disregarding those which involve affixial forms. This would mean that the use of embedded questions would be avoided because they involve a change of word order and the use of "question" *if* or *whether*. But the avoidance of constructions involving the third-person singular present-tense forms, certain plurals, or possessives would not be maintained because these only involve the addition of a suffixial -*s* in Standard English. This procedure would reduce some of the problems caused by trying to eliminate frequently occurring inflectional forms.

There is one further aspect of the alternative discussed here that should be explicated because it may not be obvious from the presentation thus far; namely, the implicit assumption that a "dialect-free" basal reader is a legitimate end-product of this method. Venezky observes:

> Reading materials for beginning reading should, in content, vocabulary, and syntax, be as dialect free (and culture free) as possible. Given the inanity of present day materials, this should not be overly difficult to achieve. (1970:343)

Although Venezky assumes that the production of dialect-free materials is a reasonable and achievable goal, the pervasiveness of dialect pattern may be considerably more extensive than he anticipates. He does not define what he means by *dialect-free,* but he presumably is referring to the fact that features that might differentiate dialects can be eliminated. That is, readers can be made "neutral" with respect to dialect. This term should not be confused with *dialect-fair,* which does not refer to neutrality, but to the adaptation of materials so that they are not biased against speakers of a given dialect. As Venezky himself admits, these terms are, in reality, reflections of the more inclusive concepts, *culture-free* and *culture-fair.* The former is highly suspect as an anthropologically valid concept because of the all-pervasive effect of cultural patterns on behavior (both linguistic and nonlinguistic), whereas the latter is an essential tenet of cultural relativism. With this in mind, we may ask if the effort to accommodate different dialects and cultures in terms of one set of materials is a naive attempt to achieve an unreal goal. At any rate, one must take these notions considerably more seriously than Venezky suggests.

Although we have described several apparent disadvantages of this alternative, we must not conclude our discussion before pointing out some potential advantages. For one, a modification of this method may eliminate some of the most salient features of Standard English that might be unfamiliar to the nonstandard-speaking child who comes to the schoolroom. Also, it would not incorporate socially stigmatized features of language, eliminating the controversy that inevitably surrounds the inclusion of nonstandard patterns in reading materials. The changes this alternative would require in materials could, in fact, be incorporated without necessarily being noticed by teachers who are using such materials.

DIALECT READERS

The final alternative dealing with linguistic aspects of the reading problem involves the use of readers that are written in the vernacular of the children. That is, every effort is made in the beginning materials to represent the cultural and linguistic content indigenous to the child. As a brief illustration of how such materials might differ from the conventional materials, we may compare two versions of the same passage, one in Standard English and one in the dialect of the children.

Standard English Version

"Look down here," said Suzy.
"I can see a girl in here.
That girl looks like me.
Come here and look, David!
Can you see that girl?" . . .

Vernacular Black English Version

Susan say, "Hey, you-all, look down here!"
"I can see a girl in here.
That girl, she look like me.
Come here and look, David!
Could you see the girl?" . . .   (Wolfram and Fasold 1969:147)

The second passage is a deliberate attempt to incorporate the features of the children's dialect into the basal readers. The absence of third-person singular -*s* (e.g., *Susan say, she look*), left dislocation (e.g., *That girl, she . . .*), *could* for *can,* and *you-all* are direct efforts to accurately represent the indigenous dialect of the child. Although it has sometimes been misunderstood by opponents of this alternative, the proposal of dialect readers does not advocate an eventual dualist reading system in American society. It is only proposed as an initial step in the adequate acquisition of reading skills. Once reading fluency has been attained in the dialect readers and the child is sufficiently confident in his ability to read, a transition from dialect to Standard English readers is made. Stewart has illustrated the several stages of transition:

STAGE 1

Charles and Michael, they out playing.

Grammatically, sentences at this stage will be pure non-standard Negro dialect. The vocabulary, also, will be controlled so that no words which are unfamiliar to the Negro dialect-speaking child will appear. Thus, all linguistic aspects of texts will be familiar to the beginning reader, and his full attention can be focused on learning to read the vocabulary. At this stage, no attempt should be made to teach standard-English pronunciations of the words, since the sentence in which they appear is not standard English.

STAGE 2

Charles and Michael, they are out playing.

At this stage, the most important grammatical features of standard English are introduced. In the example, there is one such feature—the copula. Apart from that, the vocabulary is held constant. Oral-language drills could profitably be used to teach person accord of the copula (*am, is, are*), and some standard-English pronunciations of the basic vocabulary might be taught.

STAGE 3

Charles and Michael are out playing.

Grammatically, the sentences at this stage are brought into full conformity with standard English by making the remaining grammatical and stylistic adjustments. In the example, the "double subject" of the non-standard form is eliminated. Oral-language drills could be used to teach this and additional standard-English pronunciations of the basic vocabulary could be taught.   (Stewart 1969:185)

The alternative that advocates the use of dialect readers seems to be based on three assumptions: (1) that there is sufficient mismatch between the child's system and the Standard English textbook to warrant distinct materials, (2) the psychological benefit from reading success will be stronger in the dialect than it might be if Standard English materials were used, and (3) the success of vernacular teaching in bilingual situations recommends a similar principle for bidialectal situations.

In order to evaluate the potential success of such an alternative, each of these assumptions must be discussed in more detail. Whether or not there is sufficient mismatch between even the most distinctive nonstandard dialects and the language reading materials to warrant the use of dialect readers is a thorny question. We acknowledge that there are even differences between the spoken language of the middle-class child and the written language of the reading materials, but it is clear that the lower-class child can be expected to have a considerably greater divergence than the middle-class child. We concur with Goodman that

> the more divergence there is between the dialect of the learner and the dialect of learning, the more difficult will be the task of learning to read.
> (1969:15)

But while such divergence exists, Fishman, for one, doubts whether the degree of difference is great enough to be a major problem. He cites examples of widespread literacy in countries where standard materials are used for speakers who speak dialects that are probably more linguistically divergent from the language of the readers than Standard English is from any American nonstandard dialect, and asks,

> if the distance or difference between the vernacular and the school variety is truly so central in causing reading difficulties, then how do we explain the widespread literacy not only in the same population [among impoverished pre-War *shtetl* Jews], but also among rural Japanese and Germans and Frenchmen and Swedes and Swiss-Germans and many others during the past quarter century and more? (1969:1109)

Studies such as Labov and Robins's (1965), dealing with the relation of peer-group involvement and reading failure for adolescent males in Harlem, point to a value conflict more than a linguistic conflict as the basis of reading difficulty. But it is certainly not the case that linguistic conflict plays no role whatsoever. Until empirical evidence determines otherwise, it seems reasonable to assume that language divergence is of some significance.

Before leaving our discussion of oral and written language mismatch, we must submit a word of caution about the style of dialect readers. To what extent should the beginning materials reflect the "pure nonstandard dialect" as opposed to the way in which children actually speak? In this regard, it is instructive to compare two passages, entitled "Dumb Boy" and "See a Girl," included in Wolfram and Fasold (1969:145ff.). "Dumb Boy" was simply transcribed from a dialogue as it was actually recorded and "See a Girl" was an attempt at "pure" dialect. In the former case, there is considerable variation between forms, and as Labov (1969) has observed, some of this variation cannot simply be dismissed as importation from a superposed dialect; rather, it is an inherent part of the indigenous dialect. Some of the beginning dialect materials which start with pure dialect may, in effect, be creating a new type of mismatch between written and spoken language. That is, they have made the dialect to be more divergent from Standard English in written form than it actually is in spoken form. For example, the dialect reader entitled "I Be Scared," by Davis, Gladney, and Leaverton (1969), overuses the habitual use of *be* in terms of the types of constructions in which it occurs and the relative frequency with which it occurs. Mismatch of this type must be minimized just as much as we minimize the difference between the mismatch of oral and written language for middle-class children learning to read.

The next assumption we must consider deals with the psychological reinforcement that such an approach might give to the child. Baratz observes that one of the prime advantages of this program is

> the powerful ego-supports of giving credence to the child's language system and therefore to himself, and giving him the opportunity to experience success in school.   (1969:114)

Ideally, we must concur that a program involving language familiar to the child (and, of course, an appropriate cultural setting, which must be its concomitant) will potentially hold a great opportunity for success. But if we look more closely at current attitudes toward reading materials as expressed by the community leaders and parents, we are faced with a sociopsychological fact that may force us to question these psychological advantages.

For a number of reasons, the notion of giving children nonstandard reading materials has provoked considerable controversy in communities for whom these materials have been intended. In fact, one recent attempt to experiment (one should note that this was only experimental, not curriculum revision) with dialect primers for speakers of Vernacular Black English was canceled before it ever had an opportunity to be tried. Commenting on the reasons for this cancellation, columnist William Raspberry of the *Washington Post* reported:

> Objections were made on a number of counts: Some found the text and illustrations "uninspiring" or downright offensive; others concluded that white people were trying to use black children for their dubious experiments. . . . But most of the parents, knowing that society equates facility in standard English with intelligence, do not want to risk confirming their children in "undesirable" speech patterns—a risk that advocates insist is virtually nonexistent.   (March 4, 1970: column 1)

At the heart of the rejection of dialect materials by the community (i.e., educators in lower-class schools, as well as parents and community leaders) seems to be the general attitude toward nonstandard dialects as a medium of education. The codification of a nonstandard language system may be viewed as a threat to social mobility in our society. For those who are attempting to attain middle-class status (within either the black community itself or the broader society), it may be seen as a program that implicitly attempts to "keep the black man where he is." For middle-class leaders in the black community, some of the negative reactions may be fostered by embarrassment or linguistic insecurity. Or, it may be viewed as a new type of paternalism toward the black community.

One fact that seems basic to the negative reactions toward the use of dialect in reading is the assumption that different materials for different social or ethnic groups implies the inherent incapability of these groups to learn using the traditional methods (apparently a by-product of the American "melting-pot" myth). Difference is interpreted as inferiority.

Whether the reasons for rejecting dialect readers are real or imagined, the fact remains that the sociopolitical controversy over such a program and the community's negative reactions to it may seriously impede what otherwise might be an "ego-supportive" activity. The attitudes of teachers, parents, and community leaders projected to children may be sufficiently strong to affect the children's motivation.

Finally, it is assumed on the basis of vernacular learning throughout the world that such a program can be expected to be successful. In fact, the UNESCO report on the use of vernacular languages in education specifically recommended that every pupil should begin formal education in his mother tongue (1953). For studies that compare beginning reading in the mother vis-à-vis the national language, the most predominant conclusion is that

> the youngsters of linguistic minorities learn to read with greater comprehension in the national language when they first learn to read in their mother tongue than when they receive all their reading instruction in the national language.   (Modiano 1968:9)

Nevertheless, there are still scholars who have reservations about vernacular reading for one reason or another. Bull (1955), for example, cites the vast expense (both in terms of financial considerations and curricula development) that this method may involve. Venezky (1970) cites many extralinguistic factors which bias experiments comparing vernacular and national language reading. He thus concludes that

> the native literacy approach, although possessing obvious cultural advantages over the standard language approach, has yet to be proven scholastically superior.   (1970:338)

A more relevant consideration in terms of the vernacular reading situation is the validity of using this procedure for different dialects as well as languages. A study by Österberg (1964) suggests that this alternative may be just as valid for different dialects as for different languages. Other things being equal, we would expect that the reported success of teaching reading initially in the vernacular in other situations would recommend its usage for nonstandard-speaking children. But we cannot ignore the fact that sociopsychological factors we have discussed earlier may be sufficient to impede the acquisition of reading skills. We should note in this regard, however, that in a number of bilingual situations in which reading was initially taught in the vernacular, attitudes toward the indigenous language vis-à-vis the national language are quite comparable to the attitudes toward nonstandard dialects. That is, the vernacular is overtly socially stigmatized both by the dominant class and by those who actually use the stigmatized forms. Despite these attitudes, vernacular reading materials have been reported to be successful as a bridge to literacy in the national language.

Although none of these alternatives is completely satisfactory, they do suggest the directions in which solutions to the linguistic aspects of reading problems can be found. Some combination, modification, or adaptation of one or more of them would almost certainly make a contribution to the improvement of the quality of reading instruction for the speakers of nonstandard dialects.

Teaching Writing

With regard to writing, it may be important to take a hard look at just what kinds of writing are likely to be needed by a given group of nonstandard dialect-speaking children. Perhaps it would be more realistic to focus on writing personal and business letters and on answering questions on various forms than developing the ability to write a literary critique of a short story, novel, or poem. In some of these styles, personal letters, for example, it may be unnecessary to insist that every detail of Standard English grammar be observed. If a personal letter is to be written to a peer, there would seem to be little point in writing it in a "foreign" standard dialect. However, in business letters, in filling in forms, and in other official kinds of writing, only Standard English grammar is considered appropriate and the ability to use it is a justifiable goal for an English teacher to set for all her students. In the process, it would be useful for the teacher to be able to distinguish three categories of errors. (1) There are problems in organization and logical development of arguments and similar difficulties. This kind of problem is not related to dialect differences. (2) There also are spelling and grammatical errors based on interference from a nonstandard dialect. We reviewed a set of written compositions by black inner-city students admitted to a major university, and found that over 40 percent of the errors found could have been attributed to dialect interference. (3) Finally, there are errors in spelling, punctuation, and grammar which are not traceable to dialect interference.

A variety of apparent errors in the written work of Nonstandard

English-speaking people are not errors in the strictest sense at all. They are simply the reflection in writing of the differences in grammar, pronunciation, and verbal expression between the nonstandard dialect and the standard one by which the writing is being judged. As we have pointed out, writing is a reflection of speech, so that if a student's writing contains features of his nonstandard dialect, it simply proves that his writing is fulfilling its basic function very well. In the area of grammar, when one of the university freshmen mentioned above wrote "Keith attitude" where Standard English would call for "Keith's attitude," he was merely reflecting the rules of his nonstandard grammar. According to the rules of the nonstandard dialect in question, possessive 's may be used, but does not have to be. When another of these students spelled "closest" as "closes," he revealed that his pronunciation rules allow final consonant cluster simplification. Other cases arise in which a writer uses an expression that is current in his speech community but perhaps is unknown to the teacher. When one of the university freshmen wrote "Keith had negative changes about DeVries," he was using an expression common among some black people. A teacher unfamiliar with the expression "to have changes" might well treat this expression as an error.

Other spelling, grammar, and style errors occur which cannot be traced to dialect interference and should be considered genuine errors. In the same set of compositions discussed above, the misspellings "laied" for "laid" and "tring" for "trying" were observed. There is no pronunciation feature of the nonstandard dialect involved that would account for these spellings. In grammar, the use of the clause "in which you live in" is not called for by the grammar of any nonstandard dialect. An example of what might be called a style problem is the expression "in results of this," presumably for "as a result of this." All of these usages, along with mistakes in capitalization and punctuation, are appropriately treated as errors unrelated to dialect conflict.

This division into dialect and general errors has implications for teaching writing. In a real sense, the dialect-related "errors" are not errors at all, but are correct usages based on a different grammar rule system. Because this is the case, their correction is perhaps not as urgent as the corrections of mistakes that are not founded on *any* rule system. This may mean that several writing exercises would be allowed to go by with no mention being made of the dialect-related errors. In some styles of writing—personal letters perhaps—elimination of dialect interference might not ever be appropriate.

To illustrate from a sample composition how a teacher might classify dialect features and genuine errors, let us take an example composition written by a rural sixth-grade student in south central Pennsylvania. The assignment was to write a short story from the point of view of any animal the student wished. One student submitted this composition about a cow. In the composition, we have attempted to indicate places at which a teacher might mark corrections. Because we have never been elementary school teachers, it may be that we have marked too many places or too few, but we believe it is realistic enough to illustrate the point. The errors marked with (a) numbers are general errors not related to the student's dialect. The ones marked with (b) numbers are dialect-related.

Cow

Well (1a) at first I will (2a) Iterduce myself a little bit. I am (3a) rosy the cow (4a) My (1b) favert dish is cow feed. Well (5a) Well, here I am—OUCH! Oh! oh, ah, ah, ah, there (6a) sorry for the disturbance (7a) I just bit a (2b) jager. Well (8a) here I am eating grass. Cow feed (3b) don't have jagers (9a) (10a) thats (11a) wy I like (12a) I (13a)

Here comes the farmer with the chop wagon (14a) I've got to go.

Oh no (15a) haylage again (16a) it has jagers (17a) to (18a) I wish he'd bring corn. May the corn got (4b) all. I hate jagers.... OUCH! (19a) see (20a) wath I mean (21a) (22a) bossy just got a jager. Oh (23a) here come the boy.... Hey! Hey! Get in! HEY! good-by.

Well you finally got here (24a) they just put the milker on me. It's a bother. Well (25a) good-by. See you next time.

It appears that the dialect-interference occurrences are a small minority, and that the great majority of the general errors are examples of a general punctuation problem (1a, 4a, 5a, 6a, 7a, 8a, 9a, 13a, 14a, 15a, 16a, 18a, 21a, 23a, 24a, 25a). Another very pervasive general problem is with capitalization (2a, 3a, 5a, 16a, 19a, 22a, 24a). There are several spelling errors not related to dialect (2a, 11a, 17a, 20a). There is an error involving the apostrophe in *that's* (10a) and the student seems to have temporarily lost his train of thought and to have written *I* where he intended *it* (12a). Once this student has mastered capitalization and punctuation, the only specific local flaws will be the four spelling errors, the apostrophe problem, the carelessness at 12a, and the dialect interferences. The teacher also may wish to work with organization and transition as well, but the composition impresses us as having considerable potential, considering the age of the student.

The first of the dialect errors occurs at 1b, where the spelling *favert* is doubtless far more accurate a representation of the writer's pronunciation than *favorite* would be. The word *jager* (perhaps a better spelling would be *jagger*) is a common term in the area in which this boy lives for thorns and other objects capable of causing scratches. It is not the sort of term one expects to be used in writing, but it is again an accurate reflection of the spoken language. At two places (3b and 5b) the student's writing reflects the fact that the third-person singular present tense suffix -*s* is not required by the grammar of his dialect in every situation in which the standard dialect requires it. At 4b, he uses the expression *got all* (was used up), a common expression in this region borrowed from Pennsylvania Dutch.

A teacher aware of the nature of dialect interference might well spend his efforts on capitalization, punctuation, spelling, and organization and development problems and ignore the dialect errors until much later. The composition, with improvement in the general areas and in organization, but with the dialect interference allowed to pass, might look like this.

Cow

Well, at first I will introduce myself a little bit. I am Rosy the cow. My favert dish is cow feed. Well, well, here I am—OUCH! Oh! oh, ah, ah, ah, there, sorry for the disturbance. I just bit a jagger. Well, here I am eating grass. Cow feed don't have jaggers, that's why I like it.

Here comes the farmer with the chop wagon. I've got to go.

Oh no, haylage again! It has jaggers, too. I wish he'd bring corn. Maybe the corn got all. I hate jaggers—OUCH! See what I mean? Bossy just got a jagger. Oh, here come the boy. He's yelling, "Hey! HEY! Get in! HEY!"

Well, we finally got here. They just put the milker on me. It's a bother. Well, that's all for now.

If the student showed this degree of improvement (we do not mean to suggest that the composition could not be further improved, even aside from the dialect items), he might well be worthy of praise and an A grade. It would then be time to teach him the necessity of using Standard English in written work. The two basic assumptions stressed in our discussion of both reading and writing—respect for linguistic integrity of nonstandard dialects and a realization of the primacy of speech over writing—puts a new and helpful perspective on the teaching of both these language arts.

Standardized Testing

The areas of spoken language, reading, and writing involve the problems of teaching skills to young people. The fourth area to which we turn our attention has to do not with the teaching of students, but with the evaluation of their progress by means of standardized tests. At no other time in the history of American education has the general role of standardized testing been called into such serious question as it is now. To any reader of this book, the importance mainstream American society places on testing should be readily apparent. Before we entered elementary school, we were probably given a battery of tests to determine our readiness for school. Throughout our elementary- and secondary-school education, standardized tests were given at specified intervals in order to evaluate our educational achievement. Our preparedness for college was further evaluated on the basis of the Scholastic Aptitude Test, and our potential for graduate study was measured in the Graduate Record Examination. As if this were not sufficient, our capabilities for certain types of employment may have been determined on the basis of a standardized test such as the Civil Service Entrance Examination. It is no wonder that the appropriateness of various types of standardized tests should be called into question. Given the importance attached to testing, the uses and misuses of standardized tests can hardly be scrutinized closely enough. Recent proceedings have now set a precedent for challenging the legality of certain types of tests because of their discrimination on the basis of race, class, or sex.

There is obviously a broad spectrum of subject areas for which standardized tests are used. Some of these deal directly with language while others are based on certain assumptions about language, although they deal with topics quite unrelated to language. For example, all tests assume the testee's comprehension of the instructions, and the instructions are dependent upon linguistic comprehension of some type (whether oral or written). If the testee cannot comprehend the task involved, he can hardly be expected to respond in an appropriate manner. In essence, the interpretation of the task requires matching the interpretation of the test designer on the part of the testee. From a linguistic standpoint, this involves the comprehension of sentence meanings, including the presuppositions and implications of a question. Because of certain assumptions, then, tests in a wide range of areas may indirectly involve linguistic matters. In this section, however, we will only discuss sociolinguistic aspects of several representative types of language tests.

Although we shall restrict our attention to dialect bias in current language tests, we must recognize that test bias is not limited to linguistic items. There is also the question of cultural appropriateness of the test items, the testing format, and the testing situation itself. All of these may represent more serious problems than the simple matter of dialect bias found in certain linguistic items, but these matters take us beyond the scope of this book. Because of the pervasiveness of cultural conditioning, we would seriously doubt that a culture-free test can exist. On the other hand, it does seem reasonable to suggest that the construction of culture-fair tests is a reasonable goal. Unfortunately, at this point our criticism of the biases of current testing instruments is considerably ahead of our construction of culturally and linguistically fair alternatives.

There are several different types of relevant questions that must be asked about language tests with respect to our knowledge of social dialects. (1) To begin with, we must ask what aspects of language the test *claims* to be testing. To answer this question, we must naturally read the test manual carefully. It is somewhat surprising to observe test administrators who sometimes do not know precisely what the test claims to be measuring. (2) Following our familiarization with what the test claims to be testing, we must ask what aspect of language the test is *actually* measuring. All tests that consistently differentiate groups of individuals measure something, but not necessarily what they set out to measure. As we shall see, some current language tests may be rather effective tools for measuring certain linguistic abilities, but they may not be the abilities the test was designed to measure. (3) Next, we may ask what specific problems the language test may pose for the nonstandard dialect. On the basis of our descriptive knowledge of various nonstandard dialects, we may be able to predict responses that will differ from the expected Standard English norm. In such cases, we may be dealing with tests that are systematically biased against certain dialects. (4) If we find that tests are biased against certain dialects, we must ask how the scores should be interpreted for these groups of speakers. If language development is measured according to a Standard English norm, how do we interpret the score for the nonstandard speaker who is acquiring his vernacular dialect instead of Standard English?

All of the above questions relate to the matters traditionally referred to as testing *validity* and *reliability*. Validity refers to the matter of measuring what the test purports to measure and asking the right questions to obtain this desired information. Reliability is concerned with gathering a representative, unbiased selection of data as the basis for establishing the test's norms.

LANGUAGE DEVELOPMENT TESTS

There are currently many different types of tests used to evaluate language development among preschool and kindergarten children. In most areas, there are a number of tests one can choose from in order to evaluate a child's linguistic maturation. The significance of these tests should not be underestimated, for, in many instances, they have been used as the basis for the establishment of extensive language intervention programs. In other cases, children are recommended for extended periods of speech therapy on the basis of such tests.

Aspects of language development typically dealt with in diagnostic tests include articulatory development, auditory discrimination, grammatical development, and vocabulary acquisition. In some school districts, a battery of tests covering these areas is routinely given to every child in order to determine whether or not he is progressing "normally" in his language development. In other districts, such tests are only given if there is some reason to suspect that a child is not maturing linguistically at the expected rate. Children with language disabilities are then referred to speech therapists for individual attention. The effort, then, is to diagnose speech pathologies. The fact that disproportionate numbers of children from particular dialect areas are considered to have speech pathologies should immediately raise suspicion if we take our premise in Chapter One concerning language development seriously. In many instances, children are mistakenly diagnosed as having a speech pathology simply because the tests make no provision for responses other than Standard English. This can be readily illustrated in each of the four specific areas of language development that are usually included in such test batteries.

Articulation testing is one of the areas in which dialect bias is most readily apparent. Typically, the articulation test consists of the examiner showing a series of pictures to the child. The child is told to name the item in the picture. (Already we have the potential of serious cultural bias in the types of pictures chosen to be included.) In each item, the examiner is looking for the production of certain sounds in particular positions. For example, in an item such as *run,* he may be examining the production of the initial *r* and the final *n.* Unfortunately, in most of these tests, articulatory development is measured solely in terms of Standard English norms. Thus, in a commonly used articulation test such as the Templin-Darley Test of Articulation, sounds such as the diphthong *ay* in *pie, th* in *teeth, r* in *car, st* cluster in *nest,* and *th* in *there* are all considered diagnostic in determining articulatory development. If the prescribed sound is not produced, it is scored as a "misarticulation," "substitution," or "omission." On the basis of our description of phonological features of social dialects in Chapter Six, we know that each of these items may have a realization different from the one prescribed in the test. Some of these, such as the correspondence of *f* for final *th* in *teeth* or the final *s* for *st* in *nest,* are regular realizations in certain socially stigmatized dialects; others, however, may be considered to be a part of certain regional standards, such as the monophthongization of *ay* in *pie,* or the absence of *r* in *car.* In the diagnostic form of this articulation test, there are 176 sounds that are tested. For over 70 of these items, we can expect realizations that might legitimately differ from the expected norm based on a social or regional dialect pattern. This is over one-third of all the items in the test. Now suppose an eight-year-old speaker of Vernacular Black English produces all the sounds correctly except for the items that may be different in his own dialect. (This is, of course, a hypothetical situation, because the child would probably not be expected to give all Vernacular Black English forms for all items, given the inherently variable nature of some of the items. On the other hand, we could not realistically expect him to get correct responses on all the other items.) When his score is compared with the expected norms for various age levels, we find that he falls beneath the norm (i.e., mean) for the four-year-old. Even if we realistically allow for only half of the potentially biased items to be realized in their dialectally divergent form, the child would still fall below the mean for the five-year-old. It is no wonder, then, that disproportionate numbers of children from nonstandard-speaking linguistic environments are erroneously classified as having retarded articulation development.

Although we have chosen only one articulation test for illustration, the situation is equally bleak for most of the articulation tests currently used for screening and diagnosis. Most of them indicate similar types of bias against nonstandard dialects. In some instances, evaluating diagnosticians may be aware that particular regional standard realizations should not be counted as authentic articulation problems and that speakers of socially stigmatized dialects should not be penalized for producing their dialect norms. However, on the basis of many of these tests, speakers of socially stigmatized varieties are often referred for articulation therapy.

Similar types of problems can be predicted for language-based auditory discrimination tests. Items for these tests are typically based on Standard English norms without any provision for other dialects. The problems in such tests can be readily illustrated by looking at one of the popular tests given to determine the development of sound discrimination skills; namely, the Wepman Auditory Discrimination Test. The test is based essentially on the principle of *minimal word pairs*. In this format, word pairs are given to the subject. Some of the pairs differ by one sound (the minimal word pair) while others are produced identically. The examiner gives the word pairs to the subject, who is instructed to respond whether the pairs sound the same or different. For example, the subject may be given the items *zone-zone,* to which he is expected to respond that they are the same; and *pit-pet,* to which he is expected to respond that they are different. Unfortunately, some of the items that are minimal word pairs in one dialect are homophonous in other dialects. For example, items such as *pin-pen, wreath-reef, lave-lathe,* and *sheaf-sheath* are all supposed to be perceived as different. But based on the rules we specified in Chapter Six, all of the above illustrations would be considered homophonous in various regional and social dialects.

At this point, one may suggest that even if children do not make certain phonological distinctions between words, they still should be able to perceive the difference produced by the tester. But this is not necessarily the case, because we edit items to fit our own sound system. Because of this editing process, it is much more difficult to perceive distinctions we ordinarily do not make. This difficulty can be illustrated easily by the perception problems encountered by English speakers learning the Spanish sound system. When asked to distinguish between p and b in Spanish, they typically have problems initially because they perceive the sounds in terms of the English system. In Spanish, p and b are just distinguished by voicing, but in English, *p* is usually also distinguished from *b* by aspiration [pʰ]. In many instances, it is this aspiration which is the most important identifying characteristic. Without the aspiration as a cue, introductory students want to assign Spanish *p* to *b,* although the native Spanish speaker would have no difficulty hearing the distinction. The problem for the introductory Spanish student is not primarily one of auditory discrimination, but the tendency to filter the sounds through his own system of contrasts. A similar type of filtering process can be expected by the speaker of a dialect where he does not ordinarily expect contrasts between sounds.

One should not assume that language-based auditory discrimination tests based on distinctions more gross than minimal word pairs will automatically eliminate dialect bias. In some instances, the number of expected phonological cues may differ from dialect to dialect and this may favor some varieties over others. For example, the Standard English speaker may normally expect two cues to distinguish *bull* from *build* (the vowel and the final *d*), whereas a nonstandard speaker who deletes final *d* because of his consonant cluster rule might only expect one (the vowel). It has become obvious that many children are being referred for auditory discrimination training simply on the basis of dialect-biased items.

Developmental tests for grammatical ability do not fare much better than those designed to measure various aspects of phonology. The validity of such tests in measuring *any* child's actual grammatical maturity is quite questionable. In many instances, the variables used to measure grammatical development simply do not match the variables that scholars of language acquisition point out as diagnostic for various stages of acquisition. But if the validity of these tests is questionable for Standard English-speaking children, the problems are compounded for the speaker of a nonstandard dialect. In most conventional grammatical tests, only a Standard English grammatical form is accepted as a correct response. Again we can best exemplify this point by looking at an actual test, the Illinois Test of Psycho-Linguistic Abilities (ITPA). ITPA consists of a battery of tests to measure various aspects of language development. One of the subtests dealing directly with grammar is called "grammatic closure." In this section, the child is asked to supply a missing word in a sentence as the tester points to a picture. For example, the examiner shows a picture of two beds to a child. He points to the first and says, "Here is a bed." Then he points to the two beds and says, "Here are two _____." The child is expected to respond with the form *beds* if he has acquired the grammatical category of pluralization. All of the expected forms must be in Standard English in order to be considered a correct response. Thus, the child who responds with *hisself* for *himself, mans* or *mens* for *men,* and *hanged up* for *hung up* must be scored as incorrect. Of the total of 33 actual items in this part of the test, 27 of them may legitimately have different dialect forms according to the rules of Chapters Six and Seven. Obviously, any child who does not speak Standard English cannot expect to score well in this area. Ultimately, such information is interpreted as an indication of delayed grammatical development in need of remediation.

Finally, we should mention something about vocabulary tests, even though we have not dealt with lexical differences in different social dialects of American English. Roberts (1970) suggests that vocabulary tests are generally invalid for three main reasons: (1) they tap only semantic information without measuring the child's knowledge of syntactic information associated with the test, (2) the syntactic information required is often complex and uncontrolled, and (3) only one grammatical category is typically tested—namely, nouns. In the current use of vocabulary tests, vocabulary knowledge is equated with having a particular semantic association with the word in the form of a particular image or another word. Despite the general problems with vocabulary tests, they are often used as an important measure of language development. And, in a number of cases, these tests can be translated into IQ scores.

There are a number of different ways in which vocabulary tests can be directly or indirectly biased against various dialects of English. In some cases, culture-specific vocabulary items are used. That is, the word is outside the experience of the testee. For example, the use of the term *toboggan* may clearly be outside the experience of certain social or regional groups. It is also possible that an item may be within the experience of a given subculture, but is known by a different term. A child, for example, may not be familiar with the term *spectacles,* but he may be quite familiar with this item when referred to as *glasses* or *eyeglasses.* In a tabulation of potentially culture-specific items in the Peabody Picture Vocabulary Test, one of the main standards for measuring vocabulary development in young children, Roberts (1970:21) notes that 13 of the first 50 items (26 percent) are potentially culture-specific to speakers of Standard English. Nonstandard speakers can hardly expect to compete with middle-class Standard English speakers given this sort of potential bias. In addition to these types of bias, there exists the possibility that a child may be familiar with a term only to be thrown off by the particular pronunciation of the item as given by the examiner. Thus, if *wasp* is pronounced something like *wahsp* by the examiner while the child would normally produce it something like *waws,* the child may not be sufficiently sophisticated to overcome the variation. We must remember that in an artificial testing situation, the extralinguistic and linguistic context that normally could be appealed to for comprehension are often absent.

The problems with standardized language development tests obviously could be elaborated much more than we have done here. But our citations of more tests would only repeat the pessimistic profile. At this point, the language development diagnostician may ask how he is expected to diagnose various problems in language development. Some have called for a testing moratorium until tests more fair to various dialects can be constructed. But the construction of tests appropriate for nonstandard speakers has hardly begun, and some of the newly constructed tests actually fare little better than the traditional ones. We must also realistically face the educational pressures to substantiate a particular diagnosis on the basis of "objective evidence." As we mentioned in Chapter One, there is a small percentage of children from nonstandard-speaking communities who have authentic speech pathologies, as is the case in the Standard English-speaking community. To ignore their language problems because of inadequate testing procedures would be to discriminate out of ignorance. Given the requirements for the continued use of current language development tests for one reason or another, we can simply suggest that the test selector keep in mind several potentially useful guidelines. In the first place, some tests *are* less biased than others, so that one may appeal to the principle of lesser evil. If one, for example, looks at various articulation tests in terms of the phonological features given in Chapter Six, he will find that there are tests that do not penalize the nonstandard speaker as much as others. This sort of evaluation does, of course, presume a working familiarity with the linguistic features of various dialects. Some of the more recent tests are also referencing alternative forms that may be expected from various regional or class groups. Unfortunately, some of these lists are descriptively inadequate or incomplete. The concerned diagnostician can, however, extend such a principle based on the more elaborate inventory of dialect features. On this basis, he may make appropriate changes in the procedure. In some cases, this may mean giving credit for a particular item which the directions do not recognize. In other cases, an entire item may have to be omitted. We are fully cognizant of the fact that alternative procedures assume a certain amount of initiative on the part of the diagnostician, but he has no choice until test constructors can actually produce more adequate tests to assess language development.

ACHIEVEMENT TESTS

With respect to education, achievement tests are designed to permit the student to demonstrate his acquisition of information or skills he is supposed to have learned in school. Like all other tests, there are certain preliminary assumptions about language that affect achievement tests of practically every type. Although the single most important use of achievement tests is to check the student's learning progress, they often serve as the basis for decisions ranging from academic guidance of students to crucial decisions about admissions and promotion.

Achievement tests dealing with language are usually related to some aspects of "language arts" or reading. Under the rubric of language arts, we have everything from the mechanics of punctuation to grammatical usage of various types. A number of achievement tests also deal with aspects of vocabulary, including the association of a definition with a specific lexical item, synonyms, and antonyms.

In order to illustrate the problems encountered in these types of tests, we can take a specific test and look at it in terms of the essential socio-linguistic questions we raised at the beginning of this section. As a case in point, let us look briefly at the California Achievement Test (CAT), one of the regularly administered tests purporting to measure school achievement. The test was designed for the "measurement, evaluation, and diagnosis of school achievement." Various areas are covered in the test, including reading, arithmetic, and language, although we shall consider one aspect of the language component—namely, what is referred to as "word usage." Following the manual, we find that the elements to be tested in this section include "tense, person, number, case, good usage, and parts of speech" (CAT Manual:9). To begin with, we must note that the test is administered through the medium of reading. Thus, if a child cannot read, he cannot even attempt the test. Because the Lower Primary Test is supposed to be used for grades 1 and 2, this turns out to be a rather formidable assumption. We know that a person's knowledge of tense, person, etc. is quite independent of reading ability, but there is no way to tap this knowledge unless a child can read. Many children, then, are automatically eliminated on this basis. But let us assume that the child can read the test. The test is set up in such a way so that the student must choose between alternative words in the context of a sentence. He is simply instructed to mark the alternative that is "correct." For example, given a sentence such as *We were/was told to sit down,* he is supposed to choose *were* as the correct alternative, or given the sentence *He didn't hear any/no noise,* he is to choose *any.* These two examples, as we know from Chapter Seven, are simply alternatives between Standard and Nonstandard English forms. Eighteen of the twenty-five items in the test are related to standard/ nonstandard alternatives, while the other seven items deal with items ranging from spelling to contrasts between ungrammatical and grammatical sentences for speakers of both standard and nonstandard dialects of English. Excluding the seven items that seem somewhat out of place in the test, we conclude that we have a test which taps a student's ability to recognize Standard English forms as they contrast with nonstandard ones. It is at this point that we must compare what the test claims to measure with what it actually measures. What does it evaluate for the middle-class Standard English-speaking child and his nonstandard-speaking counter-part? The Standard English-speaking child presumably comes to school already using these forms, so it really only measures his ability to recognize his own speech. He should be able to do this without any real assistance from the school. For the nonstandard-speaking child, the eighteen standard/nonstandard items may be a valid measure of the extent to which he can recognize Standard English. (It should be noted that we deliberately use the word "recognize" instead of "use.") Suppose that the child who came to school speaking a nonstandard dialect can now recognize 9 of the 18 forms. If Standard English has been taught, it may actually tap the extent to which he has learned this identification. But although it may measure this achievement for the child who originally spoke a nonstandard dialect, he is compared with the child from the standard-speaking home who should be able to recognize all eighteen forms. Quite clearly, the test will always favor the Standard English speaker.

We could list other types of achievement tests which include some aspect of grammatical usage, but the same conclusion would obtain. At the primary levels, most of these tests are concerned with the contrast between standard and nonstandard dialects. At the higher educational levels, most of these tests are concerned with the recognition of superstandard forms as opposed to informal standard ones. The reader will recall that we defined a superstandard form in Chapter One as a conservative form of the language that is preferred above others even though these forms may not be used. For example, a language achievement test may include the contrast between *shall* and *will*. The testee is required to know that *shall* is used in the first-person and *will* with other persons despite the fact that very few people actually maintain such a contrast in their speech. Or, a testee may be required to recognize the formation of conditional sentences with *were* when the conjunctions are not present, as in *Were it not for him, I should speak up.* What this requires, then, is a knowledge of older, conservative forms of the grammar which have been prescribed as the preferred forms.

A number of achievement tests in language also concern themselves with vocabulary. For the most part, achievement tests in vocabulary suffer from the same sort of inadequacies that we have specified for vocabulary tests in language development. Syntactic information and grammatical categories are typically uncontrolled, and natural context is often lacking. Again, we find that the items are very culture-specific and dependent on middle-class values about vocabulary usage. Definitions, synonyms, and antonyms for words specific to non–middle-class groups are excluded. Although some of the currently popular *soul* or *chitterling* vocabulary tests may be exaggerated somewhat, they do, by contrast, point out the culture-specific nature of vocabulary items in standardized vocabulary achievement tests. It is not by chance that scores on such tests typically correlate with socioeconomic class background.

The extent of dialect bias in reading achievement tests is largely dependent on the type of test that is given. In the more advanced stages of reading, where comprehension is directly tapped, it is very difficult to assess the specific effect that a nonstandard dialect may have on an individual's performance. On a more elementary level, where word identification is focused on, it is easier to isolate particular examples that could be biased potentially against particular dialects of English. For example, dialect differences may create legitimate alternatives not anticipated by the test designer. Whereas the Standard English speaker may use his "sounding-out" ability to discriminate between words such as *sole* and *sold* and *walk* and *walked,* the speaker of a nonstandard dialect may not have the same advantage. Because these words are potentially homophonous in some dialects, a testee may choose an alternative that uses his sounding-out ability correctly in terms of his dialect. But the test, designed for Standard English speakers, may not recognize this as a correct response. If items were kept in appropriate contexts, this sort of *interdialectal homophony* (i.e., items that sound different in one dialect but are homophonous in another) would not usually cause a problem because only one alternative might fit in the context appropriately. But all too often, context is not used in beginning reading tests. Items consistently missed by speakers of particular dialects should give reading instructors a clue as to the forms that may diverge because of a dialect difference. This information, of course, presumes that instructors receive an item-analysis of their students on achievement tests. In a preliminary study of the elementary-level Metropolitan Reading Test by Hutchinson (1971), it was shown that grades of Vernacular Black English-speaking children were raised on the average of one grade level when the test was rescored excluding some of the dialect-biased items.

Standardized spelling tests may hold similar types of problems. We may recall our discussion of dialect influence in writing by noting that some of the items may have alternative spellings if the testee attempts to arrive at a spelling by sounding out the words. The speaker of a Southern dialect who has difficulty distinguishing the spelling of *tinder* and *tender* will not be aided by trying to "sound out" the two words, because they are homophonous. Similarly, a Vernacular Black English speaker who confuses the spelling of *find* and *fine* may have been misled by the instructions to rely on sounding out these words as a clue to their spelling differences. The orthography of English favors the Standard English speaker if one is going to use the conventional type of "phonics" as a clue to certain types of spelling patterns.

Given the particular types of potential dialect bias that are encountered in various types of achievement tests dealing with language, it is a tragedy that so much emphasis is placed on those tests in our current educational system. This is even more tragic when we realistically admit that dialect bias may be one of the lesser evils when viewed in the broader perspective of cultural bias. Hopefully, educators will put such tests in their proper perspective as their inadequacies are exposed. From our criticisms, however, we must move to replace invalid instruments with more valid measurements of achievements in the language arts. Sociolinguistics is just one of the specialties that must be considered in the construction of new instruments for assessing language achievement. Its contribution must be combined with those from fields such as educational psychology, anthropology, psycholinguistics, and education in order to ensure that our future in standardized achievement testing is brighter than our past.

BIBLIOGRAPHY

The bibliography includes both works cited in the text and some additional sources of background information. For the reader with little or no linguistic background, we suggest basic introductory texts such as Langacker, *Language and Its Structure,* and Lyons, *Introduction to Theoretical Linguistics.* The reader interested in following up this presentation of social dialects in American English may consult Labov's *Sociolinguistic Patterns* and *Language in the Inner City: Studies in the Black English Vernacular.* Theoretical interests deriving from Chapter Five can be pursued in Bailey's *Variation and Linguistic Theory* and Bailey and Shuy's *New Ways of Analyzing Variation in English.* There are also several journals concerned with the types of topics we have dealt with here. *Language in Society* is devoted to a broad range of topics in sociolinguistics, whereas *The Florida FL Reporter* focuses on various types of studies dealing with Vernacular Black English.

For the convenience of the reader, we have asterisked those articles and books which we consider to be of primary importance. The judgment represents the opinion of the authors, and readers may find that other selections are more appropriate, depending on their particular interests.

AGHEYISI, REBECCA, and JOSHUA A. FISHMAN. 1970. "Language Attitude Studies: A Brief Survey of Methodological Approaches," *Anthropological Linguistics* 12, No. 5:137–57.

ALLEN, HAROLD B., and GARY N. UNDERWOOD, eds. 1971. *Readings in American Dialectology.* New York: Appleton-Century-Crofts.

ANSHEN, FRANK. 1969. *Speech Variation among Negroes in a Small Southern Community.* Unpublished Ph.D. dissertation, New York University.

ATWOOD, ELMER BAGBY. 1962. *The Regional Vocabulary of Texas.* Austin: University of Texas Press.

BAILEY, BERYL LOFTMAN. 1965. "Toward a New Perspective in Negro English Dialectology," *American Speech* 40:171–77.

BAILEY, CHARLES-JAMES N. 1972. "The Patterning of Language Variation," in *Varieties of Present-Day English,* ed. R. W. Bailey and J. L. Robinson. New York: Macmillan Co.

* ———. 1973. *Variation and Linguistic Theory.* Washington, D.C.: Center for Applied Linguistics.

BAILEY, CHARLES-JAMES N., and ROGER W. SHUY, eds. 1973. *New Ways of Analyzing Variation in English.* Washington, D.C.: Georgetown University Press.

BARATZ, JOAN. 1968. "Language in the Economically Disadvantaged Child: A Perspective," *ASHA* (April):143–45.

———. 1969. "Teaching Reading in an Urban Negro School System," in *Teaching Black Children to Read,* ed. Joan C. Baratz and Roger W. Shuy. Washington, D.C.: Center for Applied Linguistics.

BEREITER, CARL. 1965. "Academic Instruction and Preschool Children," in *Language Programs for the Disadvantaged,* ed. Richard Corbin and Muriel Crosby. Champaign, Ill.: National Council of Teachers of English.

BERKO, JEAN. 1958. "The Child's Learning of English Morphology," *Word* 14:150–77.

BERNSTEIN, BASIL B. 1964. "Elaborated and Restricted Codes: Their Social Origins and Some Consequences," in *The Ethnography of Communication, American Anthropologist* 66, No. 6, Part 2.

BICKERTON, DEREK. 1971. "Inherent Variability and Variable Rules," *Foundations of Language* 7:457–92.

BLOOMFIELD, LEONARD. 1933. *Language.* New York: Holt, Rinehart and Winston.

BROOM, LEONARD, and PHILLIP SELZNICK. 1963. *Sociology: A Text with Adapted Readings.* New York: Harper & Row.

BRYDEN, JAMES D. 1968. *An Acoustic and Social Dialect Analysis of Perceptual Variables in Listener Identification and Rating of Negro Speakers.* USOE Project No. 7-C-003.

BULL, WILLIAM. 1955. "The Use of Vernacular Languages in Fundamental Education," *IJAL* 21:228–94.

BURLING, ROBBINS. 1973. *English in Black and White.* New York: Holt, Rinehart and Winston.

California Achievement Tests. 1963.

* CEDERGREN, HENRIETTA J., and DAVID SANKOFF. 1972. "Variable Rules: Performance as a Statistical Reflection of Competence." Unpublished manuscript.

CHOMSKY, NOAM. 1965. *Aspects of the Theory of Syntax.* Cambridge, Mass.: MIT Press.

————. 1968. *Language and Mind.* New York: Harcourt, Brace & World.

DAVIS, LAWRENCE M. 1971. *A Study of Appalachian Speech in a Northern Urban Setting.* USOE Project No. 5-70-0046(509).

DAVIS, OLGA, MILDRED GLADNEY, and LLOYD LEAVERTON. 1968. *Psycholinguistics Reading Series.* Chicago: Board of Education.

DECAMP, DAVID. 1971. "Toward a Generative Analysis of a Post-Creole Speech Continuum," in *Pidginization and Creolization of Languages,* ed. Dell H. Hymes. Cambridge: At the University Press.

DILLARD, J. L. 1967. "Negro Children's Dialect in the Inner City," *The Florida FL Reporter* 5:7–10.

————. 1972. *Black English: Its History and Usage in the United States.* New York: Random House.

ERVIN-TRIPP, SUSAN M. 1964. "An Analysis of the Interaction of Language and Listener," in *The Ethnography of Communication, American Anthropologist* 66, No. 6, Part 2.

————. 1969. "Sociolinguistics," in *Advances in Experimental Social Psychology,* Vol. 4. New York: Academic Press.

FASOLD, RALPH W. 1969a. "Tense and the Form *be* in Black English," *Language* 45:763–76.

————. 1969b. "Orthography in Reading Materials for Black English Speaking Children," in *Teaching Black Children to Read,* ed. Joan C. Baratz and Roger W. Shuy. Washington, D.C.: Center for Applied Linguistics.

————. 1970. "Two Models of Socially Significant Linguistic Variation," *Language* 46:551–63.

————. 1971. "What Can an English Teacher Do about Nonstandard Dialect?" in *Studies in English to Speakers of Other Languages and Standard English to Speakers of Non-Standard Dialect,* Special Anthology Issue and Monograph 14 of *The English Record,* ed. Rudolfo Jacobson.

* ————. 1972. *Tense Marking in Black English: A Linguistic and Social Analysis.* Washington, D.C.: Center for Applied Linguistics.

* FEIGENBAUM, IRWIN. 1969. "Using Foreign Language Methodology to Teach Standard English: Evaluation and Adaptation," in *Linguistic-Cultural Differences and American Education,* Special Anthology Issue of *The Florida FL Reporter,* ed. Alfred A. Aarons, Barbara Y. Gordon, and William A. Stewart.

————. 1970a. "The Use of Nonstandard English in Teaching Standard: Contrast and Comparison," in *Teaching Standard English in the Inner City,* ed. Ralph W. Fasold and Roger W. Shuy. Washington, D.C.: Center for Applied Linguistics.

————. 1970b. *English Now.* New York: New Century.

FISCHER, JOHN L. 1958. "Social Influences on the Choice of a Linguistic Variant," *Word* 14:47–56.

FISHMAN, JOSHUA A. 1969a. "Literacy and the Language Barrier," Book Review of *Intelligence and Cultural Environment,* by Phillip E. Vernon, and *Teaching Black Children to Read,* ed. Joan C. Baratz and Roger W. Shuy. *Science* 165:1108–1109.

————. 1969b. "Bilingual Attitudes and Behaviors," *Language Sciences* No. 5:5–11.

FISHMAN, JOSHUA A., ROBERT L. COOPER, and ROXANA MA. 1971. *Bilingualism in the Barrio, Language Science Monographs,* Vol. 7. Bloomington, Ind.: Indiana University Publications.

FRANCIS, W. NELSON. 1958. *The Structure of American English.* New York: The Ronald Press.

FRIES, CHARLES C. 1940. *American English Grammar: The Grammatical Structure of Present-Day American English with Especial Reference to Social Differences or Class Dialects.* New York: Appleton-Century-Crofts.

GARVIN, PAUL, and MADELINE MATHIOT. 1956. "The Urbanization of the Guarani Language: A Problem in Language and Culture," in *Men and Cultures: Selected Papers of the Fifth International Congress of Anthropological and Ethnological Sciences.* Philadelphia: University of Pennsylvania Press.

GOLDEN, RUTH. 1963. *Effectiveness of Instructional Tapes for Changing Regional Speech.* Unpublished Ed.D. dissertation, Wayne State University.

GOODMAN, KENNETH S. 1969. "Dialect Barriers to Reading Comprehension," in *Teaching Black Children to Read,* ed. Joan C. Baratz and Roger W. Shuy. Washington, D.C.: Center for Applied Linguistics.

GORDON, DAVID, and GEORGE LAKOFF. 1971. "Conversational Postulates," *Papers from the Seventh Regional Meeting Chicago Linguistic Society.* Chicago: Chicago Linguistic Society.

GUMPERZ, JOHN J. 1966. "On the Ethnology of Linguistic Change," in *Sociolinguistics,* ed. William Bright. The Hague: Mouton.

GUTTMAN, LOUIS. 1944. "A Basis for Scaling Qualitative Data," *American Sociological Review* 9:139–59.

HAAS, MARY. 1944. "Men's and Women's Speech in Koasati," *Language* 20:142–49.

HACKENBERG, ROBERT. 1972. *A Sociolinguistic Description of Appalachian English.* Unpublished Ph.D. dissertation, Georgetown University.

HALL, ROBERT A. 1950. *Leave Your Language Alone.* Garden City, N.Y.: Doubleday.

HERMAN, SIMON R. 1961. "Explorations in the Social Psychology of Language Choice," *Human Relations* 14:149–64.

HUTCHINSON, JUNE O'SHIELDS. 1972. "Reading Tests and Nonstandard Language," *Reading Teacher* 25:430–37.

HYMES, DELL H. 1962. "The Ethnography of Speaking," in *Anthropology and Human Behavior,* ed. Thomas Gladwin and William C. Sturtevant. Washington, D.C.: Anthropological Society of Washington.

———. 1964. "Introduction: Toward Ethnographies of Communication," in *The Ethnography of Communication, American Anthropologist* 66, No. 6, Part 2.

———. 1969. "Linguistic Theory and the Functions of Speech," in *International Days of Sociolinguistics.* Rome: Palazzo Baldassini.

JOOS, MARTIN. 1962. *The Five Clocks. IJAL,* Memoir No. 22. Bloomington, Ind.: Indiana University Publications.

KOCHMAN, THOMAS. 1969a. "Rapping in the Black Ghetto," *Trans-action* 6 (February):26–34.

———. 1969b. "Social Factors in the Consideration of Teaching Standard English," in *Linguistic-Cultural Differences and American Education,* Special Anthology Issue of *The Florida FL Reporter,* ed. Alfred A. Aarons, Barbara Y. Gordon, and William A. Stewart.

KURATH, HANS. 1939. *Handbook of the Linguistic Geography of New England.* Providence, R.I.: American Council of Learned Societies.

———. 1949. *A Word Geography of the Eastern United States.* Ann Arbor: University of Michigan Press.

LABOV, WILLIAM. 1964a. "Phonological Correlates of Social Stratification," in *The Ethnography of Communication, American Anthropologist* 66, No. 6, Part 2.

———. 1964b. "Stages in the Acquisition of Standard English," in *Social Dialects and Language Learning,* ed. Roger W. Shuy. Champaign, Ill.: National Council of Teachers of English.

———. 1965. "On the Mechanism of Linguistic Change," *Monograph Series on Languages and Linguistics* No. 18, ed. Charles W. Kreidler. Washington, D.C.: Georgetown University Press.

* ———. 1966. *The Social Stratification of English in New York City.* Washington, D.C.: Center for Applied Linguistics.

* ———. 1969. "Contraction, Deletion, and Inherent Variability of the English Copula," *Language* 45:715–62.

* ———. 1970a. "The Logic of Nonstandard English," in *Georgetown Monograph Series on Languages and Linguistics* No. 22, ed. James E. Alatis. Washington, D.C.: Georgetown University Press.

———. 1970b. *The Study of Nonstandard English.* Champaign, Ill.: National Council of Teachers of English.

———. 1971. "Methodology," in *A Survey of Linguistic Science,* ed. William Orr Dingwall. College Park: University of Maryland Linguistics Program.

* ———. 1972a. "Some Principles of Linguistic Methodology," *Language in Society* 1:97–120.

* ———. 1972b. *Language in the Inner City: Studies in the Black English Vernacular.* Philadelphia: University of Pennsylvania Press.

* ———. 1972c. *Sociolinguistic Patterns.* Philadelphia: University of Pennsylvania Press.

LABOV, WILLIAM, and CLARENCE ROBINS. 1969. "A Note on the Relation of Reading Failure to Peer-Group Status in Urban Ghettos," in *Linguistic-Cultural Differences and American Education,* Special Anthology Issue of *The Florida FL Reporter,* ed. Alfred A. Aarons, Barbara Y. Gordon, and William A. Stewart.

LABOV, WILLIAM, PAUL COHEN, CLARENCE ROBINS, and JOHN LEWIS. 1968. *A Study of the Non-Standard English of Negro and Puerto Rican Speakers in New York City.* USOE Final Report, Research Project No. 3288.

* LANGACKER, RONALD W. 1967. *Language and Its Structure: Some Fundamental Linguistic Concepts.* New York: Harcourt, Brace & World.

LEAP, WILLIAM L. 1973. "Ethnics, Emics, and the New Ideology," in SAS Proceedings, No. 8, *Social and Cultural Identity: Problems in Persistence and Change.*

LEGUM, STANLEY E., CAROL PFAFF, GENE TINNIE, and MICHAEL NICHOLAS. 1971. *The Speech of Young Black Children in Los Angeles,* Southwest Regional Laboratory Technical Report No. 33. Inglewood, Calif.: Southwest Regional Laboratory.

LEVINE, LEWIS, and HARRY J. CROCKETT. 1966. "Speech Variation in a Piedmont Community: Postvocalic r," *Sociological Inquiry* 35:204–26.

———. 1967. "Friends' Influence on Speech," *Sociological Inquiry* 37:109–28.

LOFLIN, MARVIN. 1970. "On the Structure of the Verb in a Dialect of American Negro English," *Linguistics* 59:14–28.

* LYONS, JOHN. 1968. *Introduction to Theoretical Linguistics.* Cambridge: At the University Press.

McDAVID, RAVEN I. 1948. "Postvocalic /-r/ in South Carolina: A Social Analysis," *American Speech* 23:194–203.

———. 1952. "Some Social Differences in Pronunciation," *Language Learning* 4:102–116.

———. 1958. "The Dialects of American English," in W. Nelson Francis, *The Structure of American English.* New York: Ronald Press.

———. 1967. "A Checklist of Significant Features for Discriminating Social Dialects," in *Dimensions of Dialect,* ed. Eldonna L. Evertts. Champaign, Ill.: National Council of Teachers of English.

———. 1969. "Dialectology and the Teaching of Reading," in *Teaching Black Children to Read,* ed. Joan C. Baratz and Roger W. Shuy. Washington, D.C.: Center for Applied Linguistics.

MENCKEN, H. L. 1936. *The American Language.* New York: Alfred A. Knopf.

MENYUK, PAULA. 1971. *The Acquisition and Development of Language.* Englewood Cliffs, N.J.: Prentice-Hall, Inc.

* MITCHELL-KERNAN, CLAUDIA. 1969. *Language Behavior in a Black Urban Community,* Working Paper No. 23. Berkeley, Calif.: Language-Behavior Laboratory, University of California.

MODIANO, NANCY. 1968. "National or Mother Tongue in Beginning Reading: A Comparative Study." Unpublished manuscript.

NATALICIO, DIANA, and FREDERICK WILLIAMS. 1971. *Repetition as an Oral Language Assessment Technique.* Austin, Tex.: Center for Communication Research.

ÖSTERBERG, TORE. 1961. *Bilingualism and the First School Language: An Educational Problem Illustrated by Results from a Swedish Dialect Area.* Umean: Västerbottens Trycheri AB.

PEET, WILLIAM. 1973. "Omission of Subject Relative Pronouns in Restrictive Relative Clauses in Hawaiian English," in *New Ways of Analyzing Variation in English,* ed. Charles-James N. Bailey and Roger W. Shuy. Washington, D.C.: Georgetown University Press.

PELTO, PERTTI J. 1970. *Anthropological Research: The Structure of Inquiry.* New York: Harper & Row.

QUIRK, RANDOLPH, and JAN SVARTVIK. 1966. *Investigating Linguistic Acceptability.* The Hague: Mouton.

RAPH, JANE B. 1967. "Language and Speech Deficits in Culturally Disadvantaged Children and Their Implication for the Speech Clinician," *Journal of Speech and Hearing Disorders* 32:203–14.

RASPBERRY, WILLIAM. 1970. "Potomac Watch," *The Washington Post,* March 15.

REDDEN, JAMES E. 1966. "Walapai I: Phonology," *IJAL* 32:1–16.

* ROBERTS, ELSA. 1970. "An Evaluation of Standardized Tests as Tools for the Measurement of Language Development," in *Language Research Reports* No. 1. Cambridge, Mass.: Language Research Foundation.

ROSENTHAL, R., and LENORE JACOBSON. 1968. "Teacher Expectations for the Disadvantaged," *Scientific American* 218:19–23.

ROSENTHAL, MARILYN. 1973. *The Acquisition of Child Awareness of Language: Age and Socio-Economic Class Correlates.* Unpublished Ph.D. dissertation, Georgetown University.

ROSS, JOHN R. 1967. *Constraints on Variables in Syntax.* Unpublished Ph.D. dissertation, MIT.

SAMARIN, WILLIAM J. 1967. *Field Linguistics: A Guide to Linguistic Field Work.* New York: Holt, Rinehart and Winston.

SANKOFF, GILLIAN. 1972. "A Quantitative Paradigm for Studying Communicative Competence," Paper delivered at Conference on the Ethnography of Speaking, Austin, Tex.

SAPIR, EDWARD. 1921. *Language.* New York: Harcourt, Brace and Co.

SHUY, ROGER W. 1967. *Discovering American Dialects.* Champaign, Ill.: National Council of Teachers of English.

――――. 1969. "A Linguistic Background for Developing Beginning Reading Materials for Black Children," in *Teaching Black Children to Read,* ed.

Joan C. Baratz and Roger W. Shuy. Washington, D.C.: Center for Applied Linguistics.

* ———. 1972. "Sociolinguistics and Teacher Attitudes in a Southern School System," in *Sociolinguistics in Cross-Cultural Analysis,* ed. David M. Smith and Roger W. Shuy. Washington, D.C.: Georgetown University Press.

SHUY, ROGER W., WALTER A. WOLFRAM, and WILLIAM K. RILEY. 1968. *Field Techniques in an Urban Language Study.* Washington, D.C.: Center for Applied Linguistics.

SHUY, ROGER W., JOAN C. BARATZ, and WALT WOLFRAM. 1969. *Sociolinguistic Factors in Speech Identification.* NIMH Final Report, Project No. MH 15048-01.

SKINNER, B. F. 1957. *Verbal Behavior.* New York: Appleton-Century-Crofts.

* SLEDD, JAMES. 1969. "Bi-dialectalism: The Linguistics of White Supremacy," *English Journal* 58:1307–29.

———. 1972. "Doublespeak: Dialectology in the Service of Big Brother," *College English* 33:439–56.

SLOBIN, DAN I. 1967. *A Field Manual for Cross-Cultural Study of the Acquisition of Communicative Competence.* Berkeley, Calif.: University of California.

* STEWART, WILLIAM A. 1967. "Sociolinguistic Factors in the History of American Negro Dialects," *The Florida FL Reporter* 5 (Spring): 11, 22, 24, 26.

———. 1968a. "An Outline of Linguistic Typology for Describing Multilingualism," in *Readings in the Sociology of Language,* ed. Joshua A. Fishman. The Hague: Mouton.

* ———. 1968b. "Continuity and Change in American Negro Dialects," *The Florida FL Reporter* 6 (Spring): 14–16, 18, 304.

* ———. 1969. "The Use of Negro Dialect in the Teaching of Reading," in *Teaching Black Children to Read,* ed. Joan C. Baratz and Roger W. Shuy. Washington, D.C.: Center for Applied Linguistics.

———. 1970. "Foreign Language Teaching Methods in Quasi-Foreign Language Situations," in *Teaching Standard English in the Inner City,* ed. Ralph W. Fasold and Roger W. Shuy. Washington, D.C.: Center for Applied Linguistics.

TARONE, ELAINE E. 1972. *Aspects of Intonation in Vernacular White and Black English.* Unpublished Ph.D. dissertation, University of Washington.

TAYLOR, ORLANDO L. 1971. Response to "Social Dialects and the Field of Speech," in *Sociolinguistics: A Cross-Disciplinary Perspective.* Washington, D.C.: Center for Applied Linguistics.

———. 1973. "Teachers' Attitudes Toward Black and Nonstandard English as Measured by the Language Attitude Scale," in *Language Attitudes: Current Trends and Prospects,* ed. Roger W. Shuy and Ralph W. Fasold. Washington, D.C.: Georgetown University Press.

UNESCO. 1953. *The Use of Vernacular Languages in Education.* Monographs on Fundamental Education, No. 8. Paris: UNESCO.

VENEZKY, RICHARD L. 1970. "Nonstandard Language and Reading," *Elementary English* 47:334–45.

WARNER, W. LLOYD. 1949. *Social Class in America.* New York: Harper & Row.

WEBER, ROSE-MARIE. 1969. "Some Reservations on the Significance of Dialect in the Acquisition of Reading," *The Reading Specialist* 7:37–40.

* WEINREICH, URIEL. 1953. *Languages in Contact.* The Hague: Mouton.

WHYTE, W. F., and A. R. HOMBERG. 1956. "Human Problems of U.S. Enterprise in Latin America," *Human Organization* 15:11–15.

WIGGINS, M. EUGENE. 1972. "The Cognitive Deficit-Difference Controversy as a Socio-Political Struggle." Unpublished manuscript.

WILLIAMS, FREDERICK. 1973. "Some Research Notes on Dialect Attitudes and Stereotypes," in *Language Attitudes: Current Trends and Prospects,* ed. Roger W. Shuy and Ralph W. Fasold. Washington, D.C.: Georgetown University Press.

WILLIAMS, FREDERICK, J. L. WHITEHEAD, and L. M. MILLER. 1971. *Attitudinal Correlates of Children's Speech Characteristics.* USOE Research Report Project No. 0-0336.

WILLIAMS, RONALD. 1971. "Race and the Word," *Today's Speech* 19, No. 2:27–33.

WOLFF, HANS. 1959. "Intelligibility and Inter-Ethnic Attitudes," *Anthropological Linguistics* 1, No. 3:34–41.

WOLFRAM, WALT. 1969. *A Sociolinguistic Description of Detroit Negro Speech.* Washington, D.C.: Center for Applied Linguistics.

———. 1970. "Sociolinguistic Implications for Educational Sequencing," in *Teaching Standard English in the Inner City,* ed. Ralph W. Fasold and Roger W. Shuy. Washington, D.C.: Center for Applied Linguistics.

———. 1971a. "Black-White Speech Relationships Revisited," in *Black-White Speech Relationships,* ed. Walt Wolfram and Nona H. Clarke. Washington, D.C.: Center for Applied Linguistics.

———. 1971b. "Sociolinguistic Alternatives for Teaching Reading to Speakers of Nonstandard English," *The Reading Research Quarterly* 6:9–33.

* ———. 1973a. *Sociolinguistic Aspects of Assimilation: Puerto Rican English in East Harlem.* Washington, D.C.: Center for Applied Linguistics.

———. 1973b. "On What Basis Variable Rules?" in *Studies in New Ways of Analyzing Variation in English.* Washington, D.C.: Georgetown University Press.

———. [forthcoming.] "The Relationship of Southern White Speech to Vernacular Black English," *Language.*

WOLFRAM, WALT, and RALPH W. FASOLD. 1969. "Toward Reading Materials for Speakers of Black English: Three Linguistically Appropriate Passages," in *Teaching Black Children to Read,* ed. Joan C. Baratz and Roger W. Shuy. Washington, D.C.: Center for Applied Linguistics.

* WOLFRAM, WALT, and NONA H. CLARKE, eds. 1971. *Black-White Speech Relationships.* Washington, D.C.: Center for Applied Linguistics.

WOLFRAM, WALT, and MARCIA F. WHITEMAN. 1971. "The Role of Dialect Interference in Composition," *The Florida FL Reporter* 9 (Fall): 34–38, 59.

WOLFRAM, WALT, in collaboration with MARIE SHIELS and RALPH W. FASOLD. 1971. *Overlapping Influence in the English of Second-Generation Puerto Rican Teenagers in East Harlem*. Final Report, USOE Project No. 3-70-0033(508).

INDEX